Remembering Lived Lives

Remembering Lived Lives

A Historiography from the Underside of Modernity

Michael Jimenez

CASCADE *Books* • Eugene, Oregon

REMEMBERING LIVED LIVES
A Historiography from the Underside of Modernity

Copyright © 2017 Michael Jimenez. All rights reserved. Except for brief quotations in critical publications or reviews, no part of this book may be reproduced in any manner without prior written permission from the publisher. Write: Permissions, Wipf and Stock Publishers, 199 W. 8th Ave., Suite 3, Eugene, OR 97401.

Cascade Books
An Imprint of Wipf and Stock Publishers
199 W. 8th Ave., Suite 3
Eugene, OR 97401

www.wipfandstock.com

PAPERBACK ISBN: 978-1-4982-3485-6
HARDCOVER ISBN: 978-1-4982-3487-0
EBOOK ISBN: 978-1-4982-3486-3

Cataloguing-in-Publication data:

Names: Jimenez, Michael.

Title: Remembering lived lives : a historiography from the underside of modernity / Michael Jimenez.

Description: Eugene, OR: Cascade Books, 2017 | Includes bibliographical references and index.

Identifiers: ISBN 978-1-4982-3485-6 (paperback) | ISBN 978-1-4982-3487-0 (hardcover) | ISBN 978-1-4982-3486-3 (ebook)

Subjects: LSCH: Historiography. | History—Religious aspects—Christianity. | Theology, Doctrinal—Latin America. | Latin America—Church history.

Classification: BT83.57 J55 2017 (print) | BT83.57 (ebook)

Manufactured in the U.S.A.   03/30/17

When we awake each morning, we hold in our hands, usually weakly and loosely, but a few fringes of the tapestry of *lived life*, as loomed for us by forgetting.

—Walter Benjamin

Contents

Preface | ix

Introduction | 1

CHAPTER 1 The Happy Historian: Diversifying Karl Barth's Advice to History Students | 15

CHAPTER 2 Never Forget (But How Will They Forget if They Never Heard?): Challenging a Eurocentric History | 48

CHAPTER 3 History as Biography: McClendon's Use of Narrative to Create Empathy | 86

CHAPTER 4 The Newspaper in One Hand and the Remote Control in the Other: On History and Cinema | 118

Conclusion | 139

Bibliography | 151

Index | 165

Preface

Remembering Lived Lives was written with the intention to bridge the gap between the historical and theological disciplines. It was written to theologians to encourage them to incorporate more history in their work, and to historians to exhort them to utilize the vast amount of material left to human history about the topic of religion. What makes this different from similar books on this subject matter is that I intentionally focused on the historical-theological thought and experiences of figures from the third world. It is my contention that Christian historiography in particular still somewhat ignores the events and theories that originate in Latin America, Asia, Africa, and even the marginalized in North America. Furthermore, I hope this book will be used in classrooms by instructors already practicing an interdisciplinary method with history, theology, and other disciplines, and for the general reader hoping to gain some insight about history and theology.

    I do not want to assume that many teachers of history or theology do not already practice the ideas I discuss in this book. In fact, I am guessing that many theologians across the globe pause to observe the lives of figures like Oscar Romero in their classes, or that history teachers emphasize the importance of religious freedom by discussing the faith of César Chávez or Martin Luther King Jr. In fact, it was from my doctoral research that I stumbled upon the work of many of the writers I feature in this book. The book, in some sense, narrates my journey from a sole concentration on the theology of Karl Barth to an overall inclusive project of thinkers across the globe. My critique of the continual nature of Eurocentrism is guided by my own affinity for European theology, history, philosophy, and literature. To criticize Eurocentric thought does not mean I am anti-Western or suddenly stopped reading books written by Europeans. What I am attacking is the idea that the center of all academic thought begins and ends in Europe.

PREFACE

What I have done is paused or decreased my own reading of European literature in order to enjoy and to evolve from the works of non-Europeans.

The writings that guided me on this particular project are Walter Benjamin's "Theses on the Philosophy of History" and Mayra Rivera's *The Touch of Transcendence*. My focus on the underside of history through a *mestiza* consciousness, following history on the borderlands, finds inspiration from these two works. The way Rivera, for example, is able to discuss theology by way of poststructuralist, postcolonial, and Latina theologians in a just a few pages was a model I have tried, in my own inadequate way, to emulate.

As we will see, history and theology are both somewhat autobiographical. Discovering one's own historical consciousness will allow the reader to inquire about the writings that have influenced her own roots. I am approaching this study from a Christian perspective, as someone born and raised in Los Angeles. My time as a student and instructor at Biola, my graduate years at Fuller Theological Seminary, and the fact I am able to teach theology and church history at Azusa Pacific University, while teaching history at Biola, Vanguard University, and Santiago Canyon College was definitely the main experience that created the foundation of this book. My autobiography definitely shaped the way this book was written, primarily in the way that history can often times be depressing (with students telling me I have a knack for finding the most gut wrenching YouTube videos), and being aware of this Benjamin type history of the oppressed has shaped the way I currently understand my own faith. History forces theology to take stock of the lives that are often invisible. If God seems Wholly Other, what happens when amnesia strikes us with regards to those who have died? Therefore, history is one of the means to narrate these lives back into consciousness.

One note on terminology in *Remembering Lived Lives*. At times I use the term third world to identify peoples from Asia, Africa, and Latin America. This title is not meant to be offensive or blindly follow a first world typology, seeing the third world as an always developing place in constant need of first world assistance. Instead I utilize this term in accordance with the work of Vjay Prashad and Chela Sandoval. Both thinkers incorporate the term in a positive way, especially as they address the diverse connections among people across these continents. Because of the nature of my studies, my focus on third world thinkers is generally on Latin American writers even though throughout this book I highlight contributions from other writers. With an element of fear and trembling I sometimes discuss

PREFACE

figures and texts that are past my professional comfort zone, or academic concentration. For example, I am not a film studies expert, but a novice who loves movies and uses them in the classroom. It is at this level of meaning that I discuss this subject in my book.

I would like to thank the following for stimulating conversations or suggestions about ideas and sources that helped produce this study: Natasha Duquette, Howard Loewen, Judith Rood, Jacquelyn Winston, Amaryah Armstrong, Nancy Wang Yuen, Oscar Garcia-Johnson, Allen Yeh, Marika Rose, Anthony Paul Smith, and Stephen Hale. A special thanks to the staff at Wipf and Stock/Cascade Books that helped put this book together, especially to Chris, who graciously took my phone call. I would also like to thank my brother, Matthew, for editing portions of early drafts and providing important corrections.

Finally, I want to thank my wife, Lluvia, for the continual encouragement she gives me on a daily basis, and to my two sons, Lucas and Raylan, for being a constant inspiration to me. I dedicate this book to my two boys.

Introduction

"To accept one's past—one's history—is not the same thing as drowning in it; it is learning how to use it." —James Baldwin[1]

Good history moves like good cinema. If the director of the film or the author of the book has done her job, the viewer or reader will be captured by the story. However, like any form of communication, a fan base potentially materializes, limiting followers to this one type of format (for example, consider Star Wars fans who refuse to watch Star Trek, or people who only read Victorian literature). Now when it comes to science fiction or classic literature the stakes of the argument are not very high. However, when we limit ourselves to reading books or watching films solely about people like ourselves there is a greater social-political problem at hand.

At the beginning of the semester, I oftentimes have both my theology and history students watch Nigerian author Chimamanda Ngozi Adichie's TED talk "The Danger of a Single Story" because it raises consciousness about the myopic view of limiting ourselves to only familiar people, and their familiar stories.[2] She discusses the problem of being a non-European, reading only European literature as a child, and how being introduced to African literature showed her that an African woman like herself could be the protagonist of good literature. The crux of her speech is that when obsessed with a single narrative, there is the potential to have a condescending pity toward the foreign Other, whose story we only vaguely know. The single story obscures the great diversity of stories that exist. A sober view of history cannot help but see this diversity.

1. Baldwin, *Fire Next Time*, 81.
2. Adichie, "Danger of a Single Story."

Why open this book with the words of a Nigerian novelist? Is this not a book dealing with themes from history and theology? Adichie talks about stories, yet in what ways do these stories have any relevancy for academic disciplines? The theme of this book, centered on the relationship between the disciplines of history and theology, what I call historical-theological thinking, is *empathy*.[3] Empathy is at the heart of Adichie's call to soak in the narratives of others. She declares this because human beings still struggle to do this properly. Resistance to hearing other narratives displays a lack of empathy. There is a whole storehouse of knowledge that reveals evidence of this lack. Moreover, wrestling with the concept of empathy is a crucial matter, even in the way we understand theology. Listening to the diverse narratives of history helps to raise consciousness about ourselves, others, and God. Reading history empathically connects to our view of God as one who is actively concerned for creation. A deep abiding interest in faith does not concurrently allow a detached view of history. If history is filled with stories, then we should read them with real concern and care.

As much as one becomes an expert on some moment in history, it will always remain foreign. The otherness of history means we can never master it, which is why we will always need new historians. Respecting this otherness, our job as historians is to approach history as listeners. Why do we listen? One cannot properly retell a story from history without having heard what the historical moment is telling you. This takes time. Since history is Other, this means one will not comprehend its message without being open to a word or world that is different than one's own. Still, as different as the past may seem, it continues to form generations one after another.

Even more difficult for the historian is attempting to write about history that has added dimensions of otherness. For example, imagine the difficulty of a white historian trying to write about lynching in the American South or a Chinese writer discussing the bombing of Hiroshima. Cross-racial scholarship happens all the time, but scholars will often be challenged by members of the ethnic, religious, or cultural community to be fair and to be truthful. One will not be able to step into this double otherness, and be successful, without a sense of empathy. One approaches the historical material from one's own particular concern about the research project, and will be thrust into dialogue with people who narrate this history as part of their identity. In some sense, there is a sacredness to history.

---

3. See LaCapra, *History and its Limits*, 67 for his poignant discussion of the use and abuse of empathy.

INTRODUCTION

Comprehending how important histories are to people, who continue to narrate these stories to their children and grandchildren, helps to prevent the shallow appropriation of the Other's narratives. In many cases, if people get a sense that someone is trying to appropriate their history for some type of personal gain, they will (and should) speak up. It takes time and respect in order to earn the trust to be able to write and speak about a history that is not one's own, considering how history is filled with tragedy. It is only with a sense of empathy that one may approach the Other's history. So how does one gain empathy?

Empathy is not something that just springs within one's soul one day, but a value that one must be fostered intentionally. It is to purpose in one's heart to step into the shoes of another person. This is a lifelong process through which one learns to foster compassion toward other living human beings. One will not be able to really comprehend the other person in order to be empathetic if one does not at first become a listener. Pity rather than empathy results from not listening properly to the diverse stories of history especially when it comes from the Other. History as a discipline is great in producing people who pause to listen, allowing empathy time to reach one's inner being.

An example of the role empathy plays in both history and theology comes from black liberation theologian James Cone's latest work *The Cross and the Lynching Tree*. Cone meditates on the ghastly historical events of lynching and connects then to the suffering of Christ on the cross. In short, Cone presents his work focused on both history and theology, never digressing to the point where either discipline could be comfortable without the other. However, what really stands out with regard to empathy is the way Cone juxtaposes the American theologian Reinhold Niebuhr and the German theologian Dietrich Bonhoeffer, who famously was executed by the Nazis for his role in a conspiracy to assassinate Hitler. On the one hand, Cone presents Niebuhr, who wrote many important things about the tragedy of history, especially for African Americans, but never seemed to cross the line of having (enough) empathy with them. Bonhoeffer, on the other hand, quickly connected to the African American church because of empathy. Bonhoeffer shows us the greater path.[4]

Bonhoeffer's life continues to be one that fascinates people, as the growing secondary literature attests. My own decision to pursue studies on Karl Barth was a result of reading my father's Bonhoeffer books in his home

4. Cone, *Cross and the Lynching Tree*, 40–43.

library. Barth's amazing historical witness together with his theology really captured my own youthful theological imagination. What continues to fascinate me is learning about other ways Bonhoeffer's life and work continues to inspire. For example, Buddhist monk Thich Nhat Hanh credits Bonhoeffer's prison works as a motivating factor for his own spiritual journey and prophetic witness in Vietnam during the war.[5] Examples like Bonhoeffer's make studying history an ethic of hope and joy, never knowing who else it may inspire and illuminate. In fact, it is Bonhoeffer's own words that serve as a sort of blueprint of this book: "We have for once learnt to see the great events of world history from below, from the perspective of the outcast, the suspects, the maltreated, the powerless, the oppressed, the reviled—in short, from the perspective of those who suffer."[6]

Sometimes I wonder if the collective amnesia of people or the necessity of asking why is history important connects to a fear of history. Do we ignore history because we are afraid of what it will tell us about ourselves? In other words, following Bonhoeffer's advice, are we afraid of looking back at the past filled with tragedy and violence especially for the marginalized? Historical consciousness disrupts narratives of exceptionalism and purity about religion, God, and the nation-state. For some it is better to live with amnesia than have their myths annihilated. One of my goals is to awaken the reader out of their ahistorical dogmatic slumbers.

The purpose of writing this book is to explore the way we read, teach, and write history especially as it relates to Christianity. I will refer to this relationship between these two disciplines as historical-theological thinking. Special attention will be given on the way we continue to discuss Christian history and its relation to theology. My wish is that we would get to the point where we would no longer speak about history or theology in the abstract but find ways to keep them in dialectical tension. The best aspects of both disciplines are when they do not forget to remember the past. It is primarily the job of historians to keep all of us from forgetting.[7] However, this is not a nostalgic looking back to the past but a view concomitantly

---

5. King, *Thomas Merton and Thich Nhat Hanh*, 79, 153–54. King's book on the great Christian and Buddhist mystics is the type of comparative study I hope to see more of in the future.

6. Bonhoeffer, *Letters and Papers from Prison*, 17. Also see Rivera-Pagán, *Essays from the Margins*, 43–44 for the place I discovered the Bonhoeffer quote.

7. Cone, *The Cross and the Lynching Tree*, 164–65. Cone specifically recalls how the United States has a sort of collective amnesia about the history of lynching. His book is a corrective toward this type of forgetting.

toward a hopeful future. Nostalgia privileges the good ole days, but forgets to ask if those days were great for everybody. When we finally are made aware of the crises in our midst, we realize there exists a trail left in history of where the problems started. Oftentimes we have simply forgotten. Moreover, it is true that the past is littered with tears, yet we must also not fall into the fallacy of presentism in thinking that the present and the future are so much more progressive than anything in the past. Tradition does not have to be a bad word.

We will first look at a couple of recent books on the subject in order to place this book in its context before outlining the contents of this study. These books address how important history, especially Christian history, is for the person of faith. However, there is a type of forgetting and tunnel vision found in much of this literature, and thus this book will serve to take the conversation forward.

Where Are the Voices of the Underside?

Historiography plays an important role for both historians and theologians. It deals with the way historians have written history in the past. It is not the study of history, but features the way historians study history (more on this topic in chapter 1). When looking specifically at Christian historians, what one finds lacking, in general, is attention toward the so-called darker nations.[8] Agreeing with theologian James Kameron Carter's diagnosis that the Western modern imagination considers those outside the theological canon as "theologically irrelevant" and "invisible" means that in order to move forward in understanding theology and history entails a sober study of these particular materials.[9] In fact, it is rather easy to repeat these historical patterns.

Earlier Christian evangelical studies of history dealt directly with the tension of faith and history, defending the historicity of the Bible and its events.[10] Written in the late twentieth-century, these books either anticipate or attempt to answer the postmodern, relativist suspicion of history. Recent studies have moved away from such concerns, and instead now focus on the importance of history in general. For example, John Fea's book

8. See Prashad, *Darker Nations*.

9. Carter, *Race: A Theological Account*, 378.

10. For example, see Brown, *History and Faith*; and Nash, *Christian Faith and Historical Understanding*.

Why Study History is an entry-level study that takes most of its examples from Anglo-American history, and Robert Rea's study *Why Church History Matters* is both a presentation of general church history and a defense on why the discipline matters for Christian churches.[11] What both Fea and Rea share is the belief that history is worth the effort of study. Specifically addressing an evangelical audience, they advocate the important discipline of the historian. Why, however, do historians continually need to ask the *why* question about their discipline? Does this question reveal the fact that people are not that interested in the past? Moreover, this question seems to be a particularly poignant one for *evangelical* historians, revealing that evangelicals in particular are not concerned with the past.

The answer to the why question is not the object of this book. The books listed above actually do a very good job addressing this issue. My concern is that questions and answers primarily dealt with in these books do not take into account two issues: first, the impact of modern racialization and its effect on history and theology; second, the increasing global perspective of Christianity and world history. In other words, the subject matter of this book is an even more complex dimension to the why question. Writers from the third world continually remind their readers how difficult it is to think outside of a Eurocentric framework. Therefore, imagine how hard it is for those of us raised within an Anglo-American and European system of education, oftentimes limited to the single story described by Adichie! Considering we continually ask why we need history, raising the topic of a more globally conscious history might be too premature. In other words, even in the twenty-first century, historians still need to write about the importance of the discipline of history, which connects well to the fact that we all seem to suffer from a memory problem, especially forgetful toward people different from ourselves. Thus, to expect an intense dedication of history toward global awareness is perhaps asking too much. However, a couple of examples might suffice to make the case for this exploration.

An important book that I fear is somewhat forgotten in our time is C. T. McIntyre's edited anthology *God, History, and Historians*.[12] This is the book that inspired me to dedicate years navigating the writings of theologians on the topic of history. McIntyre provides writings from the twentieth century that were part of a renaissance of sorts on the subject of faith

---

11. Fea, *Why Study History*; Rea, *Why Church History Matters*.

12. McIntyre, *God, History, and Historians*. Also see his essay "Ongoing Task of Christian Historiography," 51–74.

and history. The book features famous theologians across the theological spectrum, like Karl Barth, Reinhold Niebuhr, C. S. Lewis, and Georges Florovsky. Thus, we have selections from Catholic, Orthodox, Protestants, Europeans, and Americans. However, the most surprising contributor is the Latin American liberation theologian Gustavo Gutiérrez. McIntyre also includes a helpful bibliography for further reading that features other Latin American liberation thinkers. To my knowledge, this is the only anthology on Christian faith and history to feature a theologian from the Global South among mostly European thinkers.

McIntyre's book was published in 1977, so it is, in some regards, dated, and unfortunately, absent are contributions from women or other people of color. For example, why include Gutiérrez, yet nothing from black theologians like James Cone or Martin Luther King Jr.?[13] McIntyre's anthology does, however, illustrate if one wants to talk about God and history, the best way to accomplish this is by providing a diverse array of selections. The book's failure is that his selections were not diverse enough.[14]

The case that I am making in this book is that when theologians, and often historians, talk about the relationship between God and history, the discussion tends to be very Eurocentric. Eurocentrism is the centering of knowledge in particularly Western Europe, and since some see Christianity as evolving as part of the West, then the focus of Christian scholars is solely on Western materials. For instance, the figures featured in Lawrence Wood's book *God and History* are only European men (the book cover literally is covered with numerous headshots of white men).[15] The book does a good job summarizing centuries of discussions about God and history, yet it seems that non-Europeans have nothing important to contribute to our understanding of God and history. In some sense, it follows the same logic of Karl Löwith's classic Eurocentric book *The Meaning of History*.[16] Again,

---

13. See Douglas, *Black Christ*, 37–45 and 66–69 for references to the God of history in King and Cone; also see Shulman, *American Prophecy*, 97–129 for King's theistic prophecy, preaching on the God of history.

14. Another point to be made is that even though he has included a Latin American (Peruvian) theologian with Gutierrez, he is still somewhat a Eurocentric thinker much like the rest of the major Latin American Liberation theologians. We will explore this issue further in chapter 2.

15. Wood, *God and History*.

16. Löwith, *Meaning in History*. One way to deconstruct the people behind the meaning of history is to announce the African identity of St. Augustine, who is a crucial thinker of historiography.

no one west of the Atlantic is in this book either, yet Löwith is purposely mapping a particularly European reading of history in the first place. Löwith follows the logic of the modern European philosophers, claiming through silence that people of color have nothing to contribute to the meaning of history. In general, much of the meaning in history books written in the past one hundred years are woefully Eurocentric.

Perhaps I am arguing from a position of criticizing writers for their silence when they did not mean to exclude historical thinkers, especially those identified as ethnic minorities. For example, it would be ridiculous to conclude that since Löwith did not include any Americans in his survey he therefore had a deep, subconscious hatred of Americans! The probing of historians' or theologians' psyches to determine their hidden loves and hates is dangerous. In fact, it is not the job of the historian to get to the bottom of such a thing. Historians mostly work with texts. Texts tell us things. Sometimes texts can be ambiguous so historians will dedicate years to become a specialist on specific writings. Specialization is a comfortable place to speak about matters of familiarity, so historians generally write and teach from this location. For example, for a historian trained analyzing medieval literature of the tenth century, commenting about gender history in the nineteenth century is like entering a whole new universe. There is much to praise in the historian's caution about speaking too boldly about a subject matter to which they have not dedicated adequate time. Still, this does not excuse us from at least saying something or intentionally looking for diverse voices when even analyzing ancient or medieval texts, for that matter.

A sober view of Christian history is willing to finally listen to the diversity of narratives about this history. The turn to globalized Christianity is a good start, but attention to the horrors done in the name of Christ toward countless peoples needs to be dealt with.[17] Yes, we can celebrate Paul's epistles, Aquinas's genius, Teresa's courage, and Tutu's activism. However, we must answer for forced conversions, the Crusades, the Inquisition, and the Holocaust. It is in the light of these events that Gil Anidjar states the history of Christianity is filled with blood.[18] That is why I will focus on theologians and historians primarily from ethnic minorities or from outside the Anglo-American/European world. Following Enrique

---

17. The best examples of global Christianity are Sanneh, *Whose Religion is Christianity*; Jenkins, *The Next Christendom: The Coming of Global Christianity*.

18. Anidjar, *Blood*.

INTRODUCTION

Dussel's liberation program, this is a historical-theology that privileges the oppressed, making up the "immense majority" of the global population.[19] By following this tract, we will attempt to avoid what Sathianathan Clarke calls "western methodolatry."[20] For all the recent attempts to decolonize Western thought from their works, the impossibility of historical removal looms large, forcing the writers to, at the very least, raise awareness of not slavishly utilizing the ideas from the West. Consequently, to a large extent, I stand in amazement of Christian thinkers from these worlds, especially when the memory of slavery, genocide, and colonialism is not so distant. The fact that historians and theologians from outside Europe, or as minorities within the United States or Europe, focus on the living memories of oftentimes violent histories yet remain Christian is a testament to their faith. This faith is purposely historical because their identities are formed by this history. Considering that it seems evangelicals are constantly needing to be reminded that history matters, this book is committed to helping jump start a history lesson by using thinkers across the world. However, the purpose of this book is not simply to say that there are a number of thinkers outside the Western canon that the student should read, but rather it asserts that both the theological and historical output of these diverse thinkers presents a more dynamic understanding of both faith and history than found within the existing canon.

Remembering Lived Lives serves its purpose if it points outside of one's familiar world. The book supplements the other historiography books listed above in that it aims to fill in gaps of missing narratives.[21] Whereas contextual and liberation theologies critique the theological discipline for betraying historical praxis, this book will look critically at a historiography that does not give due diligence to histories outside of the European framework. However, it is not simply a supplement, but stands on its own as a future-oriented vision for studying history and theology. This is one reason the book features a mixture of historians and theologians. Taking a cue from McIntyre, theologians write about history and often their works cause repercussions outside of its discipline. To section off the discipline of theology from history, especially when it sometimes crosses over into its

19. See the list of the oppressed in Dussel, *Underside of Modernity*, vii.
20. Clarke, *Dalits and Christianity*, 11.
21. I have done my best to cite resources for students to begin the process of examining books and articles that will hopefully start the amelioration of historiography, especially of the Christian type.

territory, demands a historical response. Only an outdated secular viewpoint would see all theological talk as "religious studies" and all historical talk bound to an empirical, positivistic lens. Religious leaders, movements, and ideas shape and continue to impact history. For better or worse, theologies of history continue to be preached and followed by many, whereas historiography books collect dust on the shelf. However, in order to not frame this as a pugnacious relationship, the transparent crisscrossing of the works of theologians and historians needs to be encouraged. The integration of both disciplines, when appropriate, suggests a healthy dialectical relationship between the two.

Chapter 1 features advice from Swiss theologian Karl Barth for the theological and historical student. What may surprise readers is his uncanny advocacy for the openness of the reader of history. Remembered mostly for his uncompromising condemnation of liberal Protestant theology, he instead wishes that students of history remember past figures in their best light. Barth is read as a follower of a pessimistic reading of history, since he was forthright in his judgment upon German progressive interpretations of history. Barth's advice is important since many undergraduates walk into a history classroom ready to denigrate their theological foe (perhaps it is John Wesley, or, on the flip side, John Calvin). For instance, a potentially inspiring research paper is the one written by the Calvinist that writes a positive account of Wesley. Instead, Barth offers what I call a *neighborliness* reading of history. Starting the book with Barth's concern is a way to initiate the kind of critical thinking that makes studying history worth the effort. In some ways what he advocates is an empathic reading of history. An empathic reading of history is open, empirical, and humble in its goals. These goals are everything a history instructor wants in her students. In fact, we will turn this critical reading upon Barth's own Eurocentrism through the use of Latin American border-thinking and *mestiza* consciousness. In short, we will broaden his understanding of neighborliness to consider a more non-European Other.

An important problem connects an empathic historiography with a specifically Christian interpretation of history. The issue deals with the subject of eschatology. Eschatology is the doctrine of the last things (or days) for Christian systematic theology. At the close of chapter 1, we will briefly explore how a deterministic eschatological vision oftentimes problematizes a more empathic understanding of history. For example, some of the problems in a specifically Christian classroom for the history instructor consist

INTRODUCTION

of encouraging students that historical events in time and space, other than the life and times of Jesus Christ and his apostles, matter and have theological significance. By finding ways for historians and theologians, and their students, to dialogue about these issues, it allows us to move ahead and question Eurocentric models of understanding history.

Chapter 2 deals specifically with the problem of Eurocentrism. Even with historians continuing to revise history textbooks to accommodate a growing awareness of global historical consciousness, Eurocentrism is still a dilemma for both theology and history. At the heart of the issue is what W. E. B. Du Bois calls the propaganda of history. Therefore, Eurocentrism is an ideological problem. Moving into the realm of ideology involves exploring the complex world of critical theory. Perhaps many theologians and historians express consternation when theory invades their respective disciplines. Nevertheless, theory remains an important part of any discipline, whether it involves the classroom pedagogy or the methodology utilized in writing a scholarly journal essay. I will focus on two important theorists who feature as important voices in the Eurocentrism debate. The first is Edward Said as the representative of the anti-Eurocentrism, and the second is Slavoj Žižek as the promoter of Eurocentrism. The point of noting Eurocentrism suggests navigating toward theorists outside of the so-called Western canon, especially if one is interested in doing research in Latin America, Asia, or Africa. However, even if one wants to research a European topic, challenging Eurocentrism means looking at the scholars outside or on the edge of its borders.

After searching the works of specifically third-world thinkers like Enrique Dussel, Hamid Dabashi, Ignacio Ellacuría, and Sylvia Wynter, among others, we will address what Tsenay Serequeberhan calls the hermeneutical horizon. What seems obvious as this chapter unfolds is the crisscrossing of European and third-world philosophies. For example, Serequeberhan's use of hermeneutics transparently borrows from German philosophers Martin Heidegger and Hans Georg Gadamer, yet uses this method in the context of African philosophy. The fractured relationship between European and third-world ideas exists today, even with appeals from the European Right of the purity of the Western tradition, or from the Global South Left of exorcising Anglo-American and European thought through the decolonial process.

Chapter 2 reveals the heart of the book—we see the underside of modernity and help history find its voice. Historical theorists from Dussel,

Wynter, and Walter Mignolo attempt to narrate history from the perspective of the Americas in its relation to the Anglo-American and European worlds. Latin American theologians, including Dussel and Ellacuría, suggest the theological ramifications a focus on the marginalized of history holds. The main obstacle in exposing Eurocentric readings consists of the ease of unconsciously practicing it again, even when attempting to intentionally to do otherwise. Thus, remembering Adichie's call at the start of the book to intentionally listen to other stories remains a path for history to illuminate the great diversity of human life. In fact, reading about past lives is a first step down this road.

The topic of chapter 3 is about historical biography. Volumes of history books contain narratives about famous figures from the past. However, what is the purpose of reading about people? Does it consist in merely memorializing some famous figure, verging on the edge of hagiography? Are biographies meant to expose the hidden truths that authorized biographies are afraid to tell?

Theologian James McClendon attempts to link theology with historical biography. In fact, the title of this book gets its idea of "lived lives" from McClendon.[22] Biographies fill his systematic theology for the purpose of guiding ethical action. Some of the examples to pursue are the stories about Catholic martyrs in El Salvador, like Archbishop Oscar Romero, Ignacio Ellacuría, and the Maryknoll Sisters, in the late twentieth-century. Numerous theological and historical works continue to grow, remembering their Christian witness for future generations. Much like the growing literature built upon the witness of Martin Luther King Jr. and Dietrich Bonhoeffer, the martyrs from late twentieth-century Latin America serve as a fresh example from the third world on the crossing of the theological and historical disciplines. The main purpose of this chapter involves making the case of encouraging general readers, and specifically students in history courses, to read biographies of figures outside one's geographical horizon. In addition, autobiographies are especially good places to witness a grasping of agency of people across the globe. Whether it is a classic like *I, Rigoberta Menchu* or Dionne Brand's *A Map to the Door of No Return*, autobiographies give the reader an entrance to both a particular and communal account of history. To understand the global nature of Christianity demands knowing the stories from people across the globe.

---

22. McClendon, *Biography as Theology*, 37.

INTRODUCTION

From McClendon's use of biography, it is important to engage our contemporary genre of telling stories in movies. Finally, chapter 4 looks at the importance of film for history. Sometimes the only history we receive at the popular level is through the television, computer, or movie screen. This is not necessarily an awful thing. Instead of seeing films as compromising the sanctity of the historical discipline, we should utilize them to raise consciousness about our own particular historicity. I have selected Roland Joffé's film *The Mission* as an example of a historical film that continues to teach viewers valuable lessons from history. The use of film is a pragmatic choice of a tool that may inspire action and critical thought about an event that might otherwise seem dead on the pages of a textbook. There are a number of films that fulfill the same goal of raising historical consciousness. Because the focus is on use, this entails that the instructor and viewer is aware of potential problems that the use of images brings to the discussion, especially if the goal is inspiring empathy. The chapter closes with a meditation utilizing critical thinkers like Simon Gikandi, Susan Sontag, bell hooks, and Jean Franco on how the different affects might come from images of suffering.

The purpose of *Remembering Lived Lives* is not shock history, a common experience of exploring events in the past that seem so ghastly to the student she is amazed such a thing actually happened. It is, instead, to take the foreignness of history to another level. The job of historians is to make past events, even the most catastrophic, alive in the memory of the present, and future. But there is a danger. Piling up horrendous events one after another leads to a type of victimology of historical actors, or what Elizabeth Martínez calls "Oppression Olympics," especially when focusing on the marginalized.[23] Victimology often leads to the cornering of the academic market on a culture or event followed by a policing on who is allowed to write or discuss this history. Again, when reading about the Other's history, it is important to practice the art of listening with empathy especially to avoid appropriation. For many ethnic minorities, the history or theology they narrate is not just for academic purposes but also something they existentially experience, or something passed on by their family and community.

The focus on historians and critical thinkers that challenge the so-called Western canon does not mean they inhabit some kind of special aura of victimhood. The appeal in this book is to the fact that their narratives

23. Martínez, *De Colores Means All of Us*, 5.

are often forgotten stories, or, at the very least, ignored writings. We are inevitably wrapped up in our past, shaping who we have become, and by whom we will ultimately be remembered. The theologians who think their historicity does not matter when writing about church ethics are trapped by abstract logic, and any type of community espoused in their dogma is a false community. In addition, the historians who only focus on their specialization do not live in a globalized world but rather one separated into compartments.

Heeding James Baldwin's words in the epigraph is crucial in understanding our own particular historicity and the way we narrate history moving forward. As an African American writer, Baldwin made it a point to insist that forgetting history was not an option. However, he is also clear that history is not deterministic. In fact, this quote illustrates a pragmatic understanding of history that pays attention to the way the past continues to shape us, without compromising our agency to live and to act with purpose toward the future.[24]

---

24. See Glaude, Jr., *In a Shade of Blue*, 66 for more on Glaude's reading of Baldwin's pragmatic history. In fact, I contend that Baldwin may be one the most important historiographical thinkers in the last one hundred years.

CHAPTER 1

The Happy Historian

Diversifying Karl Barth's Advice to History Students

"There may be a religious West, but there is not a Christian West: there is only Western man confronted with Jesus Christ . . . It could well be that one day true Christianity will be understood and lived better in Asia and in Africa than in our aged Europe." —Karl Barth[1]

"Our present is not beset by skepticism, as people often claim, somewhat superciliously. It is beset by negation." —Jacques Rancière[2]

Why Karl Barth? There are two points to answer this question. First, I have spent a number of years studying him, writing about him, and even teaching him. However, just because I have some training in Barth studies does not mean he warrants a chapter in a book, the common theme being historical-theological literature outside Europe. As a matter of fact, it is pretty obvious from even a cursory reading of Barth that he is a Eurocentric thinker extraordinaire! Moreover, he is not generally recognized as the savviest historically minded theologian. His contemporaries Bultmann, Gogarten, and the Niebuhr brothers struggled with the impact of history in relation to faith pretty much all their lives. Therefore, again,

---

1. See Busch, *Karl Barth*, 468; also see page 459 for Barth's demythologized Statue of Liberty. There is an interesting comparison for what the Statue of Liberty symbolized for Asian American immigrants; see Okihiro, *Margins and Mainstreams*, 3–30.
2. Rancière, *Figures of History*, 4.

why Barth? This leads me to my other point. The focus on Barth's statements on history writing illustrates a coming of age for writing about history, and specifically the history of theology. Thus, even though Barth often does not focus on a world outside of the Bible or Europe, there is a trace in his writings that give us this option. We will, in fact, thank Barth for the good advice, and then turn his writings critically toward him.[3] Still, I really do believe that this is good advice that needs to be retold. This retelling of Barth's ideas sets up the model for this book: examining religious figures thoughts about history. As we will see, some thinkers are too brief on the subject of history or too Eurocentric in their views. The aim is to start with Barth, a figure anticipating a revolution in theoretical study, and to move toward contemporary times focusing on a number of religious theorists who begin with their social-historical context, purposely avoiding a Eurocentric viewpoint.

When I tell people I spent years studying Barth, first at Biola and then at Fuller Theological Seminary, I am often met with a number of responses. These responses are helpful in setting up the goal of this chapter. First the positive. Some congratulate me for spending years studying a great theological mind, arguably one of the most creative. Many find his theology a source of inspiration (myself included). However, there are negative responses. For example, a few deem Barth ahistorical and abstract. One group claims he was a subtle and dangerous radical while others cannot get past how conservative he was especially on social issues. On the basis of what they do not like, some will dump Barth's multivolume corpus into the trashcan. I have seen this trashcan reaction in the classroom many times to a number of different figures. Should the strong negative reactions for some about Barth make it so that he is forgotten from history? When we consider the positive and negative perspectives on Barth, we are left to ask which Barth is the real Barth? This question is why history is so important. It is a job of a historian to make sense of the different perspectives that build up over the years. And, even though social media and blogs can be illuminating at times, the best opinions are based on critical examination of the primary and secondary sources. One should own one's perspective on Barth, but stay challenged by the fact that opinions may change in the future.

3. In some sense, Barth's close associate Dietrich Bonhoeffer is perhaps the best recent European theologian to carry this conversation further. See a number of books cited in the bibliography for further study.

THE HAPPY HISTORIAN

My choice of Barth to discuss the historical-theological method is willful, revealing elements of my own perspective on matters of faith and history. Everyone approaches history with presuppositions. The texts I choose to include here reveal many of my own perspectives on the historical world. In his historical context, Barth wrote on faith and history with an eye toward the universal Christian church at a time when Europe was in turmoil. My belief is that to carry a historical-theological message forward we must pay close attention to a more globalized concept than Barth did. This means not just paying attention to contextual theologies across the third world, but also their histories. Eurocentric historical narratives have long ignored these stories, but much has changed in recent years.

The turning point of writing history is relatively new, probably about thirty years old. Sometimes it is labeled as "revisionist" history, by a few friends but mostly by foes. Sometimes revisionist history ends up aligned with ethnic studies, or some other part of the so-called culture wars. I remember growing up and hearing warnings about this ideology that dared to try to rewrite the history textbooks. The program behind this procedure was a creeping activism that upset the balance of neutral, fact based historical accounts. As stated in the Introduction, I am not interested in the postmodern challenge to historical objectivity, which popped up around the same time, nor to those defending some form of historical orthodoxy. There are volumes on this subject, yet mostly featuring Eurocentric thinkers.[4] Instead, my aim is on historical diversity, which fits real, flesh-and-blood, concrete history. Attention to the diversity of writers and sources outside of Europe should not be relegated to the margins and labeled as contextual, activist, liberationist, or revisionist, nor managed into some multicultural textbook where diversity is celebrated for its own sake, but where ethnic minorities are still presented as *the* victims. One of the reasons critical theory is relevant is because it has been a tool that marginalized writers have used consistently in the last forty years. Thus, when some dismiss theory as muddying the waters of pure historical scholarship, it reveals an indifference to literature written by diverse set of writers.

Most of the figures covered in *Remembering Lived Lives* write their historical-theological accounts in a mode of resistance. This is why they are often called divisive, refusing to parrot accepted truths from official narratives. They articulate significant points of scholarly information that

---

4. See Gilderhus, *History and Historians*, 132–40 for more on the culture wars and postmodernism.

is critical to both the disciplines of history and theology. My point, thirty years or so later, that the mainstream will practice history (and theology) better engaging the material of non-Eurocentric writers because often it is simply better academic work and closer to actual, concrete history. These counter-histories are important because they refuse to adopt standard narratives mostly about formerly colonized territories but instead generate their own histories from another point of view. In short, for all the complaining about revisionism, if the detractors read some of these books, they might have their own minds changed. This then leads to the question of who is the one carrying along their ideology. Let me give some personal examples to make this point.

An interesting dynamic developed in the classroom of my historiography class. At a time when my focus was on German historicism and Barth's historiography, my students pursued topics from all over the global map. It was from one student in particular that the name Ronald Takaki came up. The student had read Takaki at the high school or community college level, and since the assignment was about a biography of a historian, the student chose Takaki because his writings had really challenged this particular student.[5] When the biography was presented I was excited to see that Takaki was, in fact, a magnificent historian, and someone I should thus read. At the heart of Takaki's method is an attention to a multicultural reading of mostly United States history.[6] This multiracial perspective is what my students were practicing with their projects, in essence teaching this Eurocentric teacher a lesson about diversity. Now Takaki is a go-to historian for me when I teach US history.

---

5. At this point I should thank Dr. Judith Rood from Biola University for utilizing this assignment in her historiography class when I was her Teacher's Assistant. The beauty of this assignment is twofold. One, it pays close attention to the output and methodology of a particular historian, introducing students to a world of important historical thinkers. Two, it also allows the student to see how much a historian's particular perspective plays into their work, challenging the idea of neutral, objective history.

6. See Takaki, *A Different Mirror*. To some extent it is written in the same spirit as a people's history. The most famous example of people's history is Zinn, *A People's History of the United States*.

A good example of a historical-theological reading would be to take the work of a trained historian like Takaki on the subject of the bombing of Hiroshima and Nagasaki and compare and contrast it with the theological work of post-war theologians who struggled with the ethical implications of this historical event. For example, theologians like Moltmann have continually written about this tragedy and its theological and ecological meaning. For more on this subject see Kitamori, *Theology of the Pain of God*; and Takaki, *Hiroshima*.

My other example is from a conversation I had at work. The manager at the aerospace company I worked at while finishing school often discussed history with me. Since he was Japanese-American, there were numerous times he would point out my absolutely Eurocentric views of history. Now he was not a revisionist or a radical with regards to social-political thought (he loved Ronald Reagan!), but someone who knew enough history to clue me in on my narrow view of Eurocentric history. Looking back at these conversations, I see myself once as a naïve yet genuine Christian who understood the world with the narrative structure I had been taught. This narrative was both Christian and European, thrown in with a dash of American exceptionalism. There is nothing wrong with having a Christian view of history, or in enjoying the study of European history. What was wrong in my case was being grossly ignorant about anything outside my Western Christian narrative, assuming that Chinese history was simply some information that was comfortable on the periphery. A worse mistake would be to become grossly arrogant about this narrow narrative instead of studying the historical literature outside of the West any local library provides. These two personal examples illustrate that there are always times for teachable moments. It is up to the reader to seek out the information that is there to dispel historical or theological mythologies, or to listen to other people empathically as they tell you their own narratives.

History provides a way for one's historical consciousness to evolve from the intimacy or normalcy of one's early stages to the multiple layers of reality filtered through the continuing importance of past events. One of the main reasons I start with Barth is because his works were the means to the emergence of my own historical consciousness. His theology helped to release my thinking from forms of fundamentalist thought found in North American evangelical theology. Reading Barth in the summer before my junior year in college, then exploring his work in history for a Historiography class, set me on a course to engage the relationship between history and theology throughout graduate school and beyond. His theology is called crisis theology because it challenged the nationalist and positivist theologies of the late nineteenth century that led the world into World War I. Barth's arrival in the world of theology corresponded with coordinated efforts among third-world leaders, challenging the European social-political status quo. He was not a perfect man, but history does not give us perfect people. That is one reason why history is so important because it reminds us of the messiness of human beings.

In this chapter we will witness the evidence that the discipline of theology has not generally been good at receiving teachable moments. In fact, the recent major theological thinkers of the twentieth century like Karl Barth continued the problems of a Eurocentric view. Since Barth is somewhat canonized as arguably the greatest theologian of the twentieth-century, he is the perfect candidate to develop a historical-theological reading. How does one go about developing historical-theological thinking that focuses on ethnic minorities from a clearly Eurocentric theologian? I start with Barth because there are traces of historical-theology in his work. Focusing on these traces allows us to examine Barth's insights, and to critique Barth's blindness toward concrete historical otherness and diversity. For example, theologian Mayra Rivera points out how important Barth's theology of the Wholly Other God was in the early twentieth century, challenging the nationalistic gods of the European nations. However, without building upon his insights, Barth's God ends up so distant and abstract, that it proves difficult to connect to the otherness of historical human beings.[7] Barth's theology potentially ends up in a dualistic framework between God and creation, mirrored between the relationship between the self and the Other. My way of building upon Barth is to supplement his work with *mestiza* thinkers. James Cone might offer the best statement to fit with Rivera's concern and also take Barth's theology of revelation forward:

> And so the transcendent and the immanent, heaven and earth, must be held together in critical, dialectical tension, each one correcting the limits of the other. The gospel is *in* the world, but it is not *of* the world; that is, it can be seen in the black freedom movement, but it is much more than what we see in our struggles for justice. God's word is *paradoxical*, or, as the old untutored black preacher used to say, "inscrutable," a mystery that one can neither control nor fully understand. It is here and not here, revealed and hidden at the same time.[8]

Theologians work in history. Good theologians acknowledge this fact. Yet, it must be a history that pays attention to the diversity obvious to the sober viewer. Barth's theology is sober enough to be agnostic toward a totalizing philosophy of history that saw European progress as a sign of God's

---

7. Rivera, *Touch of Transcendence*, 4–5. Barth, and other Christian theologians, would argue that it was the incarnation that bridges this gap.

8. Cone, *Cross and the Lynching Tree*, 156. Cone admits that the God of history speaks through the black freedom movement, yet also cautions against the mystery of meaning in history.

entrance into history.[9] In fact, he was conscious of this problem almost to a fault! Moreover, he shares wise advice with future theologians and historians: take an open and charitable view toward the past. I call this Barth's *neighborly* reading of history. The focus on the neighbor is everything that is good about the idea of Christianity, and everything bad in the way history is littered with examples of the violence toward the neighbor committed by Christians in history. Barth's words are good but they are unfinished because he was trapped in his own cage of Eurocentrism. Even the best philosophical or theological accounts about the ethical discourse on the neighbor are often centered in Western Europe. An ethic of the neighbor does not require us to start the discussion by making a bogeyman out of the Muslim from the East or the Latino from the South. However, a European centered narrative sees non-whites as aliens. We are past this type of ethic with the rise of cultural studies, postcolonial theory, and other critical theories that have deconstructed the type of ethic Barth was working with. This will be clear as we examine Barth's theology of the near and far neighbor to close this chapter. The way to finish and complement Barth's work is to force an engagement with theorists across the globe, the many who live and practice border thinking, who write with better empathy about historical otherness. Thus historical-theological thinking will learn to navigate from Barth's abstract theology to one that values concrete history. In turn, critiquing Barth motivates a sharper reading of Christian eschatology and any forms of supercessionism. Denying the Jewish/Middle East/Mediterranean roots of Christianity is violence toward the Other. Eschatology that ignores non-Europeans or sees them as the enemy in the East goes against the neighborliness at the heart of Christianity. Eschatology is one form of Christian theology that should be historically minded, yet oftentimes is impossibly abstract or Eurocentric. This chapter will close with some brief thoughts on the subject.

Reading History with Barth

"Any knowledge of history that proved to be merely seeing, observing, establishing, is a contradiction in itself. Certainly the knowledge of human

---

9. See Jimenez, "Power Corrupts." Again, Barth, like many other Christian thinkers, rejects any form of evolutionism in history, suspicious of the overtly positive meaning given to the present-future while essentially viewing the past as backwards and barbaric.

action—and that is what history is about—involves seeing, observing, establishing, but not in isolated theory. The theory of practice is the only possible theory where history is concerned. It is a seeing, observing, establishing where we ourselves are taken up in a particular movement, taken up in an action of our own which somehow encounters, corresponds to or even contradicts the action of another. We know history in that another's action somehow becomes a question to which our own action has to give some sort of answer. Without this responsible reaction to being questioned, our knowledge of history would be knowledge of facts, but not of living people; it would not be history but a form of science." —Karl Barth[10]

"History has always been self-serving, polemical, and, very often, simply slovenly." —Marilynne Robinson[11]

History writing is not as easy as it may appear. There is a process of picking and choosing from sources to include in one's work. The fact of this selection process implies the importance and influence of the historian. The same could be said of the theologian. Whereas the theologian works primarily on sacred texts and their interpreters, historians pull from a variety of materials from the past. There are a host of possible subjects from the past for the historian. With the sub-disciplines of intellectual and cultural history, and critical theory as necessary options for the historian, especially one willing to engage third-world writers, history writing is a whole lot more complex than simply striving to record past events in a neutral and objective manner.[12]

What do historians do with materials of a religious nature? Do they take religious figures at their word when they talk about the transcendent? How do theologians understand the historicity of their religious texts? Do the biographies of Augustine, Aquinas, and Luther matter when teaching their theology? Not every historian is trained as a church historian and not every theologian is a historical theologian. My discussion here is directed to the historical and theological disciplines in general, yet still recognizing the contributions of the academic fields of church history and historical theology. On the one hand, there are far too many instances where a

---

10. Barth, *Protestant Theology*, 1–2.
11. Robinson, *Death of Adam*, 6.
12. See LaCapra, *History and its Limits*, 13–36.

historical biography of a famous person almost totally ignores the figure's religious persuasion, or on the other hand, a biography written by a religious believer twists history like a pretzel in order to make his historical hero an evangelical! Therefore, sometimes matters get complicated when these two disciplines meet together in the arena of either history or theology. The Swiss theologian Karl Barth wrote about this very relationship that may help us to navigate understanding this relationship in the twenty-first century.

Barth opens his lectures on nineteenth-century Protestant theology with a short chapter on the task of studying past theologians. He writes this in the light of the dawn of European historicism.[13] Barth illuminates at least three points that help guide us on the study of history. First, Barth posits a subjective/existential view of history because history is a dynamic, living entity. Second, he asserts that historical study should be non-judgmental. Finally, in order to make sense of history in general, Barth insists on periodization. We shall now examine these three points in short detail.

First, Barth says that history is not closed but, in fact, features living people who speak to us in the present. He states that "Augustine, Thomas Aquinas, Luther, Schleiermacher and all the rest are not dead, but living. They still speak and demand a hearing as living voices;" even though the theologians Barth list may be physically dead, these living voices are the "subject-matter of history."[14] Because history consists of living voices, the study of history cannot conform to simply studying abstract facts. It is impossible, according to Barth, to be a passive onlooker of history. These living voices serve to question the choices and actions we make in the present. In other words, there is a sort of responsibility for which we are held accountable by voices of the past.

---

13. Davaney, *Historicism*, 1–65 for an overview. Historicism is defined by Kathryn Tanner in the Foreword as "the recognition of the conditioned, located, particular, and relative character of all human thought and experience, including the religious."

14. Barth, *Protestant Theology*, 2–3. Also see McIntire, *God, History, and Historians*, 390–442 for Henri-Irénée Marrou's and Georges Florovsky's essays on history being an encounter with living beings. Like Barth, they see the historical subject like God as the Other. My future plans is to explore the role of the Other in history among these three historical-theologians. In some sense, Florovsky could have replaced Barth in this chapter since he was a historian and follows much of what Barth advocates here. In fact, his eschatology and sense of ecclesiology in history might have been a better connecting point to third-world literature than Barth's work. However, I came to Florovsky late, and again, I am all too familiar with the positive and negative of Barth's history.

Barth's view of history focuses on the present. He claims we only care about history when it directly has some concern for us in the present. In this way Barth's presentism connects with Walter Benjamin's theses on history where he states that "every image of the past that is not recognized by the present as one of its own concern threatens to disappear irretrievably."[15] Because of the "changing" nature of the present, we must approach history as open, continually working "to begin from the beginning."[16] This is an important issue Barth raises especially toward those who wonder why we should study history? The past effects the present in powerful, but often unrecognizable ways. Barth warns that "eminent historicity" presents a problem because its nature consists of the very recent past.[17] Since recent time often features things people in the present reject, these recent living voices can be easier to resist or to dismiss. Critical theories often deconstruct and challenge the recent past in such a way that it can blind us to the fact that we are often utilizing the very theoretical tools they gave us.

How do we understand history if we do not comprehend the present? In other words, if we buy into the cynicism and skepticism of the present age then how will we be able to hear the living voices of history that Barth accounts for? We have the tendency to make the past conform with whatever preconceived notion we have of it in the present instead of listening to the real voices of the past. This is an issue that writer Marilynne Robinson writes about with great clarity. There is not only a collective amnesia toward the past that is prevalent, but also a certain prejudice toward the present against anything in the past simply because it is the past. In short, if something from the past does not agree with present sentiments then it is forgotten or attacked. Robinson counters: "A complex view of history must necessarily reincorporate in it lovely and credible things, simply because the record attests to them, as well as to venality and hypocrisy and vulgarity. It is clearly true that the reflex of disparagement is no more compatible with rigorous inquiry than the impulse to glorify."[18]

---

15. Benjamin, *Illuminations*, 255.
16. Barth, *Protestant Theology*, 2–3.
17. Ibid., 4.
18. Robinson, *The Death of Adam*, 26. Robinson shows how uncompromising readings of history affect the way we read (or do not read) certain figures. She makes this point by focusing on the way some historians like Lord Acton, Roland Bainton, and Max Weber interpret Calvin and Calvinism poorly (some discussion of Jefferson and Marx are also included). Her excellent essays on Calvin (and the fascinating character Marguerite de Navarre) illustrate the way she humanizes the stereotypical representation of

History casts a long shadow. It takes years to determine how past events might affect the future. This is one of the sober lessons of history. The present can feel like a time when many first-time events have occurred. Barth's attention to the living dimension of history reveals a neighborliness toward its characters. For history lovers this idea makes sense because it is impossible to interact with the material in a boring way. A relationship develops between the materials of history and the reader that takes on properties of a flesh and blood commitment.

Second, Barth advocates a reading of history featuring openness. Barth writes: "To hear someone else always means to suspend one's own concern, to be open to the concern of the other. Care will always be taken that this openness is not too wide. But the demand directed towards us, that we must know and may not evade, here or elsewhere, by qualifying it and weakening it, is for openness."[19] One of the reasons Barth published his work on history was to challenge his students not to be too close-minded and too condemning toward figures in the past. He feared that too many of them had become comfortable in their theological systems, missing the point of what Jacob Taubes calls Barth's "dialectical character of theology" that "must remain an open discourse and cannot close itself in a self-sufficient system."[20] The works of the figures of the past are handed down to us "defenseless" because they are dead, and thus should not "be used simply as a means to our ends."[21] Barth clearly saw a problem with his students dismissing the work of the past, many of them thinking they were faithful to his theology of crisis. However, Barth was not promoting a relativist reading of history.[22] He clearly states that both he and the other

---

Calvin for the modern reader (174–226). As someone whose faith and intellect was first challenged by a reading of Calvin's *Institutes* and his biblical commentaries, I wholeheartedly recommend Robinson's book.

19. Barth, *Protestant Theology*, 10; also, see xii.

20. Taubes, *From Cult to Culture*, 179–80. Taubes, as a Jewish intellectual, is one of my favorite Barth interpreters. See Jimenez, "Power Corrupts" for Taubes's critique of Barth's theological historicism.

21. Barth, *Protestant Theology*, 8.

22. See Ginzburg, *History, Rhetoric, and Proof*, 1–25 on the problem of relativism in historiography. He sees Nietzsche's work as the main culprit. See Jimenez, "Power Corrupts," for Barth's relationship to Nietzsche. As we will see next chapter, third world authors oftentimes criticize postmodern relativist historiography, focused as they are oftentimes on the concrete horrors of colonial violence. In some sense, the cynicism and skepticism of the present age is faithful to Nietzsche's ideas. However, much like Burckhardt's pessimism, Nietzsche's cynicism is tempered by his appreciation of classical

have a *concern*, and that this position of openness does not become too wide. As Taubes pointed out, Barth's work, both theological and historical, lived with a dialectical tension.

Barth warns us about taking one's own theological positions as the universal standard against the past. The worst type of history writing is to chronicle the past only to end up with your own position as some type of utopian end of history. For example, one could declare a person a theological heretic in an attempt to forever silence his or her voice. Barth insists that approaching history as a "proclamation of judgment" will be a "detriment" to the future of Christianity.[23] He declares that heretics, pagans, and figures from other faiths must be given a fair reading because one is not in a position to judge who is an insider for speaking to the present.[24] Barth remains consistent in criticizing any attempt at a God's eye point of view of history, because he reads history theologically.[25] One can never guess who or what God will use to speak to the present state of Christianity. Barth writes: "History is meant to bear witness to the truth of God, not to our achievements, so that we must avoid any thought that we already know what they have to say and be prepared to hear something new."[26] In short, if we only read and teach about voices from the past that we approve of, then where will the challenges come from? If we do not have an open view of the past (and the present) are we missing teachable moments about both God and humanity?

Barth's declaration of openness is a major point for *Remembering Lived Lives*. If we decide to only research or learn about the cultures we are already familiar with then we do ourselves a great disservice. We end up missing many of the resources of the globalized world. We prematurely close off historical and theological materials because they do not fit into some predetermined canon. This is one of the main points in Barth's method of a neighborly reading of history. To be truly open means to be truly willing to pause and listen to historical voices no matter the source.

---

culture (definitely not Christian culture).

23. Barth, *Protestant Theology*, 9.

24. Ibid., 3.

25. McIntire, *God, History, and Historians*, 205–23 for on the one hand, Barth's agnosticism toward any philosophy of history, and on the other hand, Barth's position on God's providence over creation from the basis of revelation not history. I cover this same material in Jimenez, "Power Corrupts." See Barth, CD III/3, 3–57 for the original source material.

26. Barth, *Protestant Theology*, 8.

Barth's agnostic caution about a philosophy of history is a necessary corrective of the view of God's judgment on history espoused in Steven J. Keillor's book *God's Judgments: Interpreting History and the Christian Faith*.[27] Keillor must be commended for at least being bold in criticizing some of the policies and actions by the United States, concluding that God's judgment is behind such events as the British Burning of Washington in 1812, the Civil War, and 9/11. Theologians throughout the centuries talk about God's judgment all the time, but for a Christian historian to make this claim is something special. Contemporary historians, even the evangelical ones, often solely dwell on the cold hard events of history, not mentioning God's potential role. In this sense, Keillor attempts to revitalize the prophetic language of Lincoln with regards to US history. However, I am suspicious of the lack of minority perspectives throughout his book. The best example of prophetic history is evident among African-American theologians like Martin Luther King Jr., James Cone, and even Malcolm X.[28] Why are their voices silent in a book that spends pages on the sin of slavery? Furthermore, when Keillor rails against liberalism and postmodernism, I suspect that he is yearning for an era where history can be read in black and white. Is this also an era where actual black voices, regardless of religious affiliation, were kept at the margins? To Keillor's credit, his advocacy of God's judgment takes aim at both conservative and liberal social-political identities, the political Right and Left, so his God does not play partisan politics. Nevertheless, there is a clear danger in being too optimistic about reading God's judgement toward one set of historical circumstances and not toward another. Perhaps I am just exercising my historian's caution about *knowing* the hand of God in history.[29]

---

27. Keillor, *God's Judgments*. The fact that dean of evangelical historians, Mark A. Noll, writes the Foreword to the book adds instant respectability. In fact, the book is a nuanced way to talk about God's judgment in history in academia as opposed to the knee jerk declarations of televangelists.

28. For a study detailing the prophetic, jeremiad voices in US history, see Shulman, *American Prophecy*.

29. In some sense, the historian (and theologian) should exercise caution in presenting God as directly involved in the events of history. The rhetorical use of this idea is found throughout history used by both prophets and presidents. However, when we resort to this language we often pick moments that are convenient to us, seeing God act in history in some moments while non-committal at other times. This forces both the historian and theologian to have to answer the why question. See Borg, *The Heart of Christianity*, 66–67 for more on the problem of divine intervention. Again, Barth's ambiguity and antipathy toward a philosophy of history (and frankly even somewhat toward a

Perhaps a better voice that might temper our enthusiasm of Barth's exhortation for openness is Barth's contemporary W. E. B. Du Bois.[30] Du Bois must be considered one of the great "superhistorians" of the recent past.[31] James Cone presents him as a "man of deep faith" with a radical concern for the plight of African Americans.[32] This *concern* was the type that did not allow him to hold a relativist understanding of history. With regards to the role of the historian, Du Bois writes that he cannot "distort the facts" especially for the nationalist "idea that evil must be forgotten, distorted, skimmed over."[33] This concern of hiding the flaws of national heroes presents a real challenge not to just each national history, but even for the narrative of Christian history. The history of textbook writing reveals sometimes a conscious effort to present a nationalist history in the best light. Focusing on the black experience in the United States, Du Bois was one of the first historians to reveal agenda driven histories. Unfortunately this type of agenda driven history is still with us today. When the absolute horrors of the American slavery system is sugarcoated with terms like "workers" instead of the word "slaves" in textbooks or when commentators state that the slaves were actually well cared for by their masters there is a not so subtle attempt to downplay the violence of the slave system and its inevitable affects across history.

According to John Barker, Du Bois envisioned "history as a tool for making history anew" by being one of the pioneers in the history of American minorities.[34] Du Bois closes his study of Reconstruction, published in 1935 around the same time Barth was giving his history lectures in Germany, illustrating the false characterization of African Americans by white historians. The trend to be non-judgmental and scientific by these historians produced an account of American slavery that glossed over the inhumanity of the institution. Discussing the history of slavery and Reconstruction by

theology of history) balances a belief that God does have the capacity to reveal Godself to creation, yet the creation cannot be absolutist or dogmatic about this revelation because of our human limitations and the mystery of the being of God.

30. See Carter, "An Unlikely Convergence" for a historical-theological comparison between Barth and Du Bois.

31. Barker, *Superhistorians*, 239–67. The fact that Du Bois is given a chapter among the typical European figures makes it a model for the type of historical works I am advocating in this book. Also see Breisach, *Historiography*, 367–68.

32. Cone, *Cross and the Lynching Tree*, 101.

33. Du Bois, *Black Reconstruction of America*, 722.

34. Barker, *Superhistorians*, 266.

American historians, Du Bois declares that "we fell under the leadership of those who would compromise with truth in the past in order to make peace in the present and guide policy in the future."[35] Therefore, Du Bois uncovers a form of propaganda of American history in his study of the written histories on the subject. In short, at what price for the peace of the present, and for whom? His historiography illustrates a picking and choosing of historical sources that betray an honest account of concrete history. Barker correctly notices that Du Bois pioneers the critique of so-called unbiased history based on the subject of race, serving as a turning point in historiography for giving agency to African Americans.

Why bring in the histories by Keillor and especially Du Bois at this point? Du Bois writes with an element of surprise and disappointment at the prejudicial view of white historians. The basic humanity of African Americans serves as a presupposition for how he read history, a fact missing from the accounts he uncovered. Therefore, there needs to be maintained a point when history, written in the present, is sometimes rightly judgmental. Barth's warnings about not judging from the vantage point of the present are important because the historian (and theologian) might think it is her duty to dismiss the past as backwards or superstitious prematurely. However, there are elements of the past that weigh heavy on the present, which arguably require conscious exorcising of its evil trace and truth telling for the betterment of humanity. For example, what benefit does it serve future generations to attempt impartiality with regards to the Holocaust, African slavery, or the Spanish conquest of the Americas? Barth's theology of crisis views God's judgment upon human history in general, but he opens himself to an interpretation of silence toward particular acts of history with his reserve toward reading God's revelation in concrete history outside of his Christological focus. Therefore, Du Bois's exhortation of ethics in history writing serves as a corrective of Barth's agnostic reading of history. Du Bois is worth quoting in full:

> If history is going to be scientific, if the record of human action is going to be set down with that accuracy and faithfulness of detail which will allow its use as a measuring rod and guidepost for the future of nations, there must be set some standards of ethics in research and interpretation. If, on the other hand, we are going to use history for our pleasure and amusement, for inflating our national ego, and giving us a false but pleasurable sense of

---

35. Du Bois, *Black Reconstruction in America*, 727.

accomplishment, then we must give up the idea of history either as a science or as an art using the results of science, and admit frankly that we are using a version of historic fact in order to influence and educate the new generation along the way we wish.[36]

Du Bois's appeal for ethics requires a sober look at the past and the present for the sake of future generations. We may not like to see our national or Christian heroes of the past judged for their sins, yet Du Bois rightly points out that historical truth telling has a liberating affect to deal with concrete human crises in history. Barth's theology of crisis similarly judged the previous generation for compromising the Christian faith for nationalist glory. However, Barth continued to critically respond with a plea for openness against those in the present who were too self-confident in their dismissal of nineteenth-century theology. Moreover, because of his focus on race, Du Bois's critique fits nicely in further challenging Eurocentric history, whereas Barth is woefully inadequate. In fact, Du Bois's sense of the prophetic, truth-telling aspect of history cautions against a neighborliness that is too abstract.

Too much neighborliness and openness can cover over the real adversarial aspects of historical events. Barth's presentism does, however, reveal a forward movement of hope to a better world. Our ethical choices occur in the present, with the past serving as a landscape of examples of the very good and the very bad. We should realize from the historical evidence that there has been progress in some areas and some regression in others. Even the sense that we talk about a more global view illustrates the openness toward history Barth speaks of even though he did not form an adequate view himself. As we will see in the next section of this chapter, Barth had a dated, uncritical view of national identity that was arguably Eurocentric.

Finally, Barth advocates periodization as means to provide order and structure to historical events. Historians use periodization in order to create a coherent narrative of events for people to study in the present. History textbooks use periods to divide chapters for students to make reading history a coherent practice. The periods we often associate with history are usually composed following a consensus by other historians. Barth writes, "In historical knowledge, periodization is always the announcement of a hypothesis the proof of which is to be given afterwards, and this proof can only be given if one works with it and in this way allows it to speak

---

36. Du Bois, *Black Reconstruction in America*, 714.

for itself."[37] A good use of periodization takes note of the real differences between the past and the present, yet views these events within a unified narrative. Barth makes this point because history is a dynamic, living thing that needs to be understood in different stages. According to Barth, the organic understanding of history as a living thing is applied to Christianity to illustrate the dynamic nature of this tradition.

The history of Christianity provides events that illustrate a unity of the past with the present and future expressions of Christianity. Christian history is given an eschatological meaning because it has a beginning and an end due to its association with biblical prophecy. The linear view of history so prevalent in the historical discipline is due to its Christian roots. Barth says that Christian history illustrates "real historical knowledge of another period must consist in an awareness of its peculiarity and otherness, of its subsidiary themes, as well as the main theme which it shares with us."[38] Periodization is a helpful tool to outline over two thousand years of Christian history, yet the historian must be aware of its "somewhat artificial" nature.[39] Concepts like the Renaissance or the Industrial Revolution are used to generalize about a number of different historical events, the historian artificially applying meaning and structure. In addition, Barth insists that "under the presupposition of the unity of the Church" we should study "the particular context" of some event in the past on its own terms.[40] Barth goes to great lengths to note that to be faithful to historical figures means to understand them on their own terms. This takes great historical attention to details since it is so easy to read into the past our own concerns of the present, twisting the words of the past to fit an agenda in the present.

Barth's periodization appears as a historical-theological explanation of historical events. He believes that a sovereign God provides a unity to the historical events that deal somehow with Christianity. Therefore, Barth claims that even figures or groups that we might not consider real or authentically Christian in our present day must still be considered part of the unity of Christian history. Again, since this is about perspective, the

---

37. Barth, *Protestant Theology*, 12. Barth advocates creating a synchronous chart of both historical and theological events to help map out the connections in history.

38. Ibid., 15.

39. See González, *Church History*, 11–22 for an example of periodization, one that pays attention to the global aspect of Christianity. A good example of this attention is his work on the events surrounding the Spanish Conquest around 1492 and the fact that many church histories ignore it; see 67–76.

40. Barth, *Protestant Theology*, 15.

historian must be willing to be open to new interpretations or texts. Stating this point illustrates the judgment call we sometimes make unconsciously about figures and events in history. If we buy into theories that true Christianity was missing from certain periods of history, then God's sovereignty over history is compromised. Again, this is a theological point about human history, a faith belief that cannot be proven through empirical means. This does not take away from the fact that many people follow Barth in viewing history from some type of faith commitment.

Barth's periodization features a particularly Protestant and European reading of history. In this sense it feels dated and unaware how, in fact, global Christianity was even in the thirties.[41] Even when he advocates a "unity of perplexity and disquiet, but also a unity of richness and hope" to Christian history, it tends to maintain diversity within the European world.[42] Therefore, in order for historical study of Christianity to progress to a place where it mirrors the multiplicity and diversity of global Christianity, future historical-theological thinkers must work with a periodization that takes seriously the figures, events, and literature outside the European canon. Moreover, it will challenge the way we define periods for the sake of a more ethical framework. For example, defining Columbus's voyages as "conquest" and not the innocuous term "discovery" takes into consideration what this event meant for most of the people living in the Americas and Africa in 1492. This is a subject we will spend great time on in the next chapter. We will close this chapter by looking at some examples of this type of historical-theological literature. In order to understand Barth's position with regards to this literature, we will need to examine Barth's theological understanding of peoples outside of his European framework.

Barth's Far and Near Neighbor at the Borderlands

The early twentieth century features at least two general narrative tracks from history. One is European; the other is from the third world. There are European philosophical continuities and discontinuities found in the third-world story. The fact that the European story comes to a screeching halt because of its global wars characterizes their track as a pessimistic reading of history. The other track is optimistic since it features the rise of third-world independence movements, giving a voice given to the wretched of the earth,

41. Sanneh, *Whose Religion is Christianity*, 1–6.
42. Barth, *Protestant Theology*, 13.

THE HAPPY HISTORIAN

the underside of modernity.[43] The third-world narrative defines itself as an emancipatory project that eventually yields the postcolonial world. Barth belongs to the European narrative, and even though he will optimistically proclaim Christ as the center of history, there is enough of a negative mood in his work that makes him very much a part of his European context.

Barth's work originates during the carnage of World War I, forever linked with other books written from a growing pessimism toward the West.[44] If Barth's name is found in history textbooks at all he is listed with such European figures as Sigmund Freud, Arnold Toynbee, José Ortega y Gasset, Martin Heidegger, and Oswald Spengler. For example, Spengler's work *The Decline of the West* summarizes well the general mood of European intellectuals at the time. When Barth exhorts his readers to turn to the Wholly Other God, he is imploring them to end European tribalism, and forsake their nationalistic gods. The sudden realization that Western society was failing and coming to an end by European intellectuals like Spengler and Freud, was music to the ears of third-world thinkers pushing for independence from European colonialism. The fact that this freedom was not going to come easy was one reason why an optimistic yet critical Marxist view of historical progress and the birth of liberation theology was rampant in the third world. In some sense, many nations of the third world convinced themselves of the applicability of a totalized view of history through its emancipatory projects, the types of systematic thinking that pessimistic Europeans were attempting to abandon. The modern project did not simply vanish, but Fascism and Stalinism were the death knell of totalizing socialpolitical projects in the West. While these totalitarian movements were the focus of reflective Europeans, third-world thinkers, like Aimé Césaire, saw European colonialism as a symptom of a "sick civilization."[45] As seen in the opening epigraph, Barth's own questioning of the legitimacy of Europe's hold on Christianity was inspiration for theologians across the globe.

43. See Prashad, *Darker Nations*; Chopp, *Praxis of Suffering*, 7–27 and 134–48; Haynes, *Religion in Third World Politics*.

44. Breisach, *Historiography*, 397–403; Löwith, *Meaning in History*, 97–100. Breisach follows McIntire in including Latin American Liberation theologian Gustavo Gutierrez in his list of Christian examples of world history. Löwith list writers Burckhardt, Nietzsche, Tolstoy, and Dostoevsky as prophets on the decline of the West, who, consequently, were all influential on the early Barth.

North American pessimism can be seen in the Beats movement of the 1950s, who read Spengler as inspiration; see Lardas, *Bop Apocalypse*, 33–77. This led to another religious vision among Kerouac, Ginsberg, and Burroughs other than white Protestantism.

45. Césaire, *Discourse on Colonialism*, 39.

Thus Karl Barth's theology had a greater impact on twentieth century intellectual thought than given credit. For example, Samuel Moyn's book on the origins of Emmanuel Levinas's concept of the Other reveals that this idea has its roots in the Protestant work of the Wholly Other God of both Søren Kierkegaard and Barth.[46] Speaking historically, this fact might interest some, but in what ways can we extend Barth's concept of the Other toward the horizontal level between human beings or specifically to the concerns of the twenty-first century?

In fact, Latin American theologians have explored ways to discuss divine and human relations utilizing Barth's terminology. For instance, Mayra Rivera's book *The Touch of Transcendence* presents a relational transcendence that features a concept of God close to Barth's understanding in his Romans commentary. However, she is careful to state that although God may be Other and different from God's creatures, this point should not ignore or dissolve the real differences among God's creatures.[47] Still, Robert McAfee Brown, one of the most important chroniclers of Latin American liberation theology, sees continuity between Barth and liberation theologians with their concern for the victims of history and the God who sides with the oppressed.[48]

Building upon Rivera's reading of Barth's God, I want to focus on the place where Barth actually deals with real differences between human beings. In some sense we can see Barth's concept of neighborliness in action. In his *Church Dogmatics* III/4, the ethical section of his doctrine of creation, Barth distinguishes between the near neighbor (in the nation) and the distant neighbor (other nations, the whole of humanity).[49] It is the relationship to the distant neighbor that I want to connect to the idea of "border thinking" as posited by Rivera, Walter Mignolo, and Gloria Anzaldúa, among others. Since the genesis of modern history was formed around the birth of the European nation-state (nationalism), studying Barth's idea of national identity is helpful in revealing his Eurocentric blindness.

Barth uses spatial concepts to distinguish the near neighbors from the distant neighbors. The near neighbors are the people you are close to in

---

46. Moyn, *Origins of the Other*, 113–63.

47. Rivera, *Touch of Transcendence*, 1–5.

48. Brown, "Good News From Karl Barth," 99–100. Also see Villa-Vilencio, *On Reading Karl Barth in South Africa* for similar use of Barth's theology in apartheid South Africa.

49. Barth, CD, III/4: 285–323.

an immediate, cultural way. The far neighbors are defined outside of this sphere. The near neighbors are not particularly one's family since Barth has addressed this relationship in an earlier section, which regards different ethical questions than simply how one is addressed by God in one's national and cultural location.⁵⁰ Therefore, Barth proceeds to define a person in a particular, historical sense through the family, followed by his or her nation. In short, speech, location, and a nation's history are what define a person's standing toward the near neighbors. It is from the place we call home that we can then encounter the far neighbors.⁵¹

Barth writes that once we are aware of our own socio-cultural place in the world we then relate "consciously or unconsciously on the borders of so many others."⁵² The nearness we experience with those close to us is measured by the peculiar world outside. Barth is careful to express that these borders are fluid and dynamic. We should always be on the way toward encountering the neighboring Other outside. In other words, there is no special "unique" identity for any particular nation at the expense of a foreign nation.⁵³ For Barth, God is the Lord of all history, including all of humanity. Therefore, Barth reveals that our concern grows from the immediate, particular experience among the near neighbor toward the external, far neighbor.

How does one actually show concern toward the foreign, distant neighbor? Barth's theology of the neighbor presents at least two examples I would like to reflect on. First, Barth asserts that one should not let language be a "barrier" to communicate with the Other. In short, he claims it is the imperative of one ethically commanded by God to take the first step toward trying to understand and comprehend the distant neighbor. He goes as far as saying that one's language should not be a "prison" for us and a "stronghold" toward the Other.⁵⁴ Would this appeal by Barth translate in citizens in the US learning Spanish efficiently enough to communicate with the ever growing Spanish speaking community? What would Barth make of Kenyan writer Ngũgĩ wa Thiong'o advocating the abandonment of English in order to escape the colonial past?⁵⁵

50. See Rashkover, *Revelation and Theopolitics*.
51. Barth, CD, III/4: 291.
52. Ibid., 287.
53. Ibid., 296.
54. Ibid., 290–91.
55. See Thiong'o, *Decolonising the Mind*; Gikandi, "On Culture and the State."

Secondly, Barth suggests the doors (not walls) of a nation should be open to the foreigner. Whether this is simply a conscious decision to have a general consciousness or concern for the neighbors across the world, without the actual, physical departure from one's home, or in the concrete openness in neighborly practice toward the visiting foreigner to one's home community, Barth is clear that one should never block the encounter with the far neighbor.[56]

Barth's concept of the near and far neighbor takes place at the center of the European world. He writes from a Swiss cultural-linguistic world. Much of his concern for expressing openness to both the near and far neighbor is his past experience of the rise of the Nazis in Germany and the way they preached a national, unique god in contrast to their enemies. Much like Emmanuel Levinas, the Nazi experience provided an ethical example of how language about the Other can be a context for much violence toward the Other. The focus on one's particular nation's history is a strong point for those who think they can naively escape it.[57]

At certain points in Barth's voluminous work he notes the sins of modern Europe toward its distant neighbors. In his *Ethics* of 1928 he proclaims:

> When members of the white race all enjoy every possible intellectual and material advantage on the basis of the superiority of one race and the subjection of many other races, and of the use that for centuries our race has made of both, I myself may not have harmed a single hair on the heads of Africans or Indians. I may be friendly toward them. I may be a supporter of missions. Yet I am still a member of the white race which, as a whole, has obviously used very radically the possibility of appropriation in relation to them. My share in the sin against Africa or Asia for the last hundred or fifty years may be very remote or indirect but would Europe be what it is, and would I be what I am, if that expansion had never happened?[58]

What Barth notes in this passage is his own complicity of white, European privilege simply from the fact of being born as a near neighbor among imperialist Europeans. Moreover, this is a history that he realizes he cannot detach himself from, but that God ethically demands he encounter. However, in his account of the near and far neighbor, race, gender, nor class

---

56. Barth, CD, III/4: 294.
57. Ibid., 295.
58. Barth, *Ethics*, 164.

have a role to play in this discussion. This illustrates how Barth's historical context, working before the cultural revolutions in the sixties, perhaps limits the application of his neighbor ethic.

Does Barth trap himself into a static, dualistic view of history by presenting it from the vantage point of one nationalist identity in relation to another nationalist identity? Is national identity really a standard to judge human relations? What about the mass differences of culture within one's nation and among one's near neighbors? Does he show his Eurocentrism by theologizing about a myth of nationhood status? Does our current globalized reality transform the proximity of the near and far neighbor? How do the cultures of the near and far neighbors translate? We will use the postcolonial terms of hybridity and border thinking to update Barth's reading of neighborliness among human beings.

Opening Barth's Eurocentric Borders

"Identity is more fragmented and fractured than unified or singular. It is constructed across different and often intersecting and oppositional positions and practices. A postcolonial theory of hybridity, then, seeks not to claim origin or roots but to claim multiple routes." —Wonhee Anne Joh[59]

"Multicultural society is a fact; there is no being for or against it."
—Tariq Ramadan[60]

Dualistic frameworks for all walks of life do not work because something ends up missing. Life is messy, full of welcomed and unwelcomed encounters. Whether it is history or theology, using a methodology based off of Europe and its Other ends up denying the reality of places like Latin America. In historian Peter Burke's recent survey *Cultural Hybridity*, he examines the historical shifts of culture across the globe that blurs any transparent or static understanding of national identity. He approaches the topic as a historical analyst yet agrees that "all innovation is a kind of adaptation and that cultural encounters encourage creativity."[61] Cultural exchange

59. Joh, *Heart of the Cross*, 9. See chapter 3 of her book for an excellent analysis of key postcolonial themes like hybridity, mimicry, and interstitial third space.
60. Ramadan, *What I Believe*, 13.
61. Burke, *Cultural Hybridity*, 6.

can come with a price, so we must discern when it seems that one culture is leeching off another. Indeed, historians are at the place where we must acknowledge that our houses are "drifting" and not stationary.[62] In light of this fact, theologian Tariq Ramadan, another famous Swiss citizen, recommends the following, which is worth quoting in full:

> One must resist the temptation to reduce one's identity to a single dimension that takes priority over every other. This can indeed be reassuring, but it is above all impoverishing and, in times of crisis and tension, it can lead to rejection, racism, and latent or passionate conflicts of identity, culture, or "civilization." We should reach a broader view of ourselves and our fellow-citizens: each one of us has multiple identities that she/he must accept, nurture, and develop. I have long been repeating to Muslims and to my fellow citizens that I am Swiss by nationality, Egyptian by memory, Muslim by religion, European by culture, universalistic by principle, Moroccan and Mauritian by adoption. This is no problem whatsoever: I live with those identities, and one or the other may take the lead depending on the context or occasion. Other dimensions should even be added to those identities: being a man, having a specific social status, a job, and so on. Our identities are multiple and constantly on the move.[63]

The concept of border thinking is a way to update and further develop Barth's Eurocentric neighbor, in much the same way Latin American theorist Enrique Dussel, for example, particularized the view of the Jewish European philosopher Emmanuel Levinas' Other in the colonial Other of Latin America.[64] Border thinking connects to the *mestiza/o* consciousness of being identified in the United States and Latin America. Chicana writer Sandra Cisneros, writing a Foreword in Virgilio Elizondo's classic book *The Future is Mestizo*, author of the famous book *The House on Mango Street*, writes that we encounter *mestizaje* if we would simply pause and observe the type of burritos we eat.[65]

---

62. See Lee, *Drifting House* for her fictional account of Koreans in a globalized world. A good book that features many of the pioneering thinkers of postcolonial literature is Olson and Worsham, *Race, Rhetoric, and the Postcolonial*. Thus, before diving into the work of Bhabha, Anzaldúa, Dyson, or Hall, this book has interviews where the authors are able to talk about their theories in a relaxed conversation-type style.

63. Ramadan, *What I Believe*, 37–38.

64. Rivera, *Touch of Transcendence*, 55–82. For a detailed study of Levinas's influence on Dussel see Barber, *Ethical Hermeneutics*.

65. Elizondo, *Future is Mestizo*, ix–xi. Also see his book *Galilean Journey*. For a good

Barth's concepts of near and distant neighbor are fluid enough to connect to recent discussion of border thinking, but it is crucial to remember the center of his talk is from continental Europe, limited in its scope of a certain blindness to colonial difference. In fact, one would be left disappointed if looking for Barth's opinions, for instance, about Latin America. In fact, Barth's theology about neighbors features some inherent problems.

Barth posits a near and far neighbor dichotomy that blurs the diversity of movement among migrant peoples. Postmodern theorists would point out that Barth clearly delineates a binary logic. Therefore, even when attempting to feature openness toward neighbors outside of his Swiss homeland, Barth's theology is so centered from the European vantage point that we do not know the thoughts or experiences of the many neighbors and foreigners that are both near and far to Barth. All these neighbors are simply Other. This is important to point out because Barth is not simply talking about being a Swiss citizen but theologizing about neighborliness in general. Theologizing about neighborliness needs to match with lived historical reality in a way that speaks to the most people on the globe or at least is honest about one's social location. Therefore, one particular way to bring Barth's theology up to date is to read it through the lens of border thinking.

What exactly is border thinking? Latin American theorist Walter Mignolo, developing his understanding from Latin American poet Gloria Anzaldúa, defines it as recognizing the colonial difference from subaltern perspectives.[66] It is important to point out the impact Anzaldúa's theory of borderlands had for academic disciplines that takes postcolonial criticism seriously.[67] Thus the pioneer of this theory represents a number of marginalized, subaltern positions. According to Mignolo, border thinking contains the "necessary epistemology to delink and decolonize knowledge, and, in the process, to build decolonial local histories, restoring the dig-

---

introduction to *mestizaje*, see De La Torre and Aponte, *Introducing Latino/a Theologies*, 37–39 and 141–45; and all the essays in Bañuelas, *Mestizo Christianity*. One word of caution about multiracial consciousness. The attention toward mixed race identity should never be a context for anti-blackness. I recommend Minelle Mahtani, *Mixed Race Amnesia: Resisting the Romanticization of Multiraciality* for more on this subject.

66. Mignolo, *Local Histories/Global Designs*, 3–6.

67. Bedford, "To Speak of God," 97. The work of Anzaldúa and Cherríe Moraga were pioneering for Latina/Chicana and lesbian literature. See Martínez, *De Colores Means All of Us*, 163–71 and 190–93 for an overview of Latina writers and causes, looking specifically at Moraga's work.

nity that the Western idea of universal history took away from millions of people."⁶⁸ It recovers a way of thinking that challenges the subordination of non-European ways of conceptualization. So when we look at Barth's markers of speech, location, and history in his discussion of the neighbor, we might want to pay attention to the colonial difference of these terms. For example, it is nice for Barth to encourage learning the Other's language, capturing the sense that much of the languages of the distant neighbors have been silenced for far too long, yet perhaps there might be caution toward the mastery of this foreign language? Moreover, according to Mignolo, it is one thing to think about borders like Barth, seeing the foreigner through the European imaginary, and another thing to live and think on the border, as modeled by Anzaldúa. Barth's view is limited by his time and his place.

What are some ways to think in relation to both the divine and human on the border? Robert S. Goizueta develops the theological idea that God's transcendent otherness, in fact, always reveals God as an alien to our conceptions about God.⁶⁹ Like Barth, he is careful to distinguish God from any type of national god. An ideology too steeped in the binary of *us* versus *them* would ignore God as Other, who is the continually present God-Self as the Other in our midst. As Elizondo points out, the gospel question today has to address a "shrinking planet" not the homegrown God on the nation-state.⁷⁰ Goizueta notes that "a genuine encounter with a transcendent God" comes when God "irrupts in our world from the other side of the border."⁷¹ Goizueta articulates a theology that presents what Nancy Bedford calls an "epistemological rupture," complicating the easy definitions we give to both God and to the various migrants we encounter.⁷² Consequently, Elizondo thinks we should understand Jesus as *mestizo*, a half-breed, challenging the hegemonic image of the blue-eyed Jesus.⁷³ By placing God outside the border, God is now concretely identified in the area where conflict and violence is located, the place of the "colonial wound," or as Anzaldúa states "where

---

68. Mignolo, *Local Histories/Global Designs*, x.

69. Goizueta, "Christ of the Borderlands," 177.

70. Elizondo, *Future is Mestizo*, xv.

71. Goizueta, Christ of the Borderlands," 192. I think that Barth's idea of Jesus as the prodigal son in the "far country" in CD IV/1 may be a fruitful place of dialogue for Barth and Latino/a theology.

72. Bedford, "To Speak of God," 110–13.

73. Elizondo, *Future is Mestizo*, 79. He makes this claim without trying to erase the historical Jewishness of the historical Jesus.

the Third World grates against the first and bleeds."[74] In many ways, these *mestizo/a* writers start their work on the margins, with the preferential perspective of the poor and outcast (a subject we will look at in more detail next chapter). They do not let a nationalist identity be the main marker of their identity, but instead point out the multiple identity markers that essentially makes each human being unique.

When one reads Anzaldúa's *Borderlands/La Frontera: The New Mestiza* one gets a firsthand experience of living among the marginalized. She continues, "Borders are set up to define the places that are safe and unsafe, to distinguish *us* from *them*."[75] Anzaldúa asserts that a "new *mestiza* consciousness" forms from this crisscrossing of identities and spaces, what she also calls "a consciousness of the Borderlands."[76] She declares, "Living on borders and in margins, keeping intact one's shifting and multiple identity and integrity, is like trying to swim in a new element, an 'alien' element."[77] Therefore, this new form of thinking fosters "a tolerance for contradictions, a tolerance for ambiguity."[78] This newness is exactly what Elizondo has in mind when he claims that a "new humanity" is formed on the border.[79] Elizondo, much like Anzaldúa, takes his own particular, autobiographical experience, growing up in San Antonio, Texas in the borderlands, and creates a universal concept of *mestizo* to analyze the changing nature of humanity across the globe.

Anzaldúa comes across as a spiritual and imaginative thinker tapping into a diverse assortment of Latin American traditions, viewing the lack of this perspective from modern Western thinkers as harmful overall. In other words, the religious and the secular binary choice does not apply to her and other *mestizo/a* thinkers. She declares: "In trying to become 'objective,' Western culture made 'objects' of things and people when it distanced itself from them, thereby losing 'touch' with them. This dichotomy is the root of all violence."[80] Here the critical *mestiza* term is most helpful because it re-

---

74. Mignolo, *Local Histories/Global Designs*, xiv; Anzaldúa, *Borderlands*, 25.

75. Anzaldúa, *Borderlands*, 25.

76. Ibid., 99. It is important to note that, for her, this is also a *"una conciencia de mujer"* as well. Also see page 43 where she writes that her "Chicana identity is grounded in the Indian woman's history of resistance."

77. Ibid., 19.

78. Ibid., 101.

79. Elizondo, *Future is Mestizo*, xiv–xv and 100–102.

80. Anzaldúa, *Borderlands*, 59. Also see Elizondo, *Future is Mestizo*, 54–56.

lates the fact that the *us* from *them* separation at borders is a violent fiction. The violence in this description is the walls separating the touch between the self and the Other.

The idea of being in touch with the Other is the key idea of Mayra Rivera's theology. Rivera forms a "postcolonial vision" on how "transformation emerges from the encounters with the otherness beyond. Thus, the realm of beyond is not a static place of separation, but a dynamic space of encounters and transformation."[81] She does not discuss otherness without making a theological point. She insists that Latin American theorist's attention to multiplicity and concrete otherness tells us much about God's otherness. Rivera writes: "Through these complex relations with otherness the otherness of God is mediated to humans."[82] In short, God's otherness is a relational transcendence that values the complexity among God's creatures, featuring the idea that God may be Other, but still in the realm to be touched. Rivera, building upon the work of Anzaldúa, enriches and deepens Barth's idea of the far and near neighbor to match the diverse and ambiguous relationships we develop with the Other. This idea can be applied to history and theology once we begin to read the works of the unfamiliar neighbors or the neighbors we assumed we knew.

Barth's neighborliness method of history with its attention to the present, openness, and periodization is corrected by the *mestizo/a* point of view. First, we acknowledge the great diversity of the past and the future from the present. To ignore this fact in the present is to betray reality. Second, Barth's concern for openness is taken to its logical conclusion toward a more inclusive, global Christianity and an awareness and respect for other beliefs. Finally, with our current diverse and global understanding of humanity, present and future historical periodization will take serious the viewpoints on non-Europeans. The point of placing Barth's historical-theological method with *mestizo/a* thinking is to note the potential of theoretical work that crosses interdisciplinary borders and challenges the Eurocentric framework.[83]

Border thinking illustrates that even Barth's far neighbor was not that distant to him as he imagined. The same applies to those in our historical

81. Rivera, *Touch of Transcendence*, 13.

82. Ibid., 79. See Rivera's new book *Poetics of the Flesh* for the further development of her theology and Copeland, *Enfleshing Freedom* for more on God, race and materiality.

83. There are already some examples of this type of theoretical work. See Diaz, *On Being Human*, where he mixes Hispanic theology thinkers with the Catholic theologian Karl Rahner; and Nava, *Mystical and Prophetic Thought*.

past. There are aspects of them found very near to us. We only realize this fact with the rise of our own historical consciousness. With the rise of cultural studies, history has been one discipline that recognizes the reality of this inter-connectivity across time and space. This literature is growing at such a rapid rate that it is only willful blindness that ignores it. However, we must also beware of cultural appropriation of this material. I will argue later about the importance of biographical and autobiographical accounts that provide historical context of peoples and cultures we might consider as the distant Other. As a student of history or theology, the point is to listen and to learn not to master or to control. This is why theology needs history to remind it of its connection to events and people across the globe. One place to correct the Eurocentrism of theology is found in voices from the theological third world.

Conclusion: The Neighbor & the End of History

Barth's discussion is contextually of a European Christian understanding of the ethical relationship between the near and far neighbor, defined by nationalistic borders created in the nineteenth century. Thus perhaps his openness toward history has Eurocentric limitations, blinded by a sense of European provincialism? Does this Christian distinction prevent a border understanding of Barth's concepts? It does not have to, but history tells a different story.

Daniel Boyarin's book *Border Lines* establishes the fact the earliest Christian lived in a borderland reality with Judaism. Boyarin suggests that until certain "border police" (heresiologists) were mostly successful in making the differences among communities more solid, "religious ideas, practices, and innovations permeated that border crossing in both directions."[84] It is naïve to suggest a retrieval of this period or to idealize it as well. However, paying attention to the real complexities of near and distant neighbors at the borders at least challenges specifically Christian traditions, with roots in heresiology, which present themselves as *the* absolute form here on earth. If we comprehend that the earliest forms of Christianity lived on the borderlands of difference before it became a symbol for a homogenous universalism, then perhaps there is potential to incorporate important dialogues with near and distant neighbors across the religious spectrum. Most important of all, we should not allow new heresiology to

84. Boyarin, *Border Lines*, 1–2.

prevent historical-theological thought to be trapped within a Eurocentric framework, unable to listen and to learn from third-world intellectuals and communities.

Boyarin's definition of heresiology helps us see the ways that Christianity in history has often distinguished itself from those outside its own religious borders. Recall that Barth's theology of crisis in the early twentieth century, with a gnostic form of transcendent revelation from above, was seen by many of his Christian contemporaries as a form of heresy.[85] However, Barth's care to separate God from any nationalism has been a helpful tool for Latin American thinkers like Rivera to build her own theory of the Other. A historical-theological reading of Barth sees the formation of a Protestant theologian, producing theology in the context of monumental changes in European history and the great suffering caused by two global wars. Barth's work betrays his suspicions of any theology that has the potential of repeating Nazism. In this sense, perhaps this is why he thinks, as noted in this chapter's epigraph, that the future of theology belongs to the European borderlands of Asia and Africa. Barth is enough of a theological pioneer that he opens the door for even his transcendent theology to aim at ethical, social change worldwide. However it will be the thinkers in the post-sixties generation that will diversify historical-theological thought. This is why a *mestiza* consciousness as described by Anzaldúa, developed further by Rivera and Mignolo, takes pride in the alien element, the ambiguity we constantly encounter on the street, challenging any heresiology that attempts to disrupt this difference.

One way to challenge heresiology in particularly Christian history is in the study of eschatology. Since heresiology historically started with Christians toward Jews, it meant that a Christian theology of history was warped from the very beginning.[86] Eschatology is the doctrine of the last things, dealing with the end of history. However, some forms of end times doctrines are so confident in their interpretation that they are fine with prophetic genocide of people groups that are not saved in their model. Taking our cue from Boyarin's warnings about heresiology, much is lost in our interpretation of eschatology when the writings of the First Testament are ignored, or the Jewish foundations of Christianity are superceded.[87] As Jew-

---

85. Lazier, *God Interrupted*.
86. Taubes, *From Cult to Culture*, 45–58.
87. See Soulen, *God of Israel*, 1–21; Taubes, *Occidental Eschatology*. Also see Westhelle, *After Heresy*, 65 for pointing out how post-eighteenth century Enlightenment

ish tradition and history was displaced in Christian eschatological visions, the danger in Eurocentric history is to continue the displacement of people from across the globe, in the name of theological purity. Whereas much late twentieth century theology has correctly kept the memory of the Holocaust in its sight, I will argue that Eurocentric history and theology must do the same with the postcolonial history of the third world.

I do not have the space dedicated in this book to explore eschatology in a significant way. Apart from the doctrine of creation, eschatology is potentially the most historically centered systematic theological topic. However, this doctrine is often presented completely divorced from real, concrete, everyday history. Much of it is articulated solely in the pages of the Bible, passages of Daniel and the Book of Revelation being privileged. If eschatology is primarily biblically based, along with theories divorced from concrete history, then any attempt to provide historical-theological readings with attention to human suffering in history will be seen as too political and too unbiblical. This is the accusation most often directed toward liberationist theology.[88]

Anticipating the argument of the next chapter, the historical-theological thinkers of the third world manage to think both biblically and historically. We will examine this in some detail with the event of early modernity, starting with the date 1492. Christian thought cannot simply work around the historical events associated with this date. In fact, I would argue eschatology cannot, as well. How can we in the present seek for Lord Jesus to come quickly, when there were moments in the past when his representatives arrived in his name in foreign lands to rape and plunder them? Could ahistorical, biblically based eschatology simply be an erasure of Christianity's bloody history toward Jewish people throughout history? Even though post-Holocaust, German, Christian theologians like Dorothee Soelle, Jürgen Moltmann, Johann Baptist Metz, and other European theologians made it a critical point to not practice Christian theology in the present and toward the future without forgetting the past event of the Holocaust, is their memory too selective? In other words, the Holocaust was a horrific event, but what about the other genocides of the past?

---

universal history was simply a Eurocentric reading of history and that European postmodern thinkers are rejecting this all too confident reading generally from a Eurocentric position.

88. See Wilmore, *Last Things First*, 35–39 and 77–96 for examples of liberation theology's eschatology and his important chapter "Eschatology in Black" focused on African-American experience/eschatology.

Moltmann shows a steady evolution in global consciousness in his theology, and is paradigmatic for those interested in eschatology. For the purposes of my argument here I highlight two key points. First, Moltmann opens his eschatology by recognizing the continual contribution of Jewish thought in order to properly understand the basis of Christianity.[89] For example, as Moltmann points out, Jewish scholar Jacob Taubes reminds the European philosophers of history that eschatological thinking is founded on Jewish apocalyptic, messianic idea of historical disruption.[90] With his eschatology formed on the basis of Jewish messianism, Moltmann avoids falling into the trap of Christian triumphalism and heresiology. Second, he includes a section on the history of European violence and conquest starting around 1492.[91] Not many even recent eschatologies try to connect the violence against the third world with Christian revelation about history, so Moltmann's book is a model for those serious about a historical-theological position.

For an eschatology that anticipates the discussion of the next chapter it is crucial to quickly highlight one book in particular. As noted in the introduction, McIntyre rightfully places a selection by Gustavo Gutiérrez in his book on faith and history.[92] In *A Theology of Liberation*, Gutiérrez reveals there is only one history, challenging the dualistic reading of the sacred/secular split. He posits the Christian God as one who especially liberates the marginalized and oppressed in this world. Latin American thinkers like Enrique Dussel and Ignacio Ellacuría, who we will look at next chapter, follow Gutiérrez's eschatology from below.[93]

As more and more scholars testify that global Christianity is being spearheaded by the so-called global south, caution is advised to not interpret this event as other forms of Christianity outside Europe finally playing catchup. To continue where the Eurocentric Barth left off, I look forward (following Mignolo) to struggle along with more theorists of the Other like Frantz Fanon, Édouard Glissant, and Abdelkebir Khatibi, who are somewhat located outside of Europe as they try to theorize in a decolonial

---

89. Moltmann, *Coming of God*, 29–46. The Jewish figures included here are Ernst Bloch, Franz Rosenzweig, Gershom Scholem, Walter Benjamin, Jacob Taubes, and Karl Löwith.

90. Taubes, *Occidental Eschatology*, 9–21.

91. Moltmann, *Coming of God*, 211–16.

92. McIntyre, *God, History, and Historians*, 133–56; Gutiérrez, *Theology of Liberation*, 86–97 and 121–40.

93. Ellacuría, *Freedom Made Flesh*, 3–19.

fashion.⁹⁴ If, as a reader of Barth, I want to utilize his theology in the twenty-first century, it has to be brought into severe confrontation with a number of voices from outside Occidentalism. Still, at the very least, we can perhaps applaud Barth's statement, written during the beginning of the Cold War, that even an iron curtain is still a curtain, so in its essence it is made both to fall and rise.⁹⁵ We are perhaps living at a time when this curtain is letting in a little light as it slowly rises exposing the violence of the modern/colonial world. Whereas Barth has his limits because he is a Eurocentric thinker, we shall now turn to the heart of *Remembering Lived Lives* to look at the way historical-theological thinkers of ethnic minorities engage history.

94. Mignolo, *Local Histories*, 49–88. Fanon yields a major influence on third world and indigenous writers in depicting its consciousness in contrast to the European Other. See these models inspired by Fanon's classic *Black Skin, White Masks*: see Dabashi, *Brown Skin, White Masks*, and Coulthard, *Red Skin, White Masks*.

95. Barth, CD, III/4: 301.

CHAPTER 2

Never Forget (But How Will They Forget if They Never Heard?)

Challenging a Eurocentric History

"The Third World was not a place. It was a project."—Vijay Prashad[1]

"'Third World Theology' begins by raising issues, not by digesting Augustine, Barth, and Rahner."—Kosuke Koyama[2]

"A people who do not preserve their memory are a people who have forfeited their history."—Wole Soyinka[3]

I would like to open this chapter on a meditation about Walter Benjamin's Angel of History. Benjamin's Angel looks back in horror at the catastrophe that is human history.[4] Here I juxtapose this image with the image of the lifeless body of the Spanish Jesuit priest Ignacio Ellacuría. I open this way because Ellacuría's goal was to force theology to take historical reality seriously. However, the history he had in mind is of the oppressed peoples, especially those in Latin America. As President of the University of Central

---

1. Prashad, *Darker Nations*, xv.
2. Koyama, *Water Buffalo Theology*, 3.
3. Soyinka, *Burden of Memory*, 58 adapted from quotes by Elie Wiesel and Danielle Mitterand.
4. Benjamin, *Illuminations*, 257–58.

America in El Salvador, he tried to shape education toward the needs of the marginalized.[5] For this, he and his associates were murdered by the Salvadoran forces in the dead of night. Philosopher and historian Enrique Dussel utilized his philosophy of liberation to carry on Ellacuría's program by writing a genealogy on how Latin America came into existence.

History as we know it is a modern invention. However, modernity is defined outside of Europe in its interaction with peoples across the globe. If we are going to expand our understanding of a historical-theological method from a Eurocentric bias, then we will accomplish this by analyzing voices from the third world. The year 1492 has poignant meaning in describing this point. Therefore, we will use 1492 as a springboard to focus our challenge of a Eurocentric history. The year 1492 is bigger than Columbus, even though he plays a key part. It stands for conquest, colonization, empire, and expulsion. At the heart of this interpretation is Christianity's role. One of the biggest critics of both Christianity and Europe, theorist Gil Anidjar, frames the argument thus: "Colonizing the world since 1492, Christianity slowly granted other communities and traditions, those it exploited or converted, massacres and 'civilized,' enslaved and exterminated, new structures of authority and domination, new and newly negotiable configurations of power."[6] The events that surrounded 1492 changed the whole globe. In order to understand the lasting implications of 1492 one must make time for Indigenous, Native American, African, Asian, Latin American, Muslim, Jewish histories before consulting the Eurocentric texts of the rise of the modern European nation-state.

As we examined last chapter, often Christian theorists of history remain in the realm of theological speculation and biblical interpretation of key texts, ignoring the events of concrete history, especially those outside Europe. Therefore, it is perhaps easy to fall back on the perennial response that violence done in the name of Christ betrays the essence of Christianity. However, Anidjar refuses to let Christianity or Europe off the hook that easy. He remarks that it is only the Christian/Europeans in concrete history that "exterminated Native Americans in the millions, enslaved Africans in their millions, gassed Jews in their millions, and so forth."[7] Yes, it can be argued (as it is oftentimes done by Christian apologists) that secularist, atheist, Hindu, Buddhist, Islamic, Jewish, and others also have a violent past;

5. See Ellacuría, "Challenge of the Poor Majority," 171–76.
6. Anidjar, *Semites*, 46.
7. Ibid., 5.

but so does Christianity. We cannot escape this history. For example, one cannot polemically hold Marxism accountable for the violence committed by totalitarian regimes, without also pointing out the violence of such events as the Crusades, Spanish conquest of the Americas, the Thirty Years War, among a host of other wars oftentimes done through the discourse of fighting in Christ's name.

Anidjar focuses his critique on his own interpretation of the essence of Christianity that has manifested itself throughout history. Recalling Barth's advice from last chapter, we would be wise to come face to face with the history of violence in Christian history, but not simply judge all of the tradition as inherently malicious. This is the type of argument for the value of the European, Western, and Christian tradition that Slovenian philosopher Slavoj Žižek will argue that is worth defending. Thus, we may also look at the voices from the underside within Christianity to realize the multiple manifestations of Christian belief in history. This chapter is not an apologetic for the destructive side of Christian history. From our current vantage point, there is absolutely no excuse for this. Anidjar is correct in saying not every society has been as violent as Christian nation-states in the past. This is why we will examine 1492 as a crucial time to explore this complex history. We will explore the understanding of 1492 by looking at the work of theorists located in the third world.

The third world, according to Vijay Prashad, was an "association" among "the darker nations" defined by such movements that met in Bandung and Belgrade.[8] While Europeans turned to a pessimistic view of history after the global wars, many figures in the third world identified with the an optimistic view of history mostly embodied in a synthesis of third-world cultures and Western Marxism. In short, an optimistic view of history from the barbarism of the colonial experience led to a type of teleological vision of history. Prashad identifies this optimism by detailing the constructive potential that was realized by third-world nations in the twentieth century. Therefore, when we explore third-world writers, both historians and theologians, it will be through the lens of the darker nations as a positive agency, and primarily through the postcolonial tradition.[9]

Modern history has generally been about the rise of Europe around the fourteenth century. For years this has been described as something exceptional about Europe. Recent history, written by postcolonial writers,

---

8. Prashad, *Darker Nations*, 96; also see Dabashi, *Can Non-Europeans Think*, xli.
9. See Nayar, *Postcolonialism*, 1–5 for the key definitions of postcolonialism.

challenges this Eurocentric narrative by presenting the view from the colonized. Edward Said's book *Orientalism* was the pioneering work critiquing this Occidental gaze on history, even though his own humanistic understanding of reality is based in European thought. Still, Said is oftentimes cited as a representative of anti-Eurocentrism. However, the postcolonial view has been challenged by late most recently by Žižek, who continues to talk about defending the Western tradition. Žižek's Eurocentrism has met with a number of responses by theorists like Walter Mignolo, Hamid Dabashi, and others. This current controversy presents a good historical lesson on where this discussion is moving. This complicated debate is important to cover since much current history and theology tends to fall in either the Said or Žižek camp.

The chapter will then deal specifically on how both Ellacuría and Dussel can help shape the discipline of history, especially religious history, toward the marginalized. The identity of Christian ecclesiastical history is captured by at least two dilemmas. The first is its Eurocentric bias. The second issue is on how to narrate its genre in light of the dualism of sacred and secular history. On the one hand, it is very easy for practitioners of ecclesiastical history to interpret secular history as the workings of the providential God. On the other hand, religious history oftentimes transforms into special, sacred history, transcending the phenomenological plane, and potentially ignoring the everyday events of secular history.

Ellacuría and Dussel address both of these issues. For Ellacuría historical reality is one, tied directly to nature. The *telos* of history, which both Dussel and Ellacuría state as the reign of God, arises internally and dynamically in history, not from a predetermined, eternally transcendent static form. God is viewed as an intra-cosmic transcendent source for the possibilities of transformative power in history.[10] When speaking about history, it is a "day-to-day" history where God is revealed not in some detached, abstract place.[11] This oneness to reality forces both thinkers to see Eurocentric narratives of history as privileging one side of the narrative, so they present counter-readings focused on the poor. We will first explore their understanding of a Eurocentric history and then close the

10. See Rivera, *Touch of Transcendence*, 41–47 for a good summary of Ellacuría's understanding of transcendence and historical reality.

11. Dussel, *History and the Theology of Liberation*, 139 and 157; see Burke, *Ground Beneath the Cross*, 206. For an essay comparing Dussel and Ellacuría, see Pivot, "Ignacio Ellacuría and Enrique Dussel," 119–33 for a phenomenological approach to both thinkers.

chapter with their presentation of Europe's Other, advocating a hermeneutic historical-theological view by relying on the work of Tsney Serequeberhan. Serequeberhan's work presents a good mixture of third world thought connected with European philosophy. It is to this synthesis of sorts that I believe historical-theological thought should move forward.

Said, Postcolonial Historian of Sorts

Postcolonial history has its roots in the historical consciousness of being the Other of European modernity. One of the first places that exposed Eurocentric history was among writers like Hichem Djaït and Edward Said. I mention Djaït in passing because he is often overlooked because of the impact of Said's book *Orientalism*, yet his book *Europe and Islam*, published around the same time as Said's, presents a historical overview of the relations between Islamic regimes and European ones, whereas Said exposes the bias of European writers toward the Orient. Djaït, for example, illustrates that the roots of European imperialism reaches back far in its history, and that the most obvious modern examples of Eurocentrism are found in Christianity and Marxism.[12] This is an important point that even Christian thinkers who are aware of and troubled by Eurocentrism must deal with as they try to think and practice a more global expression of their faith. Moreover, Djaït prophesies about the exact position Žižek takes with his defense of a Eurocentrism based on his interpretation of Christianity and Marxism.

Djaït, noting the role Spain and the *Reconquista* had on the rise of Europe, writes that "Europe's emergence into history took place—and could not have taken place otherwise–through the mediation of Islam: in the beginning by means of defensive recoil, afterward by an offensive explosion."[13] Here he points out that part of Europe's rise as a global phenomenon comes with a reactionary stance toward the Islamic world. Perhaps he may be stating the case a little too broadly, yet Islam has some historical role to play in the way Europeans set to navigate themselves around the globe. Djaït's book anticipates the arguments against Eurocentrism in this chapter, but it clearly remains Said's impact that dictated the current argument.

Said used his great knowledge of texts and of history as a means to speak out against the abuse of power in a way that made a connection with

12. Djaït, *Europe and Islam*, 18–20.
13. Ibid., 109.

thinkers across the academic world.[14] His work *Orientalism* is considered a pioneering text for postcolonial Christian literature.[15] By focusing on the Occidental gaze on the Orient, he exposes the biases of Eurocentric scholarship. The fact that he is a controversial figure illustrates in a sense how he fits into a type of prophetic tradition, but, most of all, his methods for writing history are very useful. Therefore, even though many may disagree with his conclusions, his emphasis on the duty of history writers is important.

Said's work falls into the humanist camp. Said's form of humanism is being "able to use one's mind historically and rationally for the purpose of reflective understanding and genuine disclosure" and "is sustained by a sense of community with other interpreters and other societies and periods."[16] In other words, a historian works in a public space in critical dialogue with other thinkers. The work of a humanist is based on the critical capacity of each individual thinker and not on "received ideas or approved authority."[17] Said declares that "the history of cultures . . . suggests that cultures really are not impermeable, they are open to every other culture" and thus it is the work of the student of history "to try to expose the historical roots of clashes between cultures *in order* to promote the possibility of a dialogue between cultures."[18] As a humanist, Said attempts to disenchant the types of histories that sees the Western and Eastern worlds locked in perennial combat. Instead of some type of clash of civilizations, he sees clear social-political motivations on why wars and oppressions continue across the Islamic world.

Another term that Said uses for humanist thinkers is that of the public intellectual. Reformed church historian Carl Trueman provides a helpful definition, based on Said's writings, of the role the humanist intellectual has in society; he writes that "intellectuals are not to allow themselves to be co-opted into the wider project of the imperialist establishment. They have no choice but to work within it. Yet they can offer dissenting, critical

---

14. See Nayar, *Postcolonialism*, 13–21 for Said's importance for postcolonial thought and Dabashi, *Can Non-Europeans Think*, xl and 44–61 for Said's influence on Dabashi.

15. Pui-lan, *Postcolonial Imagination and Feminist Theology*, 1–4; Raheb, *Faith in the Face of Empire*, 27–30. The texts of Frantz Fanon should also be included. It seems that Said's work came too late to influence Latin American liberation theology.

16. Said, *Orientalism*, xxiii. See Nur Musalha, "Civil Liberation Theology in Palestine," 193–214 for Said's secular humanist position. Probably the best study of religion and secularism in Said's corpus is Hart, *Edward Said and the Religious Effects of Culture*.

17. Said, *Orientalism*, xxix.

18. Said, *Power, Politics, and Culture*, 271.

voices which offer alternative narratives and possibilities of resistance to dominant powers."[19] In what way can the historian follow Said's methodology? Said suggests that one must "protect against and forestall the disappearance of the past" and in addition "present alternative narratives and other perspectives on history than those provided by combatants on behalf of official memory and national identity and mission."[20] He declares that it is the "final resistance" against dehumanizing procedures that corrupt the record of human history.[21] Again, since the subject matter of history is of human actors and players then humanity is the source for the use and abuse of social-political power. In some ways, the Latin American liberation theologians will often focus on this sociological viewpoint before turning to some type of theological expression.

I quote Trueman about Said for a reason. In his book *Histories and Fallacies*, he pursues Christian historiography in much the same way as John Fea and Robert Rea, which we discussed in the Introduction.[22] However, considering Trueman's essay on Said, one might expect a reference or a section on postcolonial history. Unfortunately no such allusion is to be found. In fact, outside of a chapter using Holocaust revisionist history as an example of historical fallacy, the attention in the book is toward proper methodology and the Protestant Reformers. Much like Fea and Rea, Trueman's book is an excellent toolbox for history writers (my History students in general loved the book), yet it is the lack of voices outside European matters, especially since Trueman had earlier advocated for a reading of Said, that needs updating.

Said's methodology in one sense sounds very much like a modernist understanding of history writing especially with his focus on the importance justice and human rights has in his humanism. In fact, Said's attitude toward Western Orientalism produces a type of anti-Orientalism, according to S. Sayyid, that deflates the definition of Islam.[23] Said is such a radical historicist that Islam has no place in actual history, just a smattering of little Islams. This leads to a big question historians rather than theologians

19. Trueman, "Uneasy Consciences," 41–42.
20. Said, *Humanism and Democratic Criticism*, 141.
21. Said, *Orientalism*, xxix.
22. Trueman, *Histories and Fallacies*.
23. Sayyid, *Fundamental Fear*, 31–40. In addition, see Amin, *Eurocentrism*, 175–77 for his critique of Said. I tend to agree with Muslim theologian Tariq Ramadan when he says that "there is one religion, one Islam, with various interpretations and several cultures." See Ramadan, *What I Believe*, 42.

often wrestle with: is there a universal type that one can discuss or do we follow Said and only focus on exposing the diverse particularities? Moreover, Gil Anidjar goes so far to argue that Said's critique of Orientalism corresponds with an anti-Christian stance since it grounds the separation of East and West.[24] In short, the overemphasis on historicizing removes the quality of the term Islam from having any meaning. The same thing occurs if we are limited to only being allowed to speak about numerous Christianities. However, there is also a postmodern element because Said eschews grand narratives and seeks to expose harmful ideologies that lurk behind examples of true history.[25] Said tries to keep this balance without falling into the postmodern trap of extreme relativism especially since he thinks the truth in history is "situational and political" in nature.[26] Said declares that he is not a "deconstructionist" in the sense that he is not afraid to pick out what is true and false in history.[27] In fact, the bulk of Said's work, as a postcolonial thinker, is in using history through the study of comparative literature in order to expose what he see are the abuses and untruths of writings within history.

We have seen Said's presentation of what a public thinker looks like and how important history writing is to his work. One of his main goals is putting everything in its particular historical context. The historian can help prevent the easy and lazy reliance on generalizations. The attack on generalizations, which hide harmful ideological systems, is what made Said a famous public intellectual in his own right. Said summarizes his main body of work: "My argument is that history is made by men and women, just as it can also be unmade and rewritten, always with various silences and elisions, always with shapes imposed and disfigurements tolerated, so that 'our' East, 'our' Orient becomes 'ours' to possess and direct."[28] Said suggests that the jargons and words used in texts do make a difference to the way people react to one another in society: "The worst aspect of this essentializing stuff is that human suffering in all its density and pain is spirited away. Memory and with it the historical past are effaced as in the common, dismissively contemptuous American phrase, 'you're history.'"[29] Thus, for

24. Anidjar, *Semites*, 39-63.
25. Walia, *Edward Said and the Writing of History*, 22.
26. Ibid., 18.
27. Said, *Power, Politics and Culture*, 271.
28. Said, *Orientalism*, xviii.
29. Ibid., xxi.

Said, the historian can illustrate that situations are more complex than the simple *Us* vs. *Them* or clash of civilizations formulas make it sound: "One can show, in the instances of most conflicts, that there are historical, real reasons for a conflict that didn't exist with that kind of intensity before, and that you can forsee and project a time when they wouldn't apply, if the sources of the conflict were addressed."[30] His appeal here to historical factors is paradigmatic for the historical-theological thinker.

Said deals with the complexity of texts and the subject of world history from an engaged position. He is clear about his feelings on world politics, and he oftentimes referred to himself as an exile, a familiar postcolonial trope. He assumes a position as someone who was outside the mainstream of things, as someone who was out of place. He proposes this poignant question: "If you're an exile [then] you always bear within yourself a recollection of what you've left behind and what you can remember, and you play it against the current experience."[31] Said is clear that one should not glamorize this position. Postcolonial writer Shelly Walia asserts that Said took on the role of the exile to speak out from an engaged position in a way that other writers would not be willing to do.[32] As a Palestinian exile, Said believes his writings are a historical record of one of the main events in twentieth-century history.[33]

Historians should be open to various avenues in the historical record in order to detect harmful ideologies. Said takes to task the idea that pure scholarship should avoid becoming too focused on the political; he notes that oftentimes a work is discredited if it has the adjective political attached to it.[34] However, one of the problems of society is its lack of historical consciousness. It remains the duty of the historian to be the voice of reason when concrete historical analysis is needed especially with regard to political issues. Said once commented on this issue with regards to the war in Iraq: "What our leaders and their intellectual lackeys seem incapable of understanding is that history cannot be swept clean like a blackboard, clean so that 'we' might inscribe our own future there and impose our own forms of

---

30. Said, *Power, Politics and Culture*, 278.

31. Ibid., 99. His existential position as an outsider is clearly seen in his autobiography *Out of Place*.

32. Walia, *Edward Said*, 8.

33. Said, *Power, Politics and Culture*, 429.

34. Said, *Orientalism*, 10.

life for these lesser people to follow."[35] Therefore, the titles "Christian," "the West," "religious," and "evangelical" are all tied to a social-political understanding. Even if one tries to divorce oneself from these labels when writing history, one's audience will inevitably associate whichever understanding they have of these terms to the historian.

History is a record of human history and the various changes that have occurred. Again, Said defines the humanity behind history: "The need now is for deintoxicated, sober histories that make evident the multiplicity and complexity of history without allowing one to conclude that it moves forward impersonally, according to laws determined either by divine or by the powerful."[36] Said's emphasis on the humanity of history opens up many questions for the Christian historian in particular since Eurocentrism is an extension of this religion. In what way can a historian who believes in the Christian God make any connection with his or her faith and human history without becoming Orientalist or even supercessionist? What are the standards that allow the historian to talk about the divine and history? Said's purely secular understanding of history, and if we agree with Anidjar, Said's hostility toward Christianity, is written to prevent theorists from dragging God into history in order to increase their positions of power. His appeal for sober yet engaged history writing is something we can learn a great deal. Said's critique hits home in many ways.

Žižek and the Challenge of Eurocentrism

"We are never steeped in history as when we pretend not to be, but if we stop pretending we may gain in understanding what we lose in false innocence. Naiveté is often an excuse for those who exercise power. For those upon whom that power is exercised, naiveté is always a mistake."
—Michel-Rolph Trouillot[37]

"Islam is the 'other' that we cannot embrace, even when we are at our most tolerant, because this other fails to accept the rules of the game—because it sees the game as a western game."—S. Sayyid[38]

35. Ibid., xviii.
36. Said, *Humanism and Democratic Criticism*, 141.
37. Trouillot, *Silencing the Past*, xix.
38. Sayyid, *Fundamental Fear*, 160.

REMEMBERING LIVED LIVES

"We should no longer address a dead interlocutor. Europe is dead."
—Hamid Dabashi[39]

There was a time that I read every book and watched every YouTube lecture by the Slovenian philosopher Slavoj Žižek. He discusses philosophy, psychology, politics, theology, film studies, and other disciplines in a such a way that critical theory comes across as exciting (well, these are subjects I found exciting at least). He found a way to relate these subjects that I had not seen before. Moreover, he began identifying as a Christian (albeit a Hegelian, Marxist-Leninist one), so I looked for ways to incorporate his philosophy and theology into my own thinking.

I am still grateful for the impact Žižek's work had on mine. For example, the utilization of film studies for the teaching of history that I will discuss in chapter 4 illustrates his abiding influence. However, other theorists have exposed a problematic feature of Žižek's corpus: his Eurocentrism; he has consistently argued along the framework of such essays titled "A Leftist Plea for 'Eurocentrism.'"[40] Instead of correcting this feature, Žižek obstinately defends his position.[41] In fact, he argues that the "Western legacy is effectively not just that of (post)colonial imperialist domination, but also that of the self-critical examination of the violence and exploitation the West itself brought to the Third World."[42] This is actually a key point that I do not think enough of his detractors are willing to acknowledge. In short, even though since 1492, European empires have brutalized areas of the third world and justified this oppression through the language of the civilizing

39. Dabashi, *Can Non-Europeans Think*, 11.
40. Žižek, *Universal Exception*, 183–208; also see his *The Fragile Absolute*.
41. See Žižek, *Living in the End Times*, 43–53 defending his attack against multiculturalism against critical theorist Sara Ahmed. I should note that because of recent controversial statements about refugees and other ahistorical observations, Žižek's academic star has fallen in recent years. These are the type of statements some of the figures I highlight in this chapter do not let slide. It goes without saying that conservative opposition to cultural studies, political correctness, and multiculturalism is a given. Conservatives reject these ideas for the sake of what they consider a unique, exceptional historical paradigm superior to competing systems. What is surprising is how Žižek is strangely close to conservative talking points, yet this remains part of his attempt of theoretical subversion, pointing out that fascist play the political correctness game better than anyone else. Even though he has a point about multiculturalism, his turn back to a Eurocentric universalism cannot solely be the solution.
42. Žižek, *First as Tragedy, Then as Farce*, 115. He explains this in the context of the Haitian Revolution.

project, there is located within this same tradition a subversive element that leads to a revolutionary critique of European hegemony.

Much of Žižek's defense is based on his canon of writers: Lacan, Freud, Marx, Lenin, and especially Hegel. For many postcolonial theorists, Hegel is often the prime suspect of Eurocentrism. Therefore, it is almost impossible for Žižek not to be Eurocentric since his philosophy is rooted solely in this Continental tradition. At times, he will criticize the canon writers of postcolonialism: Bhabha, and Said (and especially Levinas), or reinterpret Fanon to the consternation of Dabashi.

Žižek makes it a point to position himself against multiculturalism and postcolonialism. By taking a strong oppositional stance toward ideas formed among third-world thinkers, this positions him as an unabashedly Eurocentric thinker. Because of Žižek's opposition, for example, to discourse on race and gender, it spoils his insights on the ideology of global capitalism and the worldwide poverty left in its wake. Because he tends to reinterpret everything in accordance European universality, the criticism of his thought are mostly found outside Europe. The best way to show this critique of Žižek is to present a sample size of some of the most recent examples. The fact that they are coming from theorists who have written consistently against Eurocentrism helps to establish why this issue is still important. In fact, the number of Žižek's interlocutors continues to rise, illustrating that these thinkers from generally outside the West are not going away quietly.

The most famous and recent example of a critique of Žižek comes from Latin American theorist Walter Mignolo and Iranian writer Hamid Dabashi. Borrowing from the ideas of Kishore Mahbubani, a diplomat and writer from Singapore, they ask can the non-European think and read per the definitions coming from European philosophy?[43] The reasoning behind these questions remains the continual forgetfulness about philosophical thought outside the Western mainstream. Since in the realm of philosophical thought there is little alluding to thinkers outside the West, then it is assumed that non-Europeans have nothing to contribute. In addition, there

---

43. For Mignolo's Foreword to the book and Dabashi's essays, see Dabashi, *Can Non-Europeans Think*, viii–43; Mahbubani, *Can Asians Think*, 18–33. Mignolo opens his essay wondering why Muhbubani's book was generally ignored by the scholarly community. The incident that led to Dabashi's book was the listing of most influential philosophers today by Italian philosopher Santiago Zabala. Of course, Žižek happens to be on this list, yet no one outside of the West. I understand the context of Dabashi and Mignolo's reaction to Zabala's list, yet it is hard to argue the rise of Žižek's popularity.

consists an assumption among philosophers that true philosophy has to be connected to European thought in order to be valid. When Mignolo pointed out this fact to Žižek he basically dismisses him and Dabashi as somewhat inconsequential. Dabashi describes this attitude perfectly:

> The question of Eurocentrism is now entirely blasé. Of course Europeans are Eurocentric and see the world from their vantage point, and why should they not? They are the inheritors of multiple (now defunct) empires, and they still carry within them the phantom hubris of those empires; they believe their particular philosophy is "philosophy" and their particular thinking is "thinking," while everything else is—as the great European philosopher Emmanuel Levinas was wont to say—"dancing."[44]

Mignolo and Dabashi claim that there are a number of theorists outside of Europe who have contributed to critical philosophy throughout history. It is time to give them the attention they deserve. In order to do this, both theorists argue that a type of delinking of European thought is necessary to move forward. In some sense, according to Dabashi, we are moving toward a time in history where even the term postcolonialism has grown old and describes a past moment in history, one that relies too much on European thought. Decolonial projects attempt to think past Europe, claiming that they do not need Kant and Hegel to properly think! Decolonial theology would say the same about Aquinas and Barth. Whether or not this is possible or even advisable, it makes for an interesting rhetorical and theoretical program. Since the end of World War II, following the rise of the United States as the superpower, and the rise of independent movements across the third world, Europe has slowly started the process of decentering. In short, as Dabashi says in the epigraph, Europe has become forgettable.

Weighing in on the debate between Žižek and Dabashi, Aditya Nigam makes an interesting point about the discipline of philosophy and the type of theorists Dabashi (and Mignolo) lists from outside of Europe. He argues that philosophy is still considered part of the canon of Western thinkers, and in fact, will probably always remain that way. He contends: "Every time you want to do philosophy, you must demonstrate that you are ready to

44. Dabashi, *Can Non-Europeans Think*, 33. An important piece among this debate, located on the side of Mignolo and Dabashi, is Nigam, "End of Postcolonialism." Nigam suggests the importance of history to correct the type of European universalism that Žižek' proclaims. The irony of this point is that he points to Michel Foucault and Marx since they tend to think historically.

undergo plastic surgery, change the colour of your skin and with it, the mind that you possess."[45] Thus he appreciates Dabashi's attempt to think past Europe and postcolonialism by thinking differently, or in the language of last chapter, follow Mignolo by doing border thinking. Nigam suggests that thinking differently about philosophy would require a commitment to consider this discipline along with history. History messes with the lofty aspirations of European philosophical thought, dragging the canonical lineage of thought down to the nitty gritty events of history. Nigam's essay connects well with what I have argued so far in this book about the use of history toward abstract thought, philosophical or theological. Nigam points out that the drive to universalize and abstraction is located in European literature and, somewhat following Said from the last section, it is the job of the dissenting theorist to insist on historicizing.

At this point the reader might be wondering what does a debate among a European communist philosopher and a couple of non-European thinkers have to do with church history or Christian theology? Plenty. In fact, at the heart of Eurocentrism is the Christian faith and its history. Even liberation or contextual Christian theologians from across the globe have a fundamental dilemma delinking from the Eurocentric Christian worldview. In much the same language as Mignolo and Dabashi, oftentimes theologians outside of Europe learn the texts and culture of Europe in the form as a universal model. They utilize thought processes and techniques that are alien to their own historical context, unconsciously ignoring the contributions that may be found within one's own home traditions and cultures. The point is not that they are banned from using European thought, but that the tendency is to rely solely on it at the expense of their own historical context.

Since Žižek writes from a Marxist position, one might assume that liberation theologians from the third world would utilize his work. In fact, this is not generally the case. His main theological followers consist of contemporary North American or European Christian atheists or death of God theologians. Why does it seem that it is only theologians from the first world that read him? The problem for third-world thinkers, including some liberation theologians, remains his Eurocentrism. For example, from a position within Latin American liberation theology, Nelson Maldonado-Torres claims that Žižek, defending Christian and European exceptionalism, writes from a neo-Orientalist position that betrays a "universalized

---

45. Nigam, "End of Postcolonialism."

provinciality" not a true universality. His words on the subject are worth quoting in full:

> The trick of Eurocentrism is that it matches identity politics with the search for the universal, and then it opposes identity politics elsewhere as vicious forms of victimization. The search for the universal is thus tied to exclusivism and the affirmation of particularity: the highest religion, Christianity, corresponds with the highest civilization, Europe. . . . This ideological framework has been part and parcel of Western modernity. Christianity, liberalism, and Marxism for the most part define themselves within this scheme of things. Christian and Marxist orthodox oppositions to secular liberalism are thus the outcome of an intra-modern struggle for the heritage of Western exceptionalism and universality. The overall result it the *recolonization* of entire areas of thought and the suspension of dialogue.[46]

Dabashi would agree with Maldonado-Torres's label for Žižek's provincial pseudo-universalism since he concludes that even though postcolonial thinkers learned the texts and culture of Europe, their "interlocutors have never had any reason to reciprocate. They had become provincial in their assumptions of universality."[47] Dabashi's work serves as paradigmatic since he links Latin American liberation theology with Islamic movements specifically, but is also open to finding common cause with movements across the globe.[48] Whereas the Marxist Žižek drops the proverbial ball in not utilizing Latin American liberation theology, Dabashi links up Latin American, Black and Islamic forms, among others. In short, there is an appeal here to a global dimension for theory, yet one that attempts to be truly global. This is a true attack on the arbitrary boundaries set by Orientalists, heresiologists or secularists suspicious of theological or spiritual movements.

One of the worst aspects of Žižek's philosophy remains his dismissal of multiculturalism as a hegemonic discourse. On the one hand, his point generally consists of the way politically correct speech avoids direct

---

46. Maldonado-Torres, "Liberation Theology," 53. For a good overview of Latin American liberation theology, paying close attention to its Marxist roots, see Löwy, *War of Gods*, 32–80.

47. Dabashi, *Can the Non-Europeans Think*, 5.

48. Dabashi, *Islamic Liberation Theology*, 14, 251–52. The seriousness of Dabashi's understanding of liberation movements is evident by the way he opens his book with a quote by Gustavo Gutiérrez and Malcolm X.

confrontation with our biases towards the differences we have with other peoples and their culture. Because of PC talk we avoid the oftentimes deep prejudices and hostilities toward other people that reside in the collective unconscious and that are only sometimes manifested by fundamentalist movements in society. His claim is that fascist are the best at taking advantage of this multicultural hegemony. On the other hand, his reasoning provides an escape for people to not actually engage with other cultures outside the West, but to instead see these discourses as unnecessarily being utilized to stamp out one's own freedom of expression. For the sake of his Marxist reading on the universalism of global capitalism, any other critical theory that steers away from this center is dismissed.

The real hegemonic discourse exposed by Sara Ahmed and Mignolo is monoculturalism or mono-nationalism.[49] In short, what inevitably happens if we follow Žižek's reasoning consists of attacking the minority cultures within a given society for not appreciating the generosity of the dominant culture. Ahmed responds on this abused love: "Migrants enter the national consciousness as ungrateful. Ironically then racism becomes attributed to the failure of migrants to receive our love. The monocultural hegemony involves the fantasy that multiculturalism is the hegemony."[50]

---

49. Ahmed, "Liberal Multiculturalism is the Hegemony;" Dabashi, *Can the Non-Europeans Think*, xxxv–xxxvi. Also, see Elizondo, *Future is Mestizo*, 95.

50. Ibid. For readers concerned with an issue like women's rights and traditional forms of thought, this is a point that needs to be worked out in a democratic, pluralistic society. It is not always a black and white issue. There are forms of cultural-religious expressions that we would probably deem progressive by contemporary standards. For example, one can find a book written by women on the feminist value of almost any traditional, religious school. To simply equate religion with barbarism is sloppy thinking. Moreover, we should not just assume that Western secular society is automatically tolerant and the universal model. Many of the thinkers in this chapter point out that as Europe became more secular its racism actually grew worse. Still, unlike some of these theorists, I do not agree that the Western secular paradigm is completely bankrupt (nor do I agree that ancient religions need to be forgotten for the benefit of humanity like some of the new atheists argue). In fact I do think a form of secularization based on historical reason and experience is important to challenge what some see as the givens of religious faith. There is constant negotiation that needs to continue. To some extent, Žižek attempts to do this in his works on Christianity. When Žižek argues from a Hegelian-Marxist position he intentionally works toward a progressive society and one that directly challenges fundamentalisms and the abuse of a global capitalism. This is just one position among many. Its foundation goes back to the eighteenth century Enlightenment and the secularization of Western Christianity. Again, the number one problem I see with Žižek's work is that he tends to write from his universalist position, exclusionary of competing traditions.

This is the Eurocentric fantasy that cannot comprehend why theorists across the world are attempting to delink from the Western paradigm. In order to be part of the Western legacy means giving up on one's cultural roots. And when figures outside the West make this decision toward the universal, they are often pushed to the periphery of the movement.

In full agreement with Ahmed, I have witnessed both faculty and undergraduates cynically smile about university advertisement brochures featuring the multicultural staff or diverse student body. It does not take special glasses to see the marketing power of these type of brochures. However, would we want a brochure that just featured blonde, blue-eyed women or one that only had men? Is this more real? If the ethos of multiculturalism or the disciplines of the various cultural studies departments are abandoned, what are we then left with?

Perhaps the biggest pleasure in exploring the writings of Žižek's critics corresponds to the benefits in reading theological literature outside of the Western canon: discovering critical theory that matches the depth and intelligence of the major European thinkers like Nietzsche, Heidegger, and others. For example, it was reading Mignolo's books that I came across the work of Jamaican cultural theorist Sylvia Wynter. Mignolo and Wynter were the two primary writers to influence my own thoughts on teaching historical-theological thought focused on 1492. Wynter argues that 1492 represented a general upheaval of the modern formation of humanity, yet so does the recent upheavals of the 1950s-1960s that challenged the modern European mode of thinking about humanity.[51] Wynter's contemporary challenge targets the way 1492 denied rationality specifically to the people of the new world and to Africans because they were defined by the binary logic of European Christianity. Her project consists of breaking apart these binaries as they continue to surface in today's world and the way the whole world was joined together by 1492. In light of these events, we realize that humanity is inter-connected across borders. If we follow the trend set by Žižek and others, we would never be exposed to the amazing theoretical work of global thinkers. To Žižek's credit, he does engage from time to time with thinkers outside of Europe, but seems to reinterpret them through his framework of European universality. It remains for theorists like Wynter and Mignolo to argue for "diversality" rather than universality.[52]

---

51. See Wynter, "1492: A New World," 40–50. For more on Wynter, see McKittrick, *Sylvia Wynter*; and Henry, *Caliban's Reason*, 117–43.

52. Mignolo, "Geopolitics of Knowledge," 255–56. Mignolo makes this claim directly

What is one of the ways to move forward from this Žižek debate? Perhaps turning toward a quick glance at some historians and theorists who purposely write from a non-European viewpoint will illustrate that Žižek's appeal for a universalized Christian/European position needs to be discarded as a relic of a bygone era. Again, my point is not that we should now abandon European literature for the sake of being postcolonial or multicultural. My point is that because of recent history, our historical consciousness should be more attuned to the diverse global voices. Just because some writing comes from the third world does not make it automatically good literature or theory. However, there is an unfortunate gross ignorance of non-European literature especially here in the US, even though many history teachers are trying to correct this issue.

The Indian historian Dipesh Chakrabarty, in his classic book *Provincializing Europe*, illustrates how that the discipline of history features the privileging of European history.[53] Chakrabarty comes from the school of subaltern studies, which is often connected to the origins of postcolonialism. He writes that "other histories tend to become variations" about European history since the discipline was created with a European historicist ideology.[54] Thus even when writers outside of Europe attempt to narrate their history, they are caught in a web of European scholarship, including representations that do not capture the true diversity of this other place. Chakrabarty's book has the rare distinction of oftentimes being referenced in a number of historiographical books, featured as a pioneering example of subaltern studies and postcolonial historiography. It has served as a starting point for decolonial and postcolonial thinkers to try to think differently about history. Mignolo, for instance, responds to Chakrabarty's work: "If history is a European kit as far as the content of the conversation is concerned, memory should become a practice of restitution that digs into the silences of the past transcending the disciplinary of history embedded in the colonial difference and the coloniality of power."[55]

Mignolo's thoughts on the use of memory as a tool against Eurocentrism are helpful in exposing the tangled roots of the historical discipline.

---

against Žižek's universalism.

53. See Chakrabarty, *Provincializing Europe*, 3–23; Nayar, *Postcolonialism*, 75–80; see Mignolo, *Local Histories/Global Designs*, 205 and 245 on Chakrabarty's historiographical dilemma. See Žižek, *Living in the End Times*, 279–91 for his critique of Chakrabarty's position against Marxist universality.

54. Ibid., 28. For Chakrabarty's definition of historicism see 22–23 and 237–55.

55. Mignolo, *Local Histories/Global Designs*, 324.

As we have seen, some of the worst examples of racist writings came from modern historians. One could make the same argument with Western theology with regards to other religions, especially Islam.[56]

S. Sayyid in his book, *A Fundamental Fear: Eurocentrism and the Emergence of Islamism*, continues Dabashi's thoughts by challenging the overuse of the term fundamentalism. The use and understanding of the term follows a European intellectual framework. The topic of the divine reveals an important distinction between secular Eurocentrism and Islamism. He asserts: "The West sees in Islam the distorted mirror of its own past. It marks the rebirth of the God they had killed so that Man (*sic*) could live. The Islamic resurgence marks the revenge of God; it signals the return of faith, the return of all that puts into question the idea of the progressive liberation of humanity."[57] Sayyid insists:

> The battle between eurocentrism and the logic of Islamism is really a conflict about genealogies—a struggle about how to narrate the future of the world. The western discourse is a product of a number of projects which narrate the world in terms of the continuity of the West. The limit of Europe comes when groups of people begin to articulate their position on the basis of the rejection of Europe's claims to copyright.[58]

Historians on the subject of the rise of Europe tend to follow on different sides of this argument, yet recent historians are more apt to challenge any type of exceptional status in contrast to other civilizations. For example, Robert Marks illustrates a non-Eurocentric reading of modern history by showing how other countries were "more advanced" than Europe during 1500-1800.[59] Until recently, China, India, the Ottomans, the Aztecs, Mayans, and the Incas were often ignored in world history books or seen as backwards in the type of Hegelian philosophy of history texts. No one would argue that Europe becomes dominant in the nineteenth century because of industrialization, connecting to its infamous *isms* of colonialism and imperialism. Marks closes his book by declaring, "Western superiority

---

56. See Toscano, *Fanaticism*, 161–66 for Žižek's narrow view of Islam.
57. Sayyid, *Fundamental Fear*, 4.
58. Ibid., 149–50.
59. Marks, *Origins of the Modern World*, 14. To Žižek's credit he also notes the importance of China in global affairs, but tends to discuss it as a warning to the West of the so-called Asian values. Again, this terminology is severely criticized by Dabashi among others.

or preeminence has hardly been evident throughout much of human history over the past millennium," noting the "resurgence of Asia" in the twentieth century further presents problems for a Eurocentric history.[60] Eurocentric philosophers like Žižek and others simply ignore the work of historians like Marks or Peter Gran.[61] If we believe Marks' narrative then Europe is not exceptional in a Hegelian universal history sort of sense. In some regards, as we saw last chapter, Jacob Taubes and Karl Löwith will criticize the Christian exceptionalist reading of history that created Eurocentrism.

The Holocaust presents a watershed moment for Christian history especially because of the erasure of the Jewish roots of this religion. The reason Dietrich Bonhoeffer became such a recognizable name was because his opposition to the Nazis as a Christian theologian was the exception and not the rule. However, without downplaying the importance of the Holocaust for contemporary history, and the crucial plea to never forget this heinous crime against humanity, many theorists across the globe wonder why the Holocaust gains exceptional status whereas other acts of genocide are forgotten. Why did Christians become culpable for the Holocaust but not 1492 or the Atlantic slave trade? Is this a problem between the recent past and the distant past?

The Nigerian writer Wole Soyinka, famous for his *Death and the King's Horseman*, discusses the importance of memory in holding to account the injustices suffered in the past and the present, contending against appeals to quick reconciliation without some type of acknowledgment of the wrongs committed. Turning to the role of the arts, he writes that "the poet appropriates the voice of the people and the full burden of their memory."[62] Speaking on the matter of the Atlantic slave trade and the topic of reparations, he finds a certain Eurocentrism culpable:

> It is not difficult to establish an abundance of reasons why the history of slavery must continue to plague the memory of the world. Principle among these is the simple fact that the history of humanity is incomplete without its acknowledgment, and the

---

60. Ibid., 199. There is a plethora of historical literature on this subject. A good place to start is Marks's book. Other books to consult on this genre are Frank, *ReOrient*; Pomeranz, *The Great Divergence*; and Wong, *China Transformed*. Much of the historical debate centers on challenging some of the Eurocentric assumptions of the larger-than-life theories of Marx and Weber. To some extent, I would say that this goes for both the disciplines of history and theology.

61. See Gran, *Beyond Eurocentrism*, 1–22.

62. Soyinka, *Burden of Memory*, 21.

history of the African continent, including its economic history, would remain truncated. Next, objectively, the Atlantic slave trade remains an inescapable critique of European humanism. In a different context, I have railed against the thesis that it was the Jewish Holocaust that placed the first question mark on all claims of European humanism—from the Renaissance through the Enlightenment to present-day multicultural orientation. Insistence on that thesis, we must continue to maintain, merely provides further proof that the European mind has yet to come into full cognition of the African world as an equal sector of a universal humanity, for, if it had, its historic recollection would have placed the failure of European humanism centuries earlier—and that would be at the very inception of the Atlantic slave trade. This, we remind ourselves, was an enterprise that voided a continent, it is estimated, of some twenty million souls, and transported them across the Atlantic under conditions of brutality that have yet to be beggared by any other encounter between races. Reparations, then, as a structure of memory and critique, may be regarded as a necessity for the credibility of Eurocentric historicism, and a corrective for its exclusionist worldview.[63]

Soyinka, in fact, carries on a message that Jewish theologian Richard Rubenstein and Jewish historian George Mosse posited.[64] Racism is a modern phenomenon targeting primarily both Jews and Africans. The most obvious historical examples are the Atlantic slave trade and the Holocaust. As the eighteenth-century Enlightenment era dawned, racism became more respectable because it was packaged in the language of anthropology, science, and nationalist historical myths. In many ways, this corresponded with the rise of secularism in European society and the ethical impulse raised by religious traditions to care for the neighbor. Rubenstein and Mosse agree with Soyinka that it was the historic treatment of Europeans colonized people, in most cases, on the basis of their black skin, that led into the systematic attempt to cleanse European soil of the Jewish people. In short, the slave and torture system of the Nazis were based on historical examples from other European nations and the United States. It is the light of this history of racism that Aimee Césaire chastises Europe.[65] In fact, even

---

63. Ibid., 38–39; also see 90–91 for Soyinka's appeal that Africans are not jumping on the "bandwagon" for reparations but predates other examples.

64. Rubenstein, *Cunning of History*, 36–47; Mosse, *Toward the Final Solution*, xxv–xxx.

65. Césaire, *Discourse on Colonialism*, 36.

Žižek admits that "whenever we are tempted by the fascinating spectacle of Third World violence, we should always take a self-reflexive turn and ask ourselves how we ourselves are implicated in it."[66]

What do the appeals of suffering at the hands of Europeans in the past and the present matter for historical-theological thought? Christian thought in the post-war period focused on dealing with the anti-Semitism in its history, yet continues to struggle with its ties to European conquest and colonialism. Does the position of the oppressed still follow a Eurocentric logic that places the non-European in a submissive role, denying the role of historical agency? We will now explore this question by looking at the event of 1492 and its historical-theological importance for Latin American thinkers.

Challenging Eurocentrism from Latin America

"I no longer feel like enrolling (or requesting membership) in a new abstract universal project that claims a fundamental European legacy."
—Walter Mignolo[67]

What is often missing from European theorists who praise the inevitable rise of the European West is the huge role played by the conquest of the Americas. A special issue of the Catholic journal *Concilium* featured a number of Latin American theologians commemorating the 500-year anniversary of Columbus's voyage.[68] In fact, a number of books were published around 1992 in order to challenge a Eurocentric reading of 1492. One of the best examples of this literature is Luis Rivera-Pagan's book *A Violent Evangelism*.[69] His book features a historical-theological reading because it

---

66. Žižek, *Living in the End Times*, 161.

67. Mignolo, "Geopolitics of Knowledge," 256.

68. Boff and Elizondo, *1491–1992: The Voice of the Victims*. See Trouillot, *Silencing the Past*, 108-140 for an excellent study of the history of Columbus Day across the globe, closing his chapter with how activists began challenging the nobility of commemorating 1492 as an ideal. He also covers the difference between seeing this history as *discovery*, *encounters*, or *conquest*.

69. Rivera, *A Violent Evangelism*, xiii–xvii; also see Rivera-Pagan's essays in *Essays from the Margins* for shorter summaries of material presented in his book. Moreover, historian Justo González writes a short yet powerful Foreword to Rivera-Pagan's book, noting the importance of 1492 for present and future history.

illustrates the importance of Christian ideas in the historical events. He pays attention to both the history of the indigenous in the Americas and of the African slaves, while presenting the theological types arguing on how to handle this changing world. Rivera-Pagan's book should be considered part of a genealogy of historical-theological texts that takes 1492 as a starting point for modern history, detailing the history of Latin America. Pioneering books in this tradition would be Pablo Richard's *Death of Christendoms, Birth of the Church: Historical Analysis and Theological Interpretation of the Church in Latin America*, with his utilization of periodization, and Enrique Dussel's *A History of the Church in Latin America* (who we will examine below).[70] Again, the common theme in all these books is the attention given to both history and theology.

Samir Amin, who has popularized the term Eurocentrism, challenges European exceptionalism, pointing out the global significance of 1492 as a major historical turning point.[71] He is critical of some of the ideology coming from the Islamic world, but also asserts that "Eurocentrism has brought with it the destruction of peoples and civilizations that have resisted its spread."[72] José Rabasa, in his book *Inventing America: Spanish Historiography and the Formation of Eurocentrism*, calls Eurocentrism "a pervasive condition of thought" framed as universality "because it affects both Europeans and non-Europeans."[73] Books like *Year 501: The Conquest Continues* by Noam Chomsky were written with the same mentality.[74]

First Nations Christian theologian Randy Woodley, who sees life in the Americas as "better prior to 1492," frames the Eurocentric foundation of modernity thus:

> The European Enlightenment was preceded by and paralleled the European Renaissance. The Renaissance was a return to the cultural and intellectual forms of the ancient Greeks. European art, literature, architecture, and such were all influenced by the "classical" era of the Greeks, and sometimes of the Roman Empire.

---

70. Richard, *Death of Christendoms, Birth of the Church*, 15–18; Dussel, *History of the Church in Latin America*, 3–35.

71. Amin, *Eurocentrism*, 152–53 and *Global History*, 17 and 174. Also see Sayyid, *Fundamental Fear*, 127–29 for a critique of Amin's socialism.

72. Ibid., 185.

73. Rabasa, *Inventing America*, 18. Rabasa quotes from Turner's *Marx and the End of Orientalism* to warn of the Eurocentrism of even progressive and leftist writings from the Hegelian and Marxist schools.

74. Chomsky, *Year 501*, 3–32.

During the Renaissance, empire in its classical forms was glamorized and utilized in new ways. The cultural Renaissance worked well as a vehicle to transport the philosophical and democratic ideas of the Greeks and the military prowess of the Romans, in order to make empire building seem both romantic and right.[75]

Richard Twiss, another First Nations author, whom we will look at in detail next chapter, continues Woodley's thoughts:

> When the first European Christians arrived in North America, the Christianity they introduced had the devastating effect of a hostile pandemic-like religion- an aberrant representation of Jesus and a gross misrepresentation of the gospel. It was a Christianity so thoroughly contextualized to European civilization that the mixture of values of the culture with Christianity made it aberrant in terms of its net impact on the tribes here. They were perhaps well-intentioned people with noble aspirations, yet they were possessed of worldview assumptions infected with hegemonic presuppositions fueled by modernism, humanism and rationalism.[76]

Finally, writing from an African-American perspective, Michael Eric Dyson challenges the celebration of the "ideal of European discovery" divorced from the "critical social, cultural, and historical context" when declaring that "the *initial* process of genocide is *continued* when the historical acknowledgment of its implementation is concealed beneath myths of European progress, expansion, and civilization."[77]

These thoughts are in agreement about the nature of the first European explorers to the Americas in 1492. There are at least two points to summarize. First, the Renaissance is important because it illustrates the time period Europeans realized they had the technology to find and to conquer other peoples. Second, the myth of the Greco-Roman past as a particular European past denies the Mediterranean basis. Sometimes figures like Ibn Rushd (Averroes) gets credit for assisting Western rationality, yet the Islamic and Jewish contributions are oftentimes forgotten.[78] Now history written in the recent past narrate the moment of Renaissance and

---

75. Woodley, *Shalom and the Community of Creation*, 77 and 104. Woodley views life as "better" among Native Americans because of the general harmonious existence of humans with nature, integrating spirituality in everyday life rather than the dualistic worldview of Europeans.

76. Twiss, *Rescuing the Gospel from the Cowboys*, 78.

77. Dyson, *Reflecting Black*, 163–66.

78. See Ramadan, *What I Believe*, 80–84.

Discovery as bring upon the world a coming age of reason and progress. However, the question being asked today is what has the five hundred years of European expansion done to the world? Wrapped up in this question is what has Christianity also done?

Christian triumphalism is at the root of modern Eurocentrism. For example, Hegel's philosophy of history is a secularized version, casting the nation-state rather than the church as the agent of history.[79] Christian theology of history begets demythologized secular European philosophy of history. Both Dussel and Ellacuría join together in their condemnation of this narrow and privileged reading of history. Only a European based institution could be celebratory in its own success while ignoring the suffering across the globe. In order to correct this Eurocentric philosophy of history is to look at models from Latin America. Since at the roots of modern philosophy of history are theological, we will look at the way Dussel and Ellacuría map out an alternative view from the vantage point of Latin America (and Spain). Their projects consist of both continuities and discontinuities of a Christian narrative of history, beginning this reading of history with the starting point of 1492.

The focus on these two theologians attempts to follow the minority literature recommended by Dabashi and Mignolo. Dussel and Ellacuría are both Latin American religious thinkers. It is in this sense I follow the agenda laid out by Latino Christian thinkers De La Torre and Aponte:

> Traditional theology, as done by Eurocentric men, necessarily differs from the theology done by African Americans, Asian/Pacific Americans, Native Americans, or Hispanics. Yet, Eurocentric theologies have positioned themselves historically and socially as the "center" in worldwide theological thought, as though they were somehow more objective and more legitimate. Any theology constructed by others, perhaps by those on the "margins," automatically becomes a response to, or a dialogue with, the "center." Any attempt by a people to study God apart from the self-appointed center risks ridicule as "nonscholarly." Unless established "authorities" like Rahner, Bultmann, Von Balthasar, Barth, Lonergan, Niebuhr, Tillich, or Brunner are mentioned, theologies from the margins often are considered lightweight and irrelevant. Yet, theology done at the self-appointed center can continue to be relevant to all without ever having to mention, discuss, or understand

---

79. Mignolo, *Local Histories/Global Designs*, ix–xxiii.

Aquino, Elizondo, Espin, González, Isasi-Díaz, Pineda, Segovia, or Villafañe.[80]

De La Torre and Aponte point out the same double standard about theology that Dabashi and Mignolo discuss about critical theory and philosophy. Eurocentrism is a one way street. The only way to properly challenge it is to focus on those thinkers from the margins and somewhat ignore and avoid the European authorities. Therefore, in order to understand the historical-theological dimension of Eurocentrism we turn to Dussel and Ellacuría.

Regarding religious history, Dussel claims that history that has a universal church as its center has been typically Eurocentric. He writes: "The existing histories of the 'universal' Church are not histories of the 'universal' Church at all. If you don't believe me, read what they have to say about Latin America."[81] Until recently, and mostly because of the insistence of intellectuals like Dussel located in the Latin America, the focus on the universal church has transformed to the globalized church. Since both thinkers are located in the Roman Catholic tradition, they see Vatican II as the turning point, with special attention toward liberation theology.[82]

Ellacuría claims that the reason for the Eurocentrism is the problem of social place.[83] This idea is not just a sociological one but also a historical and theological question. He suggests that "the Church" has not just situated itself in the First World but also aligns itself with the dominant classes.[84] Ethna Regan points out that his theology is "historically conscious and historically responsive" because of its attention to the "weight of reality."[85] Ellacuría insists that "the existence of dispossessed majorities everywhere and the fact that Western peoples have numerous responsibilities both past and present towards them obliges every Church to look at them preferentially in all their concrete reality, or at least to consider this reality as an unavoidable horizon. That reality is, as a whole, that of a crucified humankind."[86] On this point Ellacuría joins Dussel in exposing

---

80. De La Torre and Aponte, *Introducing Latino/a Theologies*, 42–43. This book has an excellent annotated bibliography at the end for further study.

81. Dussel, *History and the Theology of Liberation*, 32.

82. Ibid., 80–81. Also see Löwy, *War of Gods*, 41 for the importance of Vatican II and the Cuban Revolution for liberation theology.

83. See Ellacuría, "True Social Place," 283–92.

84. Ibid., 288.

85. Regan, *Theology and the Boundary Discourse*, 166–67.

86. Ellacuría, "True Social Place," 291–92.

the ideology of Eurocentrism in its indifference toward the poor majority. By focusing on the social place and historical record of the third world, both thinkers criticize any language of Christian triumphalism located in Europe.

However, Christian triumphalism is attempting a comeback. This can be seen in the recent books like Brad Gregory's *The Unintended Reformation* and Michael Allen Gillespie's *The Theological Origins of Modernity*.[87] Both books feature at the very least two aims. First, they aim to show that modernity caused the breakdown of European Christian society and this had tremendous social-moral ramifications for the world. And secondly, they argue the threat of radical Islam has no counter-movement because Christianity is split into multiple segments (thank you very much, Occam and Luther). There are many problems with the overall views of both authors, but perhaps it is best we follow Walter Mignolo, who insists that Islamophobia and Hispanophobia are historically united.[88] Mignolo places these two together because he writes that the European "global design of the modern/colonial world system" formed by the Spanish conquest of the Americas and the expulsion of the Jews and Muslims from Spain.[89] In other words, as liberation movements seek to make their rights known, particularly from a postcolonial context, Christian theorists of the First World complain, through the veil of Christian piety, that their hegemony has been lost and thus true global security and universal morality as well.

Dussel presents a counter-history of modern history in his book *The Invention of the Americas*, presented on the 500-year anniversary of Columbus' voyage. His claim is that typical Eurocentric histories ignore the ramifications of the European invasion of the Americas, from the Other's perspective.[90] This is accomplished by downplaying the overall importance of both Spanish and Portuguese nations as major players in the beginning of modernity. However, his claim is that the rise of European hegemony across the globe is initiated by this event. A good way to see exactly what

---

87. Gregory, *Unintended Reformation*; Gillespie, *Theological Origins of Modernity*. Both authors point out some of the problems that came with modernity, but I would be more supportive of their case if they showed awareness of literature outside of the Western canon.

88. Mignolo, "Islamophobia/Hispanophobia," 13–28; also see Trouillot, *Silencing the Past*, 74–83 in the way European modern man was created at this time.

89. Mignolo, *Local Histories/Global Designs*, x; 21–22; 49.

90. Rivera, *Touch of Transcendence*, 66–77 for Dussel's use of the Other in his reading of history.

Dussel means about Europe's parasitic relationship to Latin America is this quote about European modernity: "Modernity has shown its double-face even to this day by upholding liberty (the essential liberty of the person in Hobbes or Locke) within Western nations, while at the same time encouraging enslavement outside them."[91]

Dussel explains that for third-world peoples the invasion by Europeans was a "genocidal shock."[92] At the heart of this historical encounter, according to Dussel, was a will-to-power, indifferent to the oppression of the Other, which sees the conquistador Cortez as the "I-conqueror" prototype for the Cartesian, European autonomous subject.[93] The Europeans finally had the technology to pursue conquest, and frame their historical evolution from 1492 as the story of universal history. Therefore, he criticizes modern European intellectuals since Hegel for ignoring this event, blinded by their own narratives of progress and development.[94] Even the so-called counter-discourse of modernity has roots in early modern Spanish Catholic thinkers like Vitoria and de las Casas and not later continental thinkers like Rousseau or Kant.[95] These Spanish Catholic voices standout to Dussel because they were mostly ignored by Eurocentric authors. After ridiculing Eurocentrism, Dussel proceeds to write a history from the experience of Latin American peoples.

History of the Poor

We have seen that specifically Christian history has been Eurocentric. The way that both Latin American thinkers answer this problem is to answer with a focus on the oppressed and the poor. In fact, according to Dussel, this is the privileged place to view history.[96] The preferential option for the poor is at the heart of the program for liberation thought, in addition to its attention to history, realizing salvation in history, and joined together with a theology of praxis.[97]

91. Dussel, *Invention of the Americas*, 123.
92. Ibid., 55–56.
93. Dussel, *Invention of the Americas*, 38 and 43; *History and the Theology of Liberation*, 79; *Underside of Modernity*, 133 and 217.
94. Dussel, *Invention of the Americas*, 19–26.
95. Dussel, *Underside of Modernity*, 135.
96. Dussel, *History and the Theology of Liberation*, 34.
97. Ellacuría, "Challenge of the Poor Majority," 175; "True Social Place," 284.

Ellacuría writes about the poor majority with an element of hopeful utopia attached. This utopian goal allows him to suggest the disruption of historical reason. He asserts: "Only in a utopian and hope-filled spirit can one believe and have enough energy to join with all the poor and oppressed of the world in order to overturn history, to subvert it and send it in another direction." Again, the subject of the university must be on "the study of the dregs our civilization" so we must be willing to respond to internal critiques.[98]

Ellacuría seemed to embody this identification with the crucified people of Latin America. Following his death a nearby community was named after him and was subsequently attacked by military forces. In this sense, the poor as Other is continually crucified. Utilizing Levinas' philosophy, Dussel particularizes the experience of the Other in Latin America to continue to remind the world of this sort of violence.[99]

There are a few points I would like to raise as soft critiques of the philosophers of liberation we have examined. First, Jon Sobrino, one of Ellacuría's best interpreters, suggests that Ellacuría's "instinctive honesty toward reality" is the reason he utilizes the idea of crucified people to awaken the West from its indifferent and inhuman slumbers.[100] However, as important for both Ellacuría and Dussel to utilize terms of Otherness or the crucified people to describe Latin American people in contrast to the European world, there is perhaps a danger of absolutizing this difference and overshadowing the various multiplicities of communities and differences in Latin America.[101] One way I believe we can broaden their perspective away from abstract Otherness is in connecting their readings of history with other histories of other religions especially on the way they also focus on the marginalized. Religious history is forever attached to historical reality and no theory of secularization, as Gil Anidjar among others has noted,

---

98. Ibid., 173.

99. See Torres, *Against War* for the basis of Dussel's use of Levinas' Other in the shadow of postcolonial thought and the work of Frantz Fanon.

100. Sobrino, *No Salvation Outside the Poor*, 7–8.

101. See Schutte, *Cultural Identity and Social Liberation*, 169–73. She is especially critical of Dussel's dualistic view of reality as totality (evil) versus alterity (good). However, Barber, in his study of Dussel's hermeneutics, thinks Dussel's critics suffer from a secularist interpretation that lead his detractors to dismiss him outright; see Barber, *Ethical Hermeneutics*, 115.

would prove otherwise.[102] It is better to realize the extent of the language of Christianity that continues to be utilized even in our so-called secular age.

Second, as much as Ellacuría and Dussel point out the problems of a Eurocentric history, both authors are at some fault for mostly utilizing European philosophies and social sciences in their critique. Performing just a cursory reading of their major texts, one would perhaps wish they would utilize the poetry and literature of Latin American writers rather than an almost exclusive use of theologians, philosophers, and social scientists (European and non-European). As Andrew Gibson has recently shown in his book *Intermittency*, literature has the potential of creating a "resisting subject" especially in the moments preceding or following traumatic historical events.[103] This criticism is not meant that Latin American movements should divorce themselves from ideas and theories based in Europe, or even from Christianity, for that matter. In fact, Ofelia Schutte declares that "a total break with Western powers in the name of strengthening nation liberation movements is to amputate part of the strength of the Latin American and Caribbean societies."[104] It is in this sense that Dussel reminds his readers that since 1492 the two continents are forever linked. Latin American theorists seem to realize this relationship whereas the so-called West needs constant reminder.

Religion, History, and Hermeneutics

"Postcolonial agency is about not forgetting the community or ethnicity, but making sure that others succeed *along with* oneself."
—Pramod K. Nayar[105]

Eurocentrism defined what was rational, natural, and historical for many years. It shaped the academic disciplines of both history and theology, among others. Border thinking, *mestiza* consciousness, liberation theology,

102. See Anidjar, *Semites*, 39–63.

103. Gibson, *Intermittency*, 275–89. I include this book here since Gibson focuses on French critical theory of the late twentieth century to the present. French critical theory was influential for Latin American liberation theology. However, in order for Latin American theology to move forward, it is best served to focus on the great fictional literature originating within its own borders.

104. Schutte, *Cultural Identity and Social Liberation*, 242.

105. Nayar, *Postcolonialism*, 188.

and other third-world ideas have challenged Eurocentrism. These philosophies focused on the forgotten Other of history. Still the formation of critical third-world thought did not exorcise the spirit of Eurocentrism even from its own foundations. This is why a hermeneutic based on an honest historical viewpoint remains a necessary procedure in the postcolonial and decolonial process. This hermeneutic, based on our readings of figures like Dussel and Ellacuría, is an ethical hermeneutic. An ethical hermeneutic frames the study of historical-theological texts in the view toward the Other.

Hermeneutics pays close attention to the view of both the author and the reader. This means things like social location, ethnicity, culture, political and religious views are important for interpretation purposes. Eurocentrism is a viewpoint that ignores or is indifferent to the hermeneutical dimension. Some third-world thinkers are fighting back using an ethical hermeneutics. Their method is sometimes called a hermeneutics of suspicion, and even the preferential option for the poor and oppressed announces its own hermeneutics.

In his book *Contested Memory*, featuring his study of the Eurocentrism of the icons of the modern Western tradition, Kant, Hegel, and Marx, Tsenay Serequeberhan writes that their "candor, in bad faith, is grounded on the epistemically untenable claim that European Modernity has found, or uncovered, the *True* and proper form of human life: the truth of Being."[106] Now one might surmise that he subsequently writes off the Western canon as something to be completely avoided. However, in his book *The Hermeneutics of African Philosophy*, Serequeberhan, borrowing much from the philosophies of the Germans Martin Heidegger and Hans Georg-Gadamer, criticizes those African philosophies that try to break themselves away from any hint of European roots. He says that the "aim is not to return to some 'true,' 'uncontaminated,' 'original,' African *arche*" but instead "to make possible the autonomous and thus authentic self-standing historicity of African existence in the context of the modern world."[107] Japanese theologian

---

106. Serequeberhan, *Contested Memory*, 162–63. In fact, Kant's blatant racism was very influential in Germany. See Mosse, *Toward the Final Solution*, 30–32; Carter, *Race*, 80–121.

Amin notes Marx's tendency toward Eurocentrism but remains convinced that Marx's thought is still useful and has enough global awareness that it does not warrant dismissal; see Amin, *Eurocentrism*, 189–93.

107. Serequeberhan, *Hermeneutics of African Philosophy*, 38. Modern hermeneutics originates with the phenomenology of Husserl and Heidegger in the early twentieth century (tracing back to the work of Schleiermacher and Dilthey). The work of the Italian philosopher Gianni Vattimo, who interprets Christianity as post-universal and

Kosuke Koyama would agree with this sentiment when he writes: "As long as people live in concrete historical world of interactions, it is obvious that there is no such thing as a 'pure, intact self-identity.' Self-identity is a concept of historical interaction. It is always 'shared identity.' We must ask the questions relating to 'shared self-identity' with all nations in the world."[108]

The idea of shared self-identity that Koyama writes about connects with Sylvia Wynter's argument against the either-or choice of the celebrants or dissidents of the birth of modernity in 1492.[109] The celebrants could generally be labeled Eurocentrists and the dissidents are usually associated with the particularity of indigenous rights. According to Wynter, what both groups fail to grasp is how the symbol of 1492 forever established humanity's interrelatedness. To continue to argue for a historical, particular exception potentially leads to further barriers between people based on such categories as race, sex, class, and gender. We must get past the point where we are only concerned about our particular identity group, forsaking the amelioration of all of humanity and the natural world.

Even though it appears impossible to reach to the pre-1492 past and retrieve these traditions in some pure form, yet it remains equally irresponsible to dismiss these traditional philosophies, myths, religions, and experiences. A good hermeneutic accepts the continuing legacy of pre-European and pre-Christian ideas that continue to shape and to inspire third-world people. For example, the poetic description of a distinctly African spirituality by Wole Soyinka illustrates that Christianity does not have a patent on the concept of tolerance.[110] Modern conceptions of rationality are no longer acceptable to dismiss these type of ideas. In fact, the third-world theologians have been especially good in incorporating this heritage and mixing it with

---

post-European is the greatest living interpreter of hermeneutics.

Serequeberhan finds problems with the work of African writers like Kwame Nkrumah, Paulin J. Hountondji, and Leopold Sedar Senghor for either relying too much on European thought or producing their own essentialist vision. Frantz Fanon and Amilcar Cabral are the two theorists that he utilizes in his emancipatory efforts for African thought.

108. Koyama, *Water Buffalo Theology*, 9.

109. Wynter, "1492: A New World View," 5–8.

110. Soyinka, *Burden of Memory*, 48; and *Climate of Fear*, 136–37. For more on the arguments over Latin American and African philosophy, and its connection to the pre-European past, see Henry, *Caliban's Reason*, 21–46; Serequeberhan, *Hermeneutics of African Philosophy*, 13–53; Gordon, *Existentia Africana*, 1–40; Nuccetelli, *Latin American Thought*, 1–68. Oftentimes European modern thought becomes the litmus test on whether African or Latin American ideas are considered real philosophy or not.

the Christian experience, much to the consternation of Christian purists. Moreover, as Serequeberhan makes clear, one may practice a hermeneutics of suspicion without having to rely on the Eurocentrist thought of Kant, Hegel, Marx, Freud, and Nietzsche.

The literature contesting and defending the subject of modernity is vast. On the one hand, the modern world consists of Europe's stamp upon it, so any shying away from this reality betrays real historicity.[111] On the other hand, African-American theorist Robin D. G. Kelley argues that the appeal of the universality of the European tradition with its roots in the Renaissance and the Enlightenment among some progressive theorists "betrays an unwillingness to take ideas seriously, let alone history" because they ignore or downplay the dark side of this heritage.[112] Thus Serequeberhan's critique of European thinkers like Kant and Marx consists of their attempt to philosophize from a non-hermeneutical standpoint divorced from historicity. He declares: "For the historicity of philosophy is always measured against its own conscious awareness—or lack thereof—of its lived presuppositions and its rootedness in a specific tradition and history."[113] In other words, European philosophy like African philosophy bases itself in history, not some timeless place beyond the clouds.

Connected to the rootedness of studying history and theology from a historical-theological hermeneutic features what theologian Marcella Althaus-Reid calls a "subverting, transgressive kind of love" or as Žižek describes this "terror" love.[114] What they mean is that Christian love has a dimension that eschews a detached, neutral view of the world. This view contains the hermeneutic among third-world thinkers speaking

---

111. Serequeberhan, *Hermeneutics of African Philosophy*, 11.

112. Kelley, *Yo'Mama's Disfunktional*, 106. See chapter 4 of Kelley's book to see his critique of the literature appealing to the universal Enlightenment project among leftist and liberal thinkers as a corrective to the culture wars and the so-called New Left.

113. Serequeberhan, *Hermeneutics of African Philosophy*, 30.

114. Althaus-Reid, "From Liberation Theology to Indecent Theology," 21; Žižek, *Living in the End Times*, 116–17. The terms subversion and terror may raise some red flags among readers especially in the light of our 9/11 world. Not all the theorists in this book ascribe to this type of language. For example, Soyinka makes two points. One, the pre-9/11 world outside the West oftentimes experienced terrorism on a daily basis. Second, he argues that Islamic terror is of a different beast than other liberationist movements. He writes: "What kind of morality of a liberation struggle deceives a fourteen-year-old child into becoming a walking bomb?" See Soyinka, *Climate of Fear*, 16–21 and 141. Now Soyinka is making this claim from Nigeria, where he also is wary of the hegemonic military-industrial power of the United States.

consciously from a tradition, acknowledging the ups and downs of human history. In order to recount the history of the oppressed people in the third world, or of those located in the first and second worlds, which are often invisible, one needs to speak from a place of love, willing to disrupt the status-quo views again from a position of love. This is why for many third-world theorists Marxist thinking was in vogue during the twentieth century. Marxism is clearly a hermeneutic that privileges the preferential option of the oppressed. However, as we saw with Žižek, and analyzed by Serequeberhan, one of Marxism's main problems is its Eurocentrism. Latin American liberation theologians in particular utilized Marxist social analysis along with attention to popular religions and *comunidades eclesiales de base*. Nonetheless, for those theologians who leaned too much on a Marxist interpretation, once the Soviet Union crumbled, much of these writings get left for the dustbin of history as a product of a past time.

One of the reasons to detail the suffering caused in history during the age of Europe (1492–1945), as discussed by theorists whose heritage mostly links to ancestors that were trapped by this violence, relates to the way the religious voices remains the global standard to talk about the meaning behind these historical events. It is often a religious historical narrative that fuels the exhortation or the prohibition for terrorist acts. European appeal to secularism blinded theorists throughout the Cold War to this religious discourse. The way to move forward in the twenty-first century consists of listening to and taking serious the message of religious thinkers. In fact, the more space given to religious thinkers speaking the language of tolerance, the better off the world may be.

The language of Otherness is the place to start for both the historian and the theologian. From the last chapter we learned that Barth's idea of the Wholly Other God, at the very least, challenged the hegemonic control that European intellectual thought had of the deity. Third-world theorists, including theologians, tend to ignore Barth's theology in general. However, the idea of the Other as developed by Jewish philosopher Emmanuel Levinas, with roots in the Wholly Other of Kierkegaard and Barth, is often utilized by third-world thinkers. For example, both Dabashi and Dussel base their historical hermeneutics off of Levinas's theories, applying them to the third-world context.[115]

---

115. Dabashi, *Islamic Liberation Theology*, 14, 244, 262, and 266; Dussel, *A History of the Church in Latin America*, 6–7; "Philosophy of Liberation," 339–43. Dussel's philosophy of liberation is built on subaltern studies, postcolonialism, and Levinas's philosophy of the Other mixed with liberation theology. There is also an appreciation of Bhabha's

With the return of religions comes along the return of the philosophies of history. In fact, so does the theologies of history. The major religions of the world find some meaning in history. Even if the end is apocalyptic, dystopian, or overall pessimistic, there is still a narrative that is crafted. In fact, historiography consists of giving meaning to historical events. Theologians, for example, continue to create these stories based on the combination of divine revelation and historical events, yet the secular world stopped taking notice. It is time for both sacred and secular histories to pay attention to each other. Recent global conflicts in the twentieth to the twenty-first century are controlled by religious historical narratives. It is not the sole factor, but it is a factor. We cannot simply blow off this fact as regressive or fundamentalist readings. Religion is an important matter that still guides a majority of humanity. This is what I have joined the historical with the theological. The dash between the historical-theological illustrates the tension that holds these two disciplines together. Thinkers among both what like to do without the other, yet as we have explored in this chapter, the times are changing.

Conclusion

"History teaches us to be aware of the excitation of the liberated and the injustices that often accompany their righteous thirst for justice."
—Wole Soyinka[116]

"Hispanics living in the United States, feminists, the marginalized, the working class of global transnational capitalism, and so on need a historical narrative to reconstruct their memories and makes sense of their struggle."
—Enrique Dussel[117]

Benjamin's Angel of history reminds us that past, present, and future history is littered with catastrophe. As thinkers of liberation, both Dussel and Ellacuría expose this violence especially among the oppressed in Latin America. They are not content with the format of historical reason declaring the world is thus. The cry for the reign of God is a cry for justice against the

---

idea of hybridity (being-in-between, borderlands) which connects well with theories of mestiza/o.

116. Soyinka, *Burden of Memory*, 16.
117. Dussel, "Philosophy of Liberation," 343.

indifference of historical reason and the violence it leaves in its wake. Within the discipline of ecclesiastical history, this is a crucial narrative because religious-based history can either ignore the oppression as outside the concerns of a Eurocentric narrative or sublimate it as simply part of the workings of a sinful world. Ellacuría and Dussel both reveal there is no modern Europe, and its Christian church, without the peoples of the Americas, and that often the roots of global oppression is found at the doorstep of Europe. Both thinkers, along with a host of other third-world theologians, articulate a history that we need to take as seriously as the historiographical genealogy of the Christian West. In fact, as historical-theological works, they correct the often ahistorical writings of European theorists.

Žižek's appeal for Eurocentrism and universal Christianity ignores the messy history that began at 1492. His work serves as an example of the way Eurocentric thinkers, even theorists who are committed to social justice, hearken back to a normative narrative in light of the rise of multiple narratives coming out of the 1960s. Because of Marxism's roots in Eurocentrism even it is susceptible to the charge of normative narrative, though activists and theorists identifying with such movements as liberation theology utilized it. Did the culture wars, critical theory, and ethnic studies take place only for a Eurocentric, normative discourse to reassert itself? Questions about the definitions of normal and abnormal have a history, and it appears that only the type of disciplines that take seriously critical theory will continue to discuss them. Moreover, this turn to narrative also happened in the world of theology. So-called contextual theologies are very much also narrative theologies. This aspect of narrative is one that can potentially be beneficial to historians.

History presents a place for rigorous questioning. Representation remains a powerful weapon, and historians who realize this will continue to critically look at texts and how they are often framed in the relation between knowledge and power. In this chapter, we looked particularly at the history that began with the symbol of 1492. The globalism formed at this date has connected peoples from across the world, but has also initiated a ranking among people based on such factors as race, sex, and gender.

Latin American figures like Ellacuria and Dussel link up with Native Americans like Twiss, Tinker, Woodley, and Black Elk who says, "God did not come to the rich, but he came to the poor people. Not only Indians, but all of the poor people."[118] The attention to suffering and the oppressed is

---

118. Quoted in Costello, *Black Elk*, 175. See Costello's excellent presentation of the

not an element of weakness, but offers the best of religious and indigenous thought. The rise of modernism featured an element of individualism, which, in some cases, presented a selfish care for one's own as an ideal. During the time of European imperialism, many convinced themselves that the catastrophes at the periphery of its borders was a natural occurrence based on the lack of civilization. How did the authors in this chapter respond? First, we have followed thinkers like Dabashi, Mignolo, Wynter, and others who have recommended delinking from the Eurocentric view because of its colonial and imperial violence; and second, we have seen the way these theorists have sought ways to link up with others from the underside of modernity. The mid to late twentieth century finally features the proliferation of voices from below. As we have seen, this below is framed by the historical above from Europe that was created in 1492. Thus we are living in a historical time when Europeans no longer have a monopoly on both historical and theological thought.

Included in the view from below is the continual importance of European thought. Philosophy, history, and theology from Europe remains relevant but should not be privileged at the expense of third-world thought. Žižek's error remains his declaration of this privilege. However, we potentially make the same error that Žižek does if we buy into the narrative that we need to stop listening completely to European theorists because they happen to be European. Any form of tribalism or exclusivism is unacceptable to the historical-theological thinker. Much of the power of third-world movements came from positive contributions by Europeans critically condemning European colonial power. For example, Levinas' impact on Dussel's work features a positive contribution. Moreover, along the same arguments I have made about third-world literature and its history, much European thought is absolutely fascinating. To ignore it because of some principle of identity politics is to miss the pure pleasure of engaging some of the masterpieces of critical thought. In addition, Žižek's challenge at least poses the question about navigating the essentialized language of the underside or the oppressed that is a staple of liberationist thought. There is no apparent reason to police these terms, yet I suggest understanding this language in the light of concrete history. It is in this sense that indigenous and third-world writers can be faithful to the communities they identify with, while at the same time, express their commitment to Christianity. Seeing Christianity, or other religious thought, as simply a foreign element

---

facets of postcolonialism and post-Western Christianity (15-18).

shackled upon people across the globe denies the agency of individuals and whole communities the choice to be or not to be religious. We will see in the next chapter theological voices from below who narrate their histories in a way that shows this interconnectivity.

CHAPTER 3

History as Biography

*McClendon's Use of Narrative
to Create Empathy*

"Stories are people, people are their stories, and stories are alive."
—Richard Twiss[1]

"We are each one of us parables."—William Stringfellow[2]

"When theology ceases to nurture the questions a people need to ask about the history they are creating, critical thought atrophies."—Marc H. Ellis[3]

The nineteenth-century German philosopher Friedrich Nietzsche tends to be a polarizing figure. Often miscast as a prototypical Nazi ideologue or a postmodern pioneer, there is little doubt about his antipathy toward Christianity. Christians have returned the favor by presenting Nietzsche as the harbinger of our so-called postmodern, nihilistic age. However, he also served as an important resource for Christian thinkers like Barth and Bonhoeffer. In fact, Nietzsche became a crucial figure for my own critical development.

1. Twiss, *Rescuing the Gospel*, 191.
2. Stringfellow, *Simplicity of Faith*, 20.
3. Ellis, *Toward a Jewish Theology*, 157.

HISTORY AS BIOGRAPHY

A number of years after my unglamorous finish to high school, I eventually worked my way back into higher education by attending community college classes at El Camino College in Torrance, California. The education I received there was great, pushing me to pursue a concentration in history. However, it was what I did along with my formal education that was formative to my methodology of uniting history and critical thought, including theology.

From listening to audio cassette tapes presenting the lives and ideas of famous philosophers (narrated by Charlton Heston no less) to reading biographies and short introductory books on their thought, I was introduced to a number of fascinating people who proved the maxim that ideas have consequences as a statement of fact.[4] The idea of consequences may sound negative, but it should instead be understood to mean that ideas can have a true and lasting effect on history. I realize there is a rumor that intellectual history is a dying art form or that the history of ideas is a relic from a bygone, Eurocentric era. I wholeheartedly disagree. My argument is that the history of ideas needs to be more inclusive. Indeed, this is what is happening.[5]

I read mostly about the European existentialist and postmodernist philosophers, spending many nights studying Albert Camus and Jacques Derrida among others. The highlight of this voracious reading was the year I read anything I could get my hands on about Kierkegaard and Nietzsche. What a couple of fascinating yet odd fellows! One biography on Nietzsche stood out to me in particular. The book spent much of its time covering his early youth as a pious Christian boy. This seemed remarkable to me because the story of this famous atheist was so genuine. Gone was the bogeyman representations found in much Christian literature. Instead, what I discovered in this book was a flesh and blood human being who abandoned his childhood faith, viewing it later as a danger for philosophical integrity in his later years. It was in that reading of Nietzsche so many years ago that I gained from an empathy I still hold toward him.

Being at least competent in theology, but somewhat a novice with regards to philosophy, I began reading about the lives of these past thinkers and it helped to make their ideas more concrete. In fact, there exists what seems like an infinite amount of secondary sources on the figures

---

4. Sproul, *Consequences of Ideas*. Sproul was actually pretty helpful in, at the very least, introducing me to the history of Western philosophy.

5. For starters, see the essays in Moyn and Sartori, *Global Intellectual History*.

I mentioned that help the novice reader to engage the material. In other words, there is no excuse not to read these figures if you have the will to do it (and a library close by).

The thinkers I covered in my own intellectual biography tend to be mostly philosophers. It was actually the writing of Philip Yancey that opened up my experience to Christian figures outside of my comfort zone of Augustine and the Protestant Reformers. His book *Soul Survivor*, for example, presented characters outside of my own Calvinist brand of Protestantism that I faithfully ascribed to at the time. Like Yancey, I believe that biographies of real people can be good for theology.[6] Reading biographies of people challenges the sweeping conclusions one often see declared by demagogues or ideological groups (such as, that *all* the Founding Fathers were Christians, or that they were *all* racists). What one finds instead is nuance and a challenge to the assumptions we are taught about history.

When I turned toward studying theologians it was generally in the classroom by lecture and textbook. What stood out to me the most was when theologians discussed the topic of history. As C. T. McIntyre makes clear, theologians in the twentieth century had a newfound respect for history.[7] Since they self-identified as Christian, many approached history with an appreciation of the religious life, challenging the radical historicism of the times. A number of Christian thinkers mused about the relationship between God's will and the history of human beings. However, if we decide to continue this trend, in what discipline do we place this subject? On the one hand, are historians qualified to discuss the theological implications of God's plan for the universe? On the other hand, are theologians out of line when they begin to analyze the contextual events in human history within the overall schema of systematic theology?

Theologians generally deal with the topic of history under the category of creation, providence, or eschatology. This could theoretically be accomplished without actually engaging events from human history.[8] Moreover, theologians will at times discuss the research of the historical Jesus because

---

6. See Yancey, *Soul Survivor*. I cannot emphasize enough how important this book was for my own entrance into the academic world. For example, his chapter on Tolstoy and Dostoevsky was the basis for much of my early undergrad research. In fact, reading Dostoevsky was the impetus to go back to college and work in some capacity in the humanities. In addition, his chapter on Nouwen pushed me to take a class at Fuller on spirituality featuring his work.

7. McIntire, *God, History, and Historians*.

8. See Balthasar, *A Theology of History* as a primary example.

of its recent importance. Historians generally avoid such discussions and would rather focus on the particular subject they spent years researching. In short, historians rarely delve into the voluminous pages of systematic theology, and theologians avoid chronicling historical events because theology has its own science to worry about. Does the lack of attention to concrete lived lives hurt the discipline of theology? Does the general indifference of historians toward theologian's theories about history, marinated in the language of religious thought, harm society's comprehension of the various faiths? Where is there the opportunity to gain empathy in either of these options?

The simple answer to these questions is to further advocate for an interdisciplinary approach. Both theologians and historians are actually by nature interdisciplinary. This is the aim of the historical-theological perspective that I have advocated in this book. Finding inspiration in the work of Baptist theologian James McClendon, this chapter will turn to the topic of biography, a favorite genre of the historical discipline. Here I follow Eddie Glaude's advice:

> Our character and capacity to act freely result not only from a past which shapes and informs who we are but also from the kinds of stories we tell ourselves about that past. In responding to the demands of life we situate ourselves by telling stories-stories not of abstracted concepts (race or nation) but of people, situated in circumstances, struggling to respond to those circumstances with the tools at hand.[9]

Glaude's words reflect McClendon's theological focus on flesh-and-blood human beings. Moreover, his words challenge Barth's abstract concept of the neighbor defined by the nation that we looked at in chapter 1. Theological thinkers concentrating on the underside of history started the process of telling these stories. As we saw in chapter 2, this history was not one that presented stories of the elite or the bourgeois, but instead the narratives of the working class and especially the poor, challenging misconceptions of groups of people based on the category of race. The evolution of historical thought shows signs of the fall of the hegemony of Eurocentric histories.

Stories about people are what makes history interesting. Church history, for example, fascinates because it shows the ups and downs of some of the great Christian thinkers in the past including their relationships to

9. Glaude, *In a Shade of Blue*, 79.

family and friends. Focus on people's lives leads to intimate details, searching through letters and diaries, and now emails and text messages. A novel aspect of history writing is the importance of hermeneutics even in the writing of a historical biography. For instance, there are numerous biographies of Luther because each writer studies Luther for a reason that is special to him or her. Some biographies become authoritative because they have impressed a large and impressive readership, setting the bar high for future books. The future will definitely feature more biographies on Jefferson, Lincoln, Martin Luther King Jr., and other famous people. In addition, there is a crucial need for more biographies of people not as famous as presidents and pastors.

The focus of this chapter will be on the particular stories of particular people especially from outside the European world, serving as a source of religious inspiration and ethical model. We will first look at the use of biography for theology in general, closing the chapter by examining diverse examples of this trend. A diverse reading of religious experience showcases a better sample size of historical reality. Gone are the days when religious expression across the world can be dismissed as simply premodern, mythical thought and practices. Modern thought centered in Europe assumed that religion is some kind of opiate, neurosis, or Nietzschean anti-nature, while at the same time, classifying non-Europeans as barbarians. In many ways religious expression especially across the third world has made a comeback in recent years. It is time to take seriously the overwhelming evidence of the importance of religious, spiritual expression in history.

Theologians, many who identify as liberationist, provide a model of combining theology as an academic discipline with the histories of the people they associate with. I turn to their work primarily because they commit themselves to write theology in accordance with the historical experience of their identity group(s). Furthermore, it is time to advocate reading biographies not simply of other Christians, but of people from other faiths as well. We will accomplish this by looking at the way some theorist use the biographies of Martin Luther King Jr. and Malcolm X as inspiration for living ethically in this world. In short, thinkers from across the globe have utilized a form of biography as theology that is only recently catching on among North American and European theologians. In this sense, they are able to teach the West how to write biography as theology in a way to produce empathy in the reader.

HISTORY AS BIOGRAPHY

Biography as Theology

"To read stories of people—their myths, legends, folktales, and real-life stories—is a liberating experience." —C. S. Song[10]

One of the reasons that I became a historian of Christianity in particular is because it allowed me to tell the stories of the fascinating characters that identify with the Christian faith. I am often caught off guard at the up and down movements of some of these biographies. Just because we are talking about some people we identify as saints does not mean their stories consist of a twenty-four-hour routine of praying and reading the Bible at a monastery. Instead, we often interact with great intellectual minds that had a messy family life or figures that wanted to live a separated life in the desert to practice piety only to be drawn into a major social-political conflict of epic proportions.

Some recent general Christian history texts do a good job in presenting the biographies of the who's who of the faith while also raising critical theological questions. For example, Diana Butler Bass's *A People's History of Christianity*, inspired by American historian Howard Zinn's famous text, presents two thousand years of Christian history purposely focused on the outsiders and those who were faithful to the Great Commandment (Luke 10:25-28).[11] Rita Nakashima Brock and Rebecca Ann Parker present the history of Christianity as a betrayal of Christ's message of love and positive hope for the renewal of the earth for instead a turn toward the hopelessness of the sinful creation and the violence of the cross in dealing with this despair.[12] Like Bass, Brock and Parker often focus on the outsiders that challenged this trend or the main initiators of Christian violence.[13] Furthermore, and on a different note, theologian David Bentley Hart's *The Story of Christianity* is helpful especially to the Western reader because of his position as an Eastern Orthodox thinker, providing accounts of figures in Syria, Ethiopia and other non-European places, and Mark Noll's *Turning Points* is perhaps one of the best generalized accounts that I would recommend

10. Song, *Believing Heart*, 66.
11. Bass, *People's History of Christianity*, 1-18.
12. Brock and Parker, *Saving Paradise*, ix-xxii.
13. Ibid., 317-25 and 342-76, for their engrossing account of the Spanish Conquest of the Americas and the North American (including Puritans) colonist wars against the Native Americans.

to the beginning student because it manages to set the historical context of two thousand years while each chapter focuses on a big event.[14] What all the above Christian history books have in common is that they are short, readable accounts of history that oftentimes ask penetrating theological questions of their readers.[15] However, we cannot limit ourselves in thinking that Christian history is only dealt with in books found in the Church History aisle at the bookstore (do these exist anymore?). The aim of this chapter is to introduce the reader to the biographies, stories, and narratives of primarily non-European people of faith found in their theological and religious works.

Historians might find James McClendon's use of biography a good meeting place with theologians. McClendon does not eschew propositional theology for the sake of promoting narrative theology, but that ideas connect to "lived experience."[16] The attention to this lived experience challenges any theology that tries to approach its subject matter as some type of pure science. Instead his method connects well with Korean American theologian Jung Young Lee's open declaration in his book *Marginality: The Key to Multicultural Theology*:

> Theology is autobiographical, but it is not an autobiography. My theology is not just a story of my life. It is the story of my faith journey in the world. It is my story of how God formed me, nurtures me, guides me, loves me, allows me to age, and will end my life. It is my story of seeking who I am in relation to the community, the natural environment, time and history, and the ultimate reality of my existence which I accept by faith. It is my story of seeking to understand how God acts in my life and in the lives of those who are part of my life. It is a faith-reflection on my life, whether it is told in poetry, in parable, or in narrative. Theology is certainly autobiographical, because I alone can tell my faith story. However, it is not an autobiography. Telling my story is not itself theology but a basis for theology, indeed the primary context for doing my theology. This is why one cannot do theology for another. If theology is contextual, it must be at root autobiographical.[17]

---

14. Hart, *Story of Christianity*; Noll, *Turning Points*.

15. For a thorough study of Christian history see especially González, *Story of Christianity*.

16. McClendon, *Biography as Theology*, 178.

17. Lee, *Marginality*, 7.

On the one hand, Lee presents an autobiographical narrative of faith that a historian can thus present as an example of the Korean-American Christian experience, giving voice to an identity group often feeling marginalized in the United States. This is the type of primary source a historian uses to create her own work. On the other hand, for the theologian, Lee's work pays attention to the ethical model in McClendon's method, illustrating a particular example of someone struggling to live his life loyal to the Christian idea of faith seeking understanding.

McClendon's attention to the ethical impulse of Christian thought being drawn from figures formed by "character-in-community" features a concrete understanding how history impacts human agents.[18] He makes a powerful point about having lived lives from history to follow rather than simply attempting to emulate Jesus Christ: "Christianity turns upon the character of Christ. But that character must continually find fresh exemplars if it is not to be consigned to the realm of mere antiquarian lore."[19] As we will see at the close of this chapter, Martin Luther King Jr serves as a great example of this principle not just for McClendon, who dedicates a chapter to him, but also for a vast number of historical-theological writers. King remains one of the most famous Christians in history, yet we must not forget the importance of the many religious figures, both from the leadership and the laity, who have left writings about their lived experience with God. Furthermore, McClendon suggests that his idea of biography as theology relates to any type of religious faith connected to community, including Jews and Muslims, or for that matter, even to secular thinkers.[20] I will follow up McClendon's suggestion at the close of this chapter by engaging Malcolm X through biography as theology.

Let us turn to some examples of McClendon's idea of biography as theology. Theologians have been following this narrative type of biography as theology for years. For example, Latin American theologians Gustavo Gutierrez and Leonardo Boff have written biography as theology books on Las Casas and St. Francis of Assisi as models for Christian life.[21] Another good example of a McClendon-type of narrative theology is Anthony Dancer's book on theologian William Stringfellow. In *An Alien in a Strange*

18. McClendon, *Biography as Theology*, 22, 29, and 202.
19. Ibid., 38.
20. Ibid., 91.
21. See Gutierrez, *Las Casas*; Boff, *St. Francis*. Gutierrez's book is a good example of a theologian writing an excellent history book.

Land, Dancer explores Stringfellow's theology through a narrative form. He first presents a chapter on the historical context of Stringfellow's life and works, followed by a chapter exploring Stringfellow's theological output. The attention to Stringfellow's historical context makes his theology less abstract, especially considering the attention toward the socio-political powers.[22] Consequently, Stringfellow writes how Christianity is "diminished, dismissed, omitted, or ignored when theology is rendered in abstract, hypothesized, propositional or academic models."[23] Therefore, Dancer follows Stringfellow's own recommendation in his historical-theological account of him.

Stringfellow, in the Preface "Biography as Theology" from his autobiography *A Simplicity of Faith*, writes about discerning the Word of God in our own lives. He sees biography and history as "biblically apropos" since the Bible is filled with both these genres.[24] His understanding is shaped by Christ's Incarnation in history. Therefore, he declares, "Biography, thus, is rudimentary data for theology, and every biography is significant for the knowledge it yields of the Word of God incarnate of in common life, whether or not the subject of the biography is aware of that significance of his or her own story."[25] It is in this sense that one's calling contains a divine value. In short, when theologians turn to biographies and histories they are in essence being good theologians.

Another example of biography as theology is found in Robert Inchausti's *Subversive Orthodoxy*. His book covers Christian thinkers, figures he calls the "orthodox avant-garde," who are found among a number of different roles and intellectual disciplines.[26] Inchausti features a number of thinkers, starting with William Blake and ending with René Girard, not typically considered theologians or historians but whose work continue to influence both disciplines. For example, he has a chapter "Macrohistorical Criticism" analyzing the biography and work of such diverse intellectuals (diverse in philosophical thought not in gender or race) like Marshall McLuhan, Northrop Frye, Jacques Ellul, Ivan Illich, and Girard. This chapter connects well with my study because all these thinkers utilize Christian

---

22. Dancer, *An Alien in a Strange Land*.
23. Stringfellow, *Simplicity of Faith*, 20.
24. Ibid., 19–20.
25. Ibid., 21.
26. Inchausti, *Subversive Orthodoxy*, 12. I found the sections on Thomas Merton and the American novelist Jack Kerouac the most fulfilling.

thought to think about human history from a macrohistorical viewpoint in order to critique the trends of contemporary culture. Inchausti shows that they illustrate the value of theology to analyze what seems like the hopeless situation of historical events. What is most helpful about Inchausti's book is the way these short little studies of famous people wet the appetitive of the reader to then engage these figures on their own.

Finally, one of the best examples of biography as theology is womanist theologian Katie Cannon's work on ethics. She frames ethics based on the historical experience of African-American women, noting her research comes from "less conventional sources but probes more intimate and private aspects of Black life."[27] She turns to the lived lives of black women to form her religious ethic. Moreover, her main ethical inspiration is Harlem Renaissance writer Zora Neale Hurston, an unabashed secular writer who has religious themes throughout her corpus because she represented the historical experience of black women. Thus Cannon proves McClendon correct that even a secular thinker can be a model of narrative ethics. This book never mentions McClendon, but it embodies the use of historical characters that he advocated as the starting point for theological ethics. Cannon finishes her book with the work of Howard Thurman and Martin Luther King Jr., so that the religious implications of her ethics and the experience of Hurston may be further developed.[28] Again, like McClendon, King is used as a witness for biography as theology. King's themes of love, community, and justice serve to show how well Hurston lived and wrote about these things too. Hurston is served well by Cannon's study, and she makes a great ethical model for aspiring writers to follow.

We will now look at a specific example of biography as theology by examining Ignacio Ellacuría and the other figures who were martyred in Latin America during the late twentieth century. The history of El Salvador and the martyrdom of Christian figures presents the dialectic between what seems like a hopeless situation and their belief in an everlasting hope. Last chapter we got a chance to review Ellacuría's historical-theological theories. Now we will see how his biography matched his theory.

---

27. Cannon, *Black Womanist Ethics*, 5. See 31–98 for a great historical study of African-American women, including endnotes, and 99–157 for an equally important biographical look at Hurston.

28. Ibid., 159–78.

The Biographies of the Martyrs of El Salvador

In order to examine the biography as theology aspect of Ellacuría's life and work we will look mostly at a recent study done on the Salvadorian martyrs written by Robert Lassalle-Klein called *Blood and Ink*.[29] If one desires a general background understanding of Latin American liberation theology before looking at Ellacuría then one might read a recent historical overview by Christian Smith or one of the many theological studies.[30] Lassalle-Klein's large volume is separated into two parts. First, the book covers the history of the Cold War (specifically the United States' involvement in Latin America), the creation and purpose of the University of Central America, the relationship of Latin American liberation theology and Catholicism in general, and finally the way Ellacuría interacted with all these things, closing this section with the reasons behind his murder.[31] Much time is dedicated to Medellín to illustrate how much Ellacuría was formed by post-Vatican II theology and became a pioneer in Latin American liberation theology. Because Lassalle-Klein writes this book as a theology as biography, the reader faces the question on what type of God did Ellacuría and his associates serve. What we find is a man sensing God's call to sacrifice his own life because of his sense of mission to take the crucified down from the crosses of suffering in today's world. Lassalle-Klein wants the reader to come away with this "untapped promise" of Ellacuría's attention to history in his theology.[32]

The second part of the book deals with Ellacuría's theology. Lassalle-Klein writes chapters on seminal figures that had a direct influence on Ellacuría: the founder of the Jesuit order St. Ignatius, the Spanish philosopher Xavier Zubiri, Archbishop of El Salvador Oscar Romero, and the German theologian Karl Rahner are all given adequate attention by the author to show how these figures taught and formed Ellacuría's biography.[33] There are

---

29. Lassalle-Klein, *Blood and Ink*. An earlier study, and one Lassalle-Klein cites often, is Whitfield, *Paying the Price*. However, this book is written more as a traditional biography with not the same detailed attention Lassalle-Klein gives to Ellacuría's theology. Therefore, *Blood and Ink* serves as my example of theology as biography.

30. Smith, *Emergence of Liberation Theology*, 11–24.

31. See Lassalle-Klein, *Blood and Ink*, 103 for resources on the suffering and brutality experienced by Catholic priests in El Salvador in the late twentieth century. For example, the author calls his book *Blood and Ink*, referencing the blood drenched copy of Jürgen Moltmann's *The Crucified God* from one of the martyred priests.

32. Ibid., 357.

33. Ibid., 196 for more details and resources on Ellacuría's theology.

some other secondary sources that explore the influence of these figures on Ellacuría's theology, but since Lassalle-Klein intentionally unites Ellacuría's history and theology, the book illustrates a perfect example of the theology as biography approach. After finishing this volume, the reader understands that Ellacuría discovered the reality of Jesus Christ in the crucified peoples of the world, highlighting his liberation theology hermeneutics, but also his attention to the people he interacted with in concrete history. Reading Lassalle-Klein, Sobrino, Whitfield, or any of the other sources by or about Ellacuría, one discovers not only a charismatic theologian, thinking deeply about God's preferential treatment of the poor, but also a pragmatic figure actively involved in negotiations between warring social-political parties in El Salvador. His ideas and his activism would unfortunately lead to his murder by his detractors in the Salvadorian military.

We have examined just a short sample of the literature of Ellacuría and the other martyrs. I contend that their stories need to be better known especially among North American audiences. In fact, it was only by accident and a little research that I learned about these people. It is from the biography of Romero that one generally stumbles upon the other martyrs.[34] However, this presents a problem of sorts. The martyrs examined were generally either from North America or Spain. Of course, a historical-theological thinker like Jon Sobrino makes it his mission to be not just an "evangelist" of the witness of Romero and Ellacuría, but also of the poor of Latin America.[35] However, we are all often guilty of focusing on the intellectual or church leader in our histories, while everyone else gets lumped into the nameless mass of the poor in need of liberation. Perhaps an outlet for future study is the type of micro-histories that would examine the concrete lived lives of peasants and families found across Latin America. Lassalle-Klein notes that the Spanish native Ellacuría, who almost completely identified with the Salvadorian people, serves as a "bridge figure" in history, presenting a moment when the leadership of the Salvadorian churches went from

---

34. For example, see Chasteen, *Born in Blood and Fire*, 309 where Romero and the four American nuns are mentioned, but the assassinated priests from the University of Central America are not. For a biography about the four murdered Maryknoll nuns see Noone, *Same Fate as the Poor*.

35 Lassalle-Klein, *Blood and Ink*, 309. Sobrino has written volumes on Romero, Ellacuría, and the poor in Latin America that features a good example of theology as biography, aiming to produce empathy in the reader. Lassalle-Klein dedicates a whole chapter on Sobrino's Christology to illustrate the impact and continuation of Ellacuría's theology in his surviving friend.

Europeans to Latin Americans.[36] Since this is the growing trend, the future focus on historical-theological study should pay attention to this dynamic.[37]

Ellacuría's life, much like Archbishop Romero's, is forever tied to the biographies of the people of El Salvador. It is impossible to understand Ellacuría's theology without putting it in the context of the history of liberation theology, the Cold War, and the history of El Salvador. In fact, liberation theologians make it a point in framing their theology from a historical context. In addition, this attention to context inevitably makes their theology biographical. We will now look at a small sample size of examples of theology as biography from thinkers across the globe who identify as liberation theologians.

Narrating Stories from Below Across the Globe

"I grew up in a family where history sat at the dinner table."
—Michel-Rolph Trouillot[38]

"How is that well-meaning and genuinely Christian people could consciously and intentionally engage in such culturally hegemonic, oppressive and later genocidal activities in the name of biblical truth—as followers of Jesus, lovers of Creator and as led by the Holy Spirit?"—Richard Twiss[39]

"The one who interprets assumes power; the one who dominates the story makes it his-story, her-story, literally creating history."—Mitri Raheb[40]

Biography as theology features a narrative approach to history. We can apply at least three ideas that make it successful for a historical-theological reading. First, the art of listening is crucial to empathize with the stories that we encounter especially the ones we are not that familiar with. Many marginalized writers reveal that their group's histories are not given the same respect as European or Christian history by the mainstream or even

36. Ibid., 190.
37. See Rodríguez, *We Live*, for numerous examples of Latina theological expressions and stories.
38. Trouillot, *Silencing the Past*, xvii.
39. Twiss, *Rescuing the Gospel*, 81.
40. Raheb, *Faith in the Face of Empire*, 21.

within their own group. The collective amnesia of history affects both the center and the peripheries. Second, the use of multiple academic disciplines opens up the imagination to explore ways to tell one's narrative. This means even mixing the use of fiction and non-fiction narratives. In fact, the narrative approach takes seriously the historicity of oral history. Oral histories feature a longer lifespan than textual history. For example, we do not have a Bible without it. Traditions and cultural nuances are passed on from generation to generation, including elements of the historical, mythical and the super-historical. We might assume that textual histories are more academically rigorous, yet this should not mean we ignore oral narratives that have eventually been preserved by text. Third, the openness that comes from listening and the use of multiple writing forms to narrate dictate that the historical-theological position is philosophically anti-foundational. This means that we are not concerned at the start with making absolute truth statements or proving without a shadow of a doubt that one narrative is truer than the other. In fact, the more narratives provided the more we understand the importance of hermeneutics as a starting point in writing and reading biography as theology. One of the best ways to examine these three points is to explore particularly theological works that are identified as specifically contextual.

Focused attention on a sample size of contextual and liberation theologians will illustrate three things. One, it will dispel the myth that these writings are dated pieces, controlled by an underlining Marxist ideology. Some definitely find inspiration from Marx but oftentimes not slavishly. Two, these works are littered with biographical and historical literature in a way that features an ethical hermeneutic that many Eurocentric based texts do not. Third, real agency is expressed in the theology coming from indigenous, third world or marginalized communities. It is a gross Eurocentrism to assume that these writers came to their faith simply because it came from the West. We must also dispute a Nietzschean cynicism that sees these authors as simply participating in some type of power play by professing a Christian faith. Most of the authors show they can be both Native American, Palestinian, or Latin American and Christian at the same time. In fact, many of these writers write autobiographically to illustrate this point. Therefore, if I can encourage the reader to ignore the stereotypes of contextual theologies as too solipsistic or too Marxist, and instead, focus on these texts as historical-theological, and in the best sense as a prophetic voice of the Other, then I have done my job.[41]

A staple of contextual and liberation theologies is the art of biography as theology. Sometimes these authors write the biographies and experiences of communities they identify with, while other times the writers narrate their own autobiographies. Liberation theologians in general are educated, well trained, academics who are experts in the field. However, since they oftentimes speak through their own experiences or from the context of their ethnicity, their approach challenges the objective, detached observer. They also maintain a clear dismissal of a historicist reading that rejects the spiritual dimension. Rather than seeing this as compromising academic rigor, it is better to view this trend as a door into primary historical-theological source material. The focus of these works tends to be less on the individual ego like modern European writings, but rather tied to the community and open to the spiritual. The community, and the spiritual help to define and challenge the ego. Moreover, instead of viewing this as a wayward theology based too much on human experience of the divine, we will see these writings as an open gate that lets us see what God is doing for various people across the globe. Their method produces empathy in the reader without even trying. We will look at examples from Korea, Palestine, First Nations peoples, and the Dalits of India.

I am not going to produce an exhaustive reading of each type, but I will generally focus on one representative thinker. The literature associated with each example continues to grow and there is simply not the space to cover it all. Instead I focus on a singular person and singular work to illustrate the use of historical-theological texts. When appropriate I footnote other materials to encourage further study.

Harold Recinos's *Jesus Weeps* serves as a paradigm for the following biographies as theology. He opens his book with his own biography detailing his life as a junkie on the streets: "For me, God was present in the street

---

41. This is not to say that Marxist interpretation was not crucial for liberation theology. In fact, the utilization of Marxist social analysis is one of the major points of contention between the Vatican and Latin American theologians. See Löwy, *The War of Gods*, 4-31 for a good overview of the use of Marx among European theorists that served as a basis for Latin American thinkers. The revolutionary voices formed in Europe were developed and broadened in the third world. Moreover, even though I opened up this chapter with my reading of Nietzsche as an example of biography, this was not meant to say that I have affinity to his philosophy. In some sense, my reading of postcolonial and decolonial works, with its attention to agency, has tempered my earlier appreciation to Euro-American postmodern thought based on Nietzsche's work.

experience of utter abandonment."[42] The aim of his study is to raise awareness about the effects of globalization not only across the third world but also in the inner cities of the United States.[43] This is a really important point because overseas or global south mission trips are oftentimes the focus of churches instead of the social-spiritual cares of local communities. He asserts: "Globalization means nothing less than honestly encountering the multicultural reality that underwrites urban history in the United States."[44] His attention to cities is evident in his second chapter where he writes about the history of the city from the underside of the US population. The next chapter is the most important since he looks at a number of ethnic minorities and their theologies for the sake of the multiplicity of perspectives one encounters in the US urban setting. In his section on Native Americans, he writes this powerful historical-theological statement, which also highlights the importance of history as storytelling:

> Christians must learn the stories of faith that speak of a God who enters human history as an act of political resistance to the few who oppress the many. Doing theology means telling the story of saving acts. Jesus taught in parables showing how the Word becomes incarnate in life's ambiguities and struggles. Christians of first-world societies need to recover a sense of storytelling that is honest about the conflict in history. God is apprehended in the life of the oppressed, who enter history as agents of a new vision of humanity and as just stewards of the created world. Telling the story of Christian participation in the struggle of the whole created order for liberation images the pattern of narrative description found in the biblical reports about the reality of God. Native Americans demand honesty from Euro-American society about history. From Native America, North Atlantic Christians can learn that God's biography is the whole of creation moving toward justice and wholeness.[45]

Thus, what we find in Recinos's book is the model for a biography as theology. He opens his book with biographical information, followed

---

42. Recinos, *Jesus Weeps*, 22.

43. Ibid., 59.

44. Ibid., 78.

45. Ibid., 95. The groups he covers (Jewish, African-American, women, Womanist-Mujerista, Native American, and Arab-American) are some of the perspectives I will be looking at in the rest of the chapter. He also bases his study off of the history from Spanish Conquest of the Americas, which we covered in the last chapter.

by historical information about the city, political policies, and the ethnic minorities effected by them. Finally, he closes with an anthropological study. Throughout the whole book Recinos theologizes in light of all this social-historical information. We will see how the following books repeat this pattern.

Korean theologian Chung Hyun Kyung's *Struggle to be the Sun Again* is a classic book on Asian women's theology. The book is helpful for the beginning student of third-world theological movements because she covers the history of their activities in detail.[46] With her focus on both the third world and women, she exposes the sexism even found in liberation movements. The way Kyung approaches the problem of patriarchy is by revealing women's storytelling as an "embodied historiography" because its roots are found in their "socio-biography."[47] Therefore, she starts her theology with "gut feelings and experiences" in order to tap into the resources of concrete socio-historical liberation, especially for women.[48]

What does this embodied historiography look like? Kyung describes this form of socio-biography based in historical-theological foundation in poetic detail:

> The power of storytelling lies in its *embodied truth*. Women talked about their concrete, historical life experience and not about abstract, metaphysical concepts. Women's truth was generated by their *epistemology from the broken body*. Women's bodies are the most sensitive receiver for historical reality. Their bodies record what has happened in their lives. Their bodies remember what it is like to be a *no-body* and what it is like to be a *some-body*.[49]

Kyung spends much of her book focused on the "gut feelings and experiences" of a variety of Asian women to illustrate her historiography. Her method is important because the experiences and the bodies of Asian women are oftentimes absent from the chronicles of history and the theories of theology. Without an assertive embodied historiography these experiences would continue remaining silent. There is no hesitancy in her historical-theological work that Asian women can write theology![50]

---

46. Kyung, *Struggle to be the Sun Again*, 11–21. For more on the use of history by feminist theologians see Pui-lan, *Postcolonial Imagination and Feminist Theology*, 31–38.

47. Ibid., 104–5.

48. Ibid., 110.

49. Ibid., 104.

50. See Mahbubani, *Can Asians Think*, 18–33 on this philosophical question.

Moreover, Kyung notes that Asian women feel confident to express this embodied historiography as crucial for theology because of their view that God is the Lord of history. Her own appeal to syncretism at the end of her book is a way to challenge the "*copyright* on Christianity" by "Western theologians."[51] She declares that Korean women "know the God of history takes sides with the oppressed as witnessed in Exodus, Jesus' life, and the many unbeatable people's movements in Asia. With their trust in this God, Asian women draw their strength for their struggle for justice."[52] Kyung frames the concentration of the biographies of Asian women as a necessity of survival.

Another marginalized group struggling for survival is the Dalits in India. James Massey attempts to articulate a Dalit theology by focusing on three ideas: history, solidarity and theology. He points out that the history of Dalits are narrated by the oppressors so there needs to be a hermeneutics from the underside to trace over thousands of years of either marginalization or oppression by either the elites in India or the European colonizers. Therefore, he looks to other liberation theologies from across the globe as a roadmap for Dalit theology.[53] Building on the attention on history from below by liberation theology, Massey writes "history is very important, because till now historians either in general, or particularly Church or religious historians have not represented the views of our people."[54] What makes Massey's work biographical or interested in "stories and testimonies" is that because of the lack of historical narrative over thousands of years, he advocates the cataloguing of present and future experience among Dalits.[55] He declares that "Dalit theology will help us in placing our past and present actions in theological context, which will ultimately liberate by destroying the value systems which have contributed in making us captives."[56] Massey's Dalit theology sees Christian liberationist theology as a means to challenge and rewrite the official history that ignores the Dalits. Massey's

---

51. Kyung, *Struggle to be the Sun Again*, 113. At the end of this chapter, I will explore a similar historical-theological syncretism with regards to liberationist thought.

52. Ibid., 49.

53. Massey, *Roots of Dalit History*, 73–87. He concentrates on three major liberation theologians: Gustavo Gutierrez (Latin American); James Cone (African American); Eleazar Fernandez (Filipino, Theology of Struggle). For an additional source on Dalits, see Clarke, *Dalits and Christianity*.

54. Ibid., 81.

55. Ibid., 84, 88–102.

56. Ibid., 87.

work features an intentional connection among one third-world historical-theological experience with other marginalized religious groups.

One religious group that is surprisingly forgotten considering their location are Christians in Palestine. How could Christians in the place where Jesus lived be ignored? Lutheran Palestinian theologian Mitri Raheb, in his autobiographical book *I Am a Palestinian Christian*, points out why there is such gross ignorance about Arab Christians: "A complicating factor is that texts like history books and catechisms do not touch on the Arab origin and roots of Christianity. As a result, Christians are rendered illiterate, ignorant of their deep Middle Eastern roots and their cultural roles in the history of Christianity. This alienation from their own roots and history is important in attracting Palestinian Christians to the West."[57]

The absence of a people's history from the history books produces myths about these missing persons. The book portrays Raheb's own experience going through the major events of the conflict between Israel and Palestine, interpreting the Bible through this context. Similar to Raheb, Naim Stifan Ateek, an Episcopal Palestinian minister, opens *Justice, and Only Justice: A Palestinian Theology of Liberation* with both a personal account of his family's removal from their home and a historical/political background of the overall conflict; stereotyping of the people involved only complicates matters.[58] For both these Palestinian theologians, the forced removal from their homes contains the starting point to writing about both God and humanity. Thus Raheb insists that human history "is nothing but a chain of successive emigrations" so any appeal to timeless truths denies how theology is rooted in historical context.[59]

There are major historical-theological implications with regards Raheb's work. He calls out "church history" in particular as being presented as "Western history" even though he is as critical with so-called secular historians of the region.[60] At the heart of the problem, he notes the complicated relationship Europe has with the Palestinian region. He suggests that European guilt over the Holocaust dictates the way the dialogue between Western Christians and Jews leave out Palestinian Christians.[61] He advocates taking a *longue durée* approach that locates Palestinian history back to

57. Raheb, *I Am a Palestinian Christian*, 24.
58. Ateek, *Justice, and Only Justice*, 7–49.
59. Raheb, *I Am a Palestinian Christian*, 18, 61.
60. Raheb, *Faith in the Face of Empire*, 9–10.
61. Raheb, *I Am a Palestinian Christian*, 57–59, and *Faith in the Face of Empire*, 11.

the history of the Bible, reviewing the numerous empires that made claims to the land.[62]

Jewish liberation theologian Marc H. Ellis is a connecting figure to contextual and liberation theology. His autobiography *Practicing Exile* is filled with stories of his interaction with figures like Pablo Richard, Gustavo Gutierrez, Dorothee Soelle, and James Cone to name a few.[63] He contends that Jewish theology needs to build a bridge with other movements that struggle for justice, considering the complicated relationship Israel has with Palestine.[64] A good example of this is his discussion of the relationship of African-Americans and the Jewish community in post-war United States.[65] His book *Toward a Jewish Theology of Liberation* is strong on biography since he focuses on testimonies of the Holocaust, the musings of post-Holocaust theologians, and theorists discussing the pros and cons of the state of Israel in a position of empowerment. His perspective pays attention to Jewish history as sometimes in the position as the oppressed and now recently as in the position of the oppressors. Ellis warns: "By carrying our own history we bequeath insight to contemporary struggles. If we are overwhelmed, though, by history and seek to overwhelm others, our memory becomes a wedge of anger and insularity, a blunt instrument rather than a delicately nurtured memory."[66]

Ellis reminds Christian movements that their almost universal use of the Exodus narrative is, first and foremost, a contribution of Jewish thought. His bridge analogy serves as an important point toward dialogue among movements that takes history seriously. For example, Ellis features other liberationist theologies as a model for Jewish liberation theology, yet, because of the continual threat of a potentially resurfacing anti-Semitism, prefaces this discussion with Jewish trepidation for immediately joining

---

62. Raheb, *Faith in the Face of Empire*, 9–11.

63. Ellis, *Practicing Exile*, 89–93 (Maryknoll sisters), 110–15 (Soelle), 117–27 (Cone), and 136–53 (Richard). One of the best parts of the book is his discussion of his relationship with the Jewish philosopher Gillian Rose and her concept of the broken middle; see 75–86 and Rose, *Love's Work*.

64. Ellis, *Toward a Jewish Theology of Liberation*, 127. For more on Ellis, see Ateek, *Justice, and Only Justice*, 69–71, and Raheb, *Faith in the Face of Empire*, 32–33.

65. Ellis, *Practicing Exile*, 78.

66. Ellis, *Toward a Jewish Theology of Liberation*, 121. One way he has a biographical/theological focus is his understanding of Holocaust violence through the diaries of Etty Hillesum and the tension of the state of Israel with the Palestinian people in the work of Martin Buber.

with Christian thought, even third-world liberationist movements. Therefore, Ellis declares that "Christian movements today are authentic only insofar as they carry the memory of their victims with them."[67] In this sense, he sees violence in South Africa and Latin America, with Jewish complicity involved in some facet, as a way to make connections between third-world violence and the Holocaust experience.[68] A recurring phrase Ellis uses to raise historical consciousness of violence against the oppressed is that of "burning children."[69] Not enough theology or history pays attention to the "burning children" because they are part of the underside of history. As we will see in the final chapter of this book, the images of "burning children" in even recent history, so omnipresent because of photographic technology, upsets the abstract theologies that try to ignore them.

Ellis's work is paradigmatic among contextual and liberation theologies because he is so interactive with this genre. The amount of travelling that he did and his various life experiences led him to theorize about the connections between some of the most violent moments of recent history and the marginalized that experienced them: "In my travels I began to wonder whether the masses of poor and destitute people in Africa, Latin America, and Asia were so different from those of my dead in the Holocaust."[70]

We have already seen in the previous chapter how much the insight of Native peoples from North America complete the narrative about the birth of modernity among Latin American thinkers like Enrique Dussel and Walter Mignolo. Richard Twiss presents his theology, focusing on the experience of Native Americans, as a "historical correctionist" to Eurocentric theology; in fact, Twiss's book, filled with narratives from First Nations Christians, shows one of the best examples of biography as theology.[71]

Twiss stresses the power of racial reconciliation but frames his work in the difficulty of raising historical consciousness in the United States:

> If I was a spiritual optometrist, I would say that in the area of cross-cultural sensitivity and awareness, many people suffer serious

---

67. Ibid., 92. He concentrates on the liberation theology of James Cone, Gustavo Gutierrez, and Minjung theology in general. In addition, Ellis does theology and history, focusing on the victim, in the light of the work of Jewish philosopher Walter Benjamin.

68. Ibid., 73–90.

69. Ibid., 90 and 122.

70. Ellis, *Practicing Exile*, 9.

71. Twiss, *Rescuing the Gospel*, 93–129.

HISTORY AS BIOGRAPHY

cases of impaired vision. Sometimes I find a confused mixture of culture and gospel. Some identify the abundance of America and her free-market economy, democracy, capitalism, and even the injustices of "manifest destiny" as necessarily being Christian or being God's will. There has been little effort in this nation to get inside the minds of Native or ethnic peoples in order to genuinely understand and empathize with their pain and experiences. Native American history is viewed with very little compassion; as a result there is still estrangement between Anglo and Native people and their culture.[72]

What Twiss points out continues to be the problem of both mainstream historians and theologians. Anything that is not part of the mainstream (white) framework is considered fringe or syncretistic.[73] In theological language, if one is going to convert to Christianity then one must adopt the mainstream, white culture and forsake one's own culture. Twiss points out that even well-intentioned, white ministers oftentimes never see themselves as part of a culture but, because of a lack of historical consciousness, see themselves as representing Christianity universally.[74] According to indigenous scholar Taiaiake Alfred, indigenous people in particular are frustrated because "white people are ignorant of history."[75] Thus, Twiss frames his argument by representing "Indigenous theologizing" in contrast to "Eurocentric theology" because it "presupposes superiority and condescension toward Christian theologies developed in Africa, Asia or Central and South America."[76] Therefore, he writes his biography as theology by detailing his own experience as a Native American and his conversion to Christianity.[77] His concern stems from the fact that so much attention toward the Native people by missionaries yielded so little conversions.[78] Why is this a historical fact?

---

72. Twiss, *One Church Many Tribes*, 163–64. Also see, Rah, *Next Evangelicalism*, 155–57.
73. Twiss, *Rescuing the Gospel*, 31.
74. Twiss, *One Church Many Tribes*, 33–35.
75. Alfred, *Peace, Power, Righteousness*, 122.
76. Twiss, *Rescuing the Gospel*, 236.
77. Twiss, *One Church Many Tribes*, 28, 37–48. Twiss closes this section with some recorded narratives of the abuses of the boarding schools (or what he calls bad haircuts as a cultural genocide).
78. Twiss, *Rescuing the Gospel*, 25–28.

At the heart of Twiss's program is for Native American Christians to be able to worship the Christian God without abandoning their cultures. He gives examples, especially among indigenous Christian groups across the globe, to show the freedom to worship God in this way, not accepting that conversion to Christianity means becoming a European or Anglo-American as well. However, he points out two problems with the relationship between Native Christians and others in the United States. First, he reveals that the history of the suffering of Native Americans is still either handled with indifference or ignorance by the majority of Christian churches in the US.[79] Second, Twiss contends that until Christians in general in the United States recognize the cultural genocide committed against Native peoples, the spreading of the gospel will suffer.[80]

Even though I have stressed the compatibility among third-world religious experiences primarily because of their postcolonial experience, there are points of divergence. For example, whereas African Americans and Jewish liberation theologians see the Mosaic narrative of freedom from Egypt as a source of liberation, the use of the Exodus event as a symbol in history is treated as suspect among First Nations and Palestinian writers.[81] This reaction is built on a whole different experience on land being taken away for the purpose of nationalistic ideology like manifest destiny and the New Jerusalem, the city upon the hill. Indeed it is a dangerous place to be cast as the role of the Canaanites, and that is what has happened to both Native Americans and Palestinians in history.

As we have seen from this small sample size I presented, liberation and contextual theologies awaken a recent sense of historical consciousness among peoples who have been denied a narrative for many years or for those who are captured by the single story narrative. It pays attention to the biographies and experiences of not just the leaders and intellectuals of the various movements but also the narratives of everyday women and men. To read history from below requires two things: first, a new critical hermeneutic for all past historical sources; second, the sober attention toward the present and future experiences of marginalized voices. I claim

---

79. Twiss, *One Church Many Tribes*, 18.

80. Ibid., 49 and 170. He suggests that generational racism and sin, based on his reading of the Bible, must be acknowledged by Christians in the present and make concrete amends toward Native peoples for these acts.

81. Twiss, *Rescuing the Gospel*, 88–89; Raheb, *Faith in the Face of Empire*, 32.

this is recent since the phenomenon of histories from below is less than one hundred years old.

With all the attention toward the underside of modernity, we might take for granted the biographies of famous historical figures. One thing that a historical-theological reading of biographies cannot do is simply accept the general narrative. Moreover, there are figures who we know because they are famous in the popular media but have not really grasped their potential for historical-theological purposes. We will thus close this chapter review the biographical material of Martin Luther King Jr. and Malcolm X.

Experiment in Theology as Biography: Malcolm & Martin

The idea of pairing Martin Luther King Jr. and Malcolm X is nothing new in the world of theology. The most significant example is James Cone's book *Martin and Malcolm and America*.[82] Cone's book is a superb example of historical-theological literature with its exploration of the life, actions, and words of these two great civil rights, religious leaders. Kelly Brown Douglas also features a chapter on the two modern religious icons.[83] Michael Eric Dyson has published individual studies of both, as well.[84] However, in keeping with the theme of this chapter, I will look at the way both figures have been used as historical biography in theology. Both figures are constantly utilized as historical paradigms, inspiring generations to follow in their paths.

King and Malcolm X are two of the most recognizable figures in United States history. However, when it comes to the theological discipline, their ideas are somewhat absent. In fact, I agree with Johnny Bernard Hill's insight that King may be memorialized in monuments but rarely is granted a "footnote" in contemporary Christian and academic literature.[85] If King is handled in this manner, how do you think Malcolm X is regarded? Cone

---

82. Cone, *Martin and Malcolm and America*, 1–17. Discussing African American history, Cone claims that King represents black integrationism and Malcolm black nationalism, one appealing to the American dream and the other reflecting on the American nightmare. See Dyson, *Reflecting Black*, 250–63 for a judicious review of Cone's book.

83. See Douglas, *Black Christ*, 35–52.

84. See Dyson, *I May Not Get There With You*, and *Making Malcolm*.

85. Hill, *Prophetic Rage*, 51–52. Since Hill's subject matter is prophetic, postcolonial theology (his dissertation focusing on King and Desmond Tutu) he engages with both King and Malcolm X in his book.

declares why we need to continue to wrestle with the words and actions of both: "We need Martin and Malcolm today precisely because many people think we have moved beyond the need to talk about race. Nothing could be further from the truth."[86] This is a point I have tried to make throughout this whole book with regards to both the historical and theological disciplines. It is one thing to make this point with regards to diverse voices among third-world liberation theologians, and quite another matter to rethink these disciplines through the paradigm of King and Malcolm X!

My point is that black theologians like Cone, Douglas, and Hill critically assess the biographies and theories of iconic religious figures like King and Malcolm X. Why is work of these figures almost exclusively dealt with by black scholars? Nobody can debate their influence on either the historical or theological disciplines, yet if these icons are avoided for whatever reason, what about the countless narratives from the underside of history?[87] The utter lack of attention given to both these theologians illustrates the primary focus of this book. It is imperative of teachers and readers of history and theology to actively look outside one's discipline or area of focus, in order to dialogue with important voices that are being ignored.

Starting with James McClendon's account of King reveals a counterexample from the unfortunate norm. McClendon is useful in at least two ways because, first, he sets up the model of "theology as biography" so important in this chapter; and two, he utilizes his theory on King, providing an example of the type of historical-theological study advocated in this book.[88] McClendon sees in King someone who held the tension between humanity's role in history with the "role of the God of history."[89] In short, holding to this tension allowed King to advocate action and not simply to encourage passive reliance on a distant God. Speaking of tension, Cone places King with Malcolm X in order to avoid this semblance of passivity. He writes that "Malcolm keeps Martin from being turned into a harmless American hero. Martin keeps Malcolm from being an ostracized black hero."[90] What

---

86. Cone, *Martin and Malcolm and America*, x. Cone's account is not hagiography. In fact, he includes a whole chapter highlighting some of their faults, especially toward women; see 272–87.

87. For example, see Roberts, *Bonhoeffer and King*, 134 where he points out Christian ethicist Stanley Hauerwas admitting to him that Martin Luther King Jr. has no place in contemporary Christian ethics.

88. McClendon, *Biography as Theology*, 65–86.

89. Ibid., 85.

90. Cone, *Martin and Malcolm and America*, 316.

Cone does with the Martin and Malcolm dialectic is the applicability of the theology as biography model McClendon claims was open to other faith traditions.[91] Moreover, McClendon's work influenced theologian J. Deotis Roberts to write his own "theology as biography" on Martin Luther King Jr. and Dietrich Bonhoeffer.[92] Roberts opens up the book with his own autobiography in relation to both theologians, transitioning to their biographies afterward.

As rewarding as reading the biographies of figures like King and Bonhoeffer, the biography of non-Christian or even figures that are somewhat hostile to Christianity may be as useful in today's world. If Martin Luther King Jr. is arguably the most important and influential Christian thinker in North American history, then Malcolm X has to be its most famous Muslim. Do we generally think of Malcolm X in this way?

Hamid Dabashi's focus on Malcolm X as a key figure in his Islamic Liberation theology presents a constructive historical account for the purposes of theology. His life serves as an example of a Muslim perspective of biography as theology. Dabashi claims this is important since Islam is presented in binary terms of Islam versus the West, revealing the continual unfortunate legacy of Orientalism. Since the biography of Malcolm X was constructed by being located in both Islam and in the West, his historical narrative presents a powerful witness for contemporary liberation theology. Addressing the contemporary situation, Dabashi declares the importance of Malcolm X for Islamic history stating that "no Muslim revolutionary comes even close to Malcolm X in the liberating, global, and visionary grasp of his faith and its place in facing the barefaced barbarity of economic and military world domination."[93] It is in this prophetic light that Cone declares "Malcolm X is the best medicine against genocide."[94]

The key aspects of Malcolm X's life present a historical learning lesson for liberation theology. According to Dabashi, from his origin among the "disenfranchised poor in the US" to his historic Hajj pilgrimage, which led to his break with the narrow views of the Nation of Islam, Malcolm X's

91. McClendon, *Biography as Theology*, 91.

92. Roberts, *Bonhoeffer and King*, 3–17. Chapter 2 of Roberts's book is titled "Biography as Theology." In fact, the book is one long comparative study and an exercise in biography as theology.

93. Dabashi, *Islamic Liberation Theology*, 243. Dabashi compares Malcolm X with a contemporary Muslim radical Sayyid Qutb, concluding that Malcolm X represents a more progressive form of Islam.

94. Cone, *Martin and Malcom and America*, 317.

biographical narrative provides the tools to critique binary systems that try to explain away the diversity and complexity of history.[95] His growing international consciousness came from his historical-theological experiences.[96] Dabashi writes: "The closer we look at the episodic moves in Malcolm X's short but tumultuous life the more we notice the heroic shifts that he initiated in his thinking and activism. With each move, he expanded his horizons, widened his vision, and embraced a more global conception of what needed to be done."[97] Furthermore, Dabashi cites the witness of Malcolm X to serve as a bridge among all forms of liberation movements especially in the globalized world. Dabashi writes that "Islamic liberation theology must learn from Christian liberation, and vice versa" and thus "must come into coalition and conversation, not combative rivalry."[98] This is an important claim that is unfortunately not made enough among Christian theologians. Instead of engaging liberation theological movements outside the Christian tradition or the important influence of the most famous American Muslim in history, oftentimes there is a collective silence with regards to anything non-Christian. In our age of heightened aggression between Christians and Muslims across the globe, this is an unacceptable position to take. Even progressive Christian liberation theologians tend to work with theories from secular and atheist thinkers rather than read figures from other faith traditions. A turn to history and experience suggests following the work of theologian Paul Knitter who claimed that historical "awareness" in the "suffering Other" (liberation theology) ultimately connects to interest of the "religious Other."[99] In short, liberation theology reminds us not to make the oppressed invisible, while a theology of religions illuminates the globe of multiple religious expression. Both theologies rely on history.

Dabashi's work serves as an example of the type of non-Christian liberation theology, one that follows a historical-theological understanding of reality, which Christians and other faiths can use to begin studying the subject. Another good place to start is with literature produced by people who

95. Dabashi, *Islamic Liberation Theology*, 246.
96. Cone, *Martin and Malcolm and America*, 205–7.
97. Dabashi, *Islamic Liberation Theology*, 246.
98. Ibid., 250. For more thoughts on the relationship between Christian liberation theology and Islamic movements, see Amin, *Eurocentrism*, 83–86.
99. Knitter, *Jesus and the Other Names*, xi–xv, 27–36, and 93–98. Also see Borg, *Heart of Christianity*, 208–11 on how North American Christianity must realize the growing multiplicity of religious expressions since the rise of immigration during the nineteen-sixties.

identify as Muslim or perhaps who at the very least identify with an Islamic community. For example, Marjanie Satrapi's graphic novel (and subsequent film) *Persepolis* presents a great example of autobiographical work featuring a young women's experience of growing up in Iran during the 1980s (post-revolution Tehran). In addition, probably one of the most recognizable Muslims in the world is Tariq Ramadan, whose nickname is the Martin Luther of Islam. His books *What I Believe* and *The Quest for Meaning* are very readable for the novice.[100] To some extent, both of Ramadan's books feature a biography as theology method, along with a historical-theological framework.

We have examined how important historical biographies are for theology. This presents a clear example of when history and theology meet. When James McClendon presented his method of biography as theology he used Martin Luther King Jr. as one of his figures. However, since we are more aware of our global world, and the impact that Islam continues to make on the planet, Dabashi's utilization of Malcolm X's biography for his Islamic theology is a key complimentary text to add the idea of biography as theology. Dabashi points out what we discover from Malcolm X's biography is a growing global consciousness of what Fanon called the wretched of the earth through the prism of his Islamic faith.[101] Martin Luther King Jr. made similar discoveries through his Christian faith. What both American theologians present is the way an evolving historical consciousness deepened their theological commitments.[102]

Conclusion

"Globalization as contextualized Christian experience in the multicultural, multiracial, and class-diverse context of the city gives the church a new compass for understanding human diversity in history."
—Harold Recinos[103]

---

100. Ramadan, *Quest for Meaning* and *What I Believe*. A suggested future book study, which is out of the scope of this book, would consist of comparing and contrasting Christian and Muslim historical-theological thought. It should be noted that Dabashi is a critic of Ramadan's work; see Dabashi, *Islamic Liberation Theology*, 132–38.
101. Dabashi, *Islamic Liberation Theology*, 252.
102. Cone, *Martin and Malcolm and America*, 317–18.
103. Recinos, *Jesus Weeps*, 98.

The great twentieth century Protestant theologian Paul Tillich, in his history lectures on history of Christian thought, makes an important distinction that connects well with the focus on biographies in this chapter:

> Yesterday I read a hymn to be sung by a congregation of Southern Negroes or Midwestern peasants which included Socrates in it, besides Christ and Luther. I do not think it wise to bring theology into a hymn in this way. If people like Zwingli and Calvin speak of revelation and salvation in men like Socrates and Seneca, they are making a mistake. The mistake is that they choose only certain representatives of pagan piety. However, pagan piety is exactly the same as Christian piety in this respect that it is just as intensive in the common people who are really pious in their knowledge of God, and people in this class should have been mentioned just as much. But since they were good humanists, they mentioned only their sociological class, people who were not only great men but who also belonged to the intelligentsia. If you are ministers, it is better to decide not to incorporate such things into a hymn. Although I have given you as much Socrates and Plato as I can, nevertheless, I do not sing to them.[104]

Tillich points out that oftentimes the focus for theology has been on the "great men" of historical thought. He illustrates this by showing how the Greek philosopher Socrates is cited in a Christian hymn. But how does Socrates relate to the common people, worshipping on a Sunday morning? As Tillich notes, Socrates is arguably one of the most important philosophers of history, but why is he in a Christian hymn? The inclusion of Socrates serves as the exclusion of the numerous but nameless Christians throughout history. For this particular hymn writer, philosophical thought highlighted in intellectual history outweighed the experiences of the common believers. In this sense, Tillich's example provides the reason why historical-theological thought needs to correct the previous historical methodology of Eurocentrism and the focus on the "great men" by finally giving attention to the underside of history and religion. This chapter has focused on both great figures like Martin Luther King Jr. and nameless Korean mothers as an example of taking Tillich's advice seriously. Paying attention to minority histories, especially those written by third-world religious writers, illustrates how the social-historical context and the experience of communities influence even the way people worship the divine.[105]

---

104. Tillich, *History of Christian Thought*, 258.
105. See Cone, *The Spirituals and the Blues* as an example of taking the musical

HISTORY AS BIOGRAPHY

As Tillich observes: "Reality precedes thought; it is equally true, however, that thought shapes reality. They are interdependent; one cannot be abstracted from the other."[106] In short, historical context greatly matters for theology and religious studies. If we take context seriously it should then match reality as best as possible.

Studying the biographies of people, especially famous writers, helps put their ideas in historical context. It illustrates the way historical events and the various people they encountered shaped the person that we read about. It means to take seriously Barth's advice to read about figures from the past with a sense of charity and empathy. Western theology in particular will grow and develop if and when it pays better attention to the biographies of Christians across the earth. In addition, Christian thinkers in general will be in better position to dialogue with people of other faith traditions, if perhaps they read biography as theology in other religions. For example, imagine if Martin Luther King Jr. convinced himself not to read Gandhi's writings because he was not a Christian? Would King's commitment to nonviolent resistance wavered without Gandhi's historical experience?

My recommendation of reading third-world theological writings by means of McClendon's biography as theology is not to advocate the appropriation of this literature. It rather means to purposely read literature from outside the West and non-Christian writings as a way to gain empathy for other people and cultures and to actually gain insight for one's own intellectual development. Too often Christians make public statements about people of other faiths that transparently illustrate willful ignorance. What do we miss out when we avoid reading materials out of our faith tradition or even the discipline we work under? It is up to the historians of the next generation to take seriously the life and works of religious figures. It is up to the theologians of the future to engage these readings.

McClendon's theory about biography as theology contains an ethical impulse. The lived lives of people from the past better serve as examples of ethical choices than abstract theories. Inchausti makes an excellent point about King's biography, especially as the premier philosopher of nonviolence, as a way to formulate one's own sense of spirituality: "Those who wish to get closer to King's vision will have to undergo their own set of spiritual exercises and live for years with the contradictory facts of King's

---

contributions of African-Americans, both inside and outside the church, seriously.
106. Tillich, *History of Christian Thought*, xxxvi.

life."[107] In other words, King's story may continue to inspire us, both his accomplishments and his faults, but eventually our own narratives take on a responsibility that only we will be accountable for. King and Malcolm were great religious leaders, but they are not ahistorical representatives of their religions. Their lives are historical samples we may learn from, but both Christianity and Islam are bigger than these two figures. There are millions of religious believers that have lived before and after them. As Cone points out King and Malcolm X "show us what ordinary people can accomplish through intelligence and sincere commitment to the cause of justice and freedom."[108] Moreover, it is my hope that we develop a biography as theology that continues to acknowledge the work of King, but will now concentrate on other figures like Ellacuría, Twiss, Kyung, and others I highlighted in this chapter. Borrowing from a recent book title, rather than ponder what it would be like to utilize European postmodern philosophers in a Christian church community, taking Derrida and Foucault to church, the more appropriate question is what would it look like if we concretely brought Kyung, Twiss, and Raheb into a North American Christian church? Historians of religion and theologians have no excuse to ignore the voluminous writings of people from diverse ethnic identities and experience. Again, radical historicism that dismisses these figures maintains a prejudice against the real, concrete events of lived history.

The contemporary narrative approach only works if it follows a postcolonial and decolonial methodology because of the problem of Eurocentrism. I claim this because there is a reason why when talking about history, theology or even global politics there tends to be a center and the periphery. Guess which groups make up the peripheries? I continue to raise the issue of Eurocentrism because it is so easy to get walled in by this master historical narrative. To apply a real sense of otherness requires purposeful attention to the unfamiliar. Therefore, the reading of these historical narratives potentially raises the consciousness of the Anglo-American and European world of the danger of Adichie's singular story. With regards to the Christian world, this is an attempt to face what Christena Cleveland calls the "disunity in Christ." The history of Christianity is filled with stories of disunity. Some of the narratives we examined in this chapter noted the feeling of being left outside mainstream Christianity. Cleveland points out that the

---

107. Inchausti, *Subversive Orthodoxy*, 111. For a similar conclusion see Yancey's chapter on King in *Soul Survivor*, 11–41.

108. Cone, *Martin and Malcolm and America*, 315.

"homogenous, culturally isolated church, denomination or organization is not truly participating in the body of Christ" especially since "categorizing" convinces people that they have nothing to learn from others they differ from in either beliefs or ethnicity.[109] Encountering narratives from people we deem different makes us face the reality of the diverse, wonderful world, and, at the same time, opening up the awareness of the violent and oppressive events done in the name of religion across the world or even in our own backyard (or even so-called nation-building). The modern civilizing project centered in European thought largely ignored the stories of the people from the periphery. That is why the agency illustrated in the biographies and autobiographies from those once classified by modern European intellectuals as the barbarians need to be studied with utmost urgency by both historians and theologians. The fact that this is concrete history presented by religious believers across the world, featuring a diverse sample of experiences, helps to prevent an easy escapism into the purity language of tradition.

We will now look at the way historical biographies show up in the world of cinema. Movies are not only produced in Hollywood. In fact, films are being made across the world, providing an important lens into understanding global culture. For example, Hollywood obviously affects the way movies are made in Iran, yet there is also a unique aspect to these films that remain independent of American influence. In short, movies are such a big part of the cultural life of almost all the nations across the world. We will now examine the way to utilize films for both the disciplines of theology and history.

109. Cleveland, *Disunity in Christ*, 39 and 74.

CHAPTER 4

The Newspaper in One Hand and the Remote Control in the Other

On History and Cinema

"History, in one of its dimensions, is cinematographic"
—Ortega y Gasset[1]

"History does not belong only to its narrators, professional or amateur. While some of us debate what history is or was, others take it in their own hands"—Michel-Rolph Trouillot[2]

Vietnamese Buddhist monk Thich Nhat Hanh writes: "Movies are food for our eyes, ears, and minds."[3] Much like eating a healthy, nutritional diet is good for the body and soul, watching a good film can create values like empathy and compassion in the viewer. A good film may lead to constructive discussion and thought about the past, present, and future. However, watching bad films can be toxic. The idea of what constitutes a good film versus a bad one is highly subjective, so I will not entertain what I think is a good film. Oftentimes the consensus on a website like *Rotten Tomatoes* is a good indicator of what is truly an awful film, or something worth spending money on.

1. Ortega y Gasset, *Man and Crisis*, 176.
2. Trouillot, *Silencing the Past*, 153.
3. Hanh, *Heart of Buddha's Teaching*, 33.

The world of the church and the world of movies betray a fractured relationship. In some ways, not the most obvious, I sympathize with James Baldwin's account in *The Devil Always Works* of quitting movies for the good work of God.[4] There was a time I thought the church and the movies required an either/or choice. Any given Sunday one might walk into a church to hear the preacher warn about the immorality of Hollywood or Disney (little did I know that this conversation was also taking place in the academy). Since movies market the values of the fallen world, then one should avoid exposure to them at all cost. I recall being told by a pastor, "what would you say if someone you were trying to witness the gospel of Christ saw you leaving the movie theater" (like it was as seedy as coming out of a stripper joint). Now the churches I attended in the past presented some compromises like watching movies that oftentimes predated the 1960s, or watching exclusively Christian movies. However, once you have watched what are considered by many as good movies even once in your life, then the realization of being given a poor supplement will kick in.

I eventually made it back to the movie theater, or at least to the local Redbox, and have not stopped going since. I still attend church on a weekly basis as well, so what exactly changed in my understanding of this relationship? The change consisted on coming to terms with the complex nature of both history and theology. History and biblical literature present stories that if they were told through the medium of cinema would be banned in the churches I used to attend. The denial of movies for Christians captures them inside a protective dystopia, sealing them off from the stories of peoples across the world. Of course there are awful movies made on a yearly basis, many depicting the worst stereotypes of all races, classes, and genders, so individual discretion and sense of personal taste have a huge role to play when choosing what to watch next. In fact, Ella Shohat and Robert Stam, in their book *Unthinking Eurocentrism: Multiculturalism and the Media*, point out that cinema was born during the height of European imperialism and played a part showing Western audiences what the White Man's Burden looked like.[5] In other words, Eurocentrism can be found all

---

4. Baldwin, *Devil Finds Work*, 32–34.

5. Shohat and Stam, *Unthinking Eurocentrism*, 100. The sad thing about this book is that it is in constant need of updating. The idea of white savior or whitewashing continues to be a recurring theme (for example, see controversy about recent movies *The Great Wall*, *Exodus: Gods and Kings*, *Ghost in the Shell*, and *Aloha* to name a few). The fact that there is a level of outrage and disbelief as a response to these films illustrates the rise of historical consciousness in the public and the media. Still, these type of movies continue to be produced.

over the history of cinema. This is not a problem in the past, but one that is continually being pointed out even today especially by marginalized voices (for example, quite often a white actor plays a lead role set in Asia). It is this realization that I hope will guide the reader in making choices in viewing entertainment.

My goal in this chapter consists of finding ways to make movies, history, and theology work together. My disclaimer is that I am by no means a film studies expert, so in some sense my use of film is that of a novice. I am looking at movies and photos by means of the historical discipline. In chapter 3 we examined how real life stories in human history makes theology more dynamic and more faithful to life. This chapter focuses on the way the visual stories of photographs, art, and movies transforms our understanding of history and theology.

One major reason to insist on the medium of cinema reflects the revolution of the camera for history. The video camera and movies in general are a rather recent phenomenon, unlike the historical discipline, which goes back centuries.[6] The camera revolutionizes the way history is recorded. It is a great leveler in that the camera "records what it has been told to record."[7] In short, anyone can record history. According to the French philosopher Jacques Rancière, we are living in a democratic stage of history: "Historical time is not just the time of great collective destinies. It is the time where anyone and anything at all make history and bear witness to history."[8] For example, in our age of the camera phone, the amount of visual records replaces that of the text. The importance of the text shall never die, but it is time to recognize the prevailing value of the visual record. The fact that the camera, especially from a phone, stretches across classes and cultures provides a way for the democratic representation of image recording.

Just because the camera can record history as Rancière points out, this does not mean that it is not prone to manipulation. As James Baldwin poignantly says "the camera sees what you want it to see."[9] Therefore, talk about the importance of the camera, the photograph, or cinema must be tempered with warnings about its potential ideological function. For example, Edward Said, in his book *Orientalism*, notes how fictional accounts

6. Davis, *Slaves on Screen*, 5.
7. Rancière, *Figures of History*, 6.
8. Ibid., 69.
9. Baldwin, *Devil Finds Work*, 35.

of the East present stereotypes in the movies: "Slave trader, camel driver, moneychanger, colorful scoundrel: these are some traditional Arab roles in the cinema."[10] Reading Jasbir Puar's *Terrorist Assemblages* illustrates how since 9/11, the terrorist is a constant image.[11] In addition, Chicana activist Elizabeth Martínez points out that "the kitchen maid is never blonde" in discussing the limited roles for Latinas in movies and television.[12] These tropes are common throughout cinematic history, yet one place they are challenged is through historically themed films. Now one should be careful when a film opens with the statement that is based on true events. Not every historical film, in fact, is faithful to history. Still, it seems that recent movies are getting better at historical authenticity. Moreover, the fact that cinema is globalized presents a counterchallenge to these tropes. However, I have found that Hollywood is primarily the only place where my students think movies are made.

Films are an important cultural medium for both instructors and students to engage in. In fact, critical theorist bell hooks discovered that her students were learning more from going to the movies than in her classroom. Therefore, she suggests "cinema assumes a pedagogical role in the lives of many people. It may not be the intent of a film-maker to teach audiences anything, but that does not mean that lessons are not learned."[13] Michel-Rolph Trouillot notices the same phenomenon as hooks:

> Most Europeans and North Americans learn their first history lessons through media that have not been subjected to the standards set by peer reviews, university presses, or doctoral committees. Long before average citizens read the historians who set the standards of the day for colleagues and students, they access history through celebrations, site and museum visits, movies, national holidays, and primary school books.[14]

Since films relate to a wide audience and connect people across culture, even forms culture in many ways, it serves a purpose to open passionate

10. Said, *Orientalism*, 287.

11. Puar, *Terrorist Assemblages*, 37–78.

12. Martínez, *De Colores Means All of Us*, 54. See 49–54 for her fascinating discussion of the controversial film on race *Follow Me Home*. In addition, see Elizondo, *Future is Mestizo*, 39–40 on representations of Mexicans in history textbooks and movies.

13. hooks, *Reel to Real*, 2–3.

14. Trouillot, *Silencing the Past*, 20. Also, see Martínez, *De Colores Means All of Us*, 21–48 for a thought provoking discussion on the construction of history textbooks and the silencing of minority voices.

dialogue better than textbooks. The particular example of historical themed movies provides a pedagogical tool for students.

Historically based films, not always the most accurate, have been made since the beginning of movie making. In fact, historical films are a staple of Oscar-nominated films. For example, in 2014 *12 Years A Slave* won best picture, and in 2015 historical films like *The Imitation Game*, *Selma*, *The Theory of Everything*, and *American Sniper* were among the nominees. Thus historically based films are often recognized for their artistic quality. Sometimes these films bring commercial success to the producers. These films general attempt at historical accuracy goes against the loosely based historical movies of the distant past. Films like *A Song to Remember* about pianist and composer Frédéric Chopin and novelist George Sand and *Rhapsody in Blue* about George Gershwin, both released in 1945, are entertaining enough, yet steer away from real biographical history for the sake of plot development, making sure instead to teach its audience some type of moral lesson.[15]

Historians may balk at the notion of movies as a medium to teach history. The issue of the truthfulness of the film's narrative is oftentimes questioned by probing historians. Thus, if the movie director adds a little fiction for dramatic purposes, then the movie is unredeemable for the historian. The question then remains why do people find history boring, yet movies continue to be made from events in history? Likewise, does film have a role to play in learning theology?

Theologian Wonhee Anne Joh's book on Christology is rare in the way she dedicates a large section to film analysis in order to develop her theological themes and the Korean concepts of *han* and *jeong*, examining both the Korean and Korean-North American experience.[16] This is one of the best ways to connect the Korean experience with both its history and theology, and a place for a non-Korean to grasp this experience. In addition, Brazilian theologian Leonardo Boff praises the producers of the novella *El Clon* for featuring "the grandeur and the beauty of Arab culture."[17] *El*

---

15. Both films were released in 1945, so that must have been the year to come out with a film about a great pianist, only to spin the story into a morality play where the protagonist basically collapses on his piano because of exhaustion. These movies were my initial experience not to take for granted when a film attempts to portray a historical person based on true events, but to always do historical research on the figure.

16. Joh, *Heart of the Cross*, 30–48. Joh's book could also be added to the autobiographical, historical-theological tradition examined in the last chapter of this book.

17. Boff, *Fundamentalism*, 82. Of course, what Boff sees as beauty someone else

Clon presents its own set of problems featuring the exotification of Arab culture, yet Boff's example of a South American narrative between the Brazilian and Moroccan worlds illustrates the way media provides materials for constructive dialogue. In short, we are past the time where TV shows, movies, YouTube videos, and other forms of media are simply dismissed by both historians and especially theologians.

One of the best aspects of historical films like *Gandhi, Mandela*, and *Selma* is to witness the figures surrounding the "great figure" of history. In fact, it is a visual way of seeing that no human being is an island. Moreover, there is a historical-theological dimension to all these particular films, denying through historical events the fictional wall that separates religious belief from the public square.

Part of the appeal of movies and photographs is that they represent something other than the text. For example, how often has a book cover been the first aspect of the book to capture our gaze? Once drawn in by the image, we then notice the book's title and perhaps preview its pages. However, as symbols, images are never completely severed from textual imagination. Everything is interpreted from our hermeneutical horizon. The film or the picture forces the viewer's imagination to think on the spot. Pictures cry out to be discussed, as does films, both good and bad. It is the particular job of the historian to discuss the historical context of the images.

History textbooks, at least the good ones, are filled with images. At some point, the book moves from sketches to paintings, until finally the photograph becomes the prominent image. These images have a specific function. They are strategically placed to correspond to the author's historical narrative.

What is being advocated in this chapter is the appeal of the image, both the photograph and the film. Textbooks use them, as well as college instructors. However, oftentimes most students' papers are completed with no utilization of images. It is like the use of a photo or movie clip suddenly ruins the potential scholarship of the essay. Again, referencing the camera phone, students are not only bombarded with images on the screen, but oftentimes produce their own countless images. The discussion on whether this is some narcissist turn does not appeal to me. Instead I am more interested in the history that is being produced whether it is by video or by photograph. We will examine the way historical films are a necessary tool

---

might view as a type of Orientalism. Still, as a Christian thinker, Boff clearly states his opposition to Islamophobia; see 17–20.

to discuss the impact history has on the present-future world by looking specifically at a historically based film on a religious subject Roland Joffé's *The Mission*, and then close with a discussion about the power of the photograph on the viewer.

The Mission: A Historical-Theological Study

> "Because of the power of film, movies with historical themes affect public perceptions of the past more deeply than do scholarly reconstructions. Filmmakers and historians search for meaning in separate ways, but their quests can converge." —James Schofield Saeger[18]

Joffé's 1986 movie *The Mission* tells the story of the defense of the Guarani missions in South America from Spanish and Portuguese control. This defense turned into a small war between the European forces and a combined effort of Guarani and a few Jesuit priests. The film starts Jeremy Irons and Robert DeNiro (and a young Liam Neeson in a supporting role) as the Jesuit priests who live among the Guarani. The film is mostly famous for its beautiful cinematography and musical score. In addition, one interesting aspect of the film is that one of the actors and consultants on the film is the Irish-American activist priest Daniel Berrigan.

One characteristic of the movie that is good for theological discussion is the film's ending. The film shows the Guarani war as a total and complete slaughter. Many of my students are absolutely shocked by the end of the film since they are used to the Hollywood ending where the underdog, against all odds, wins the battle. Instead, the viewer is presented an ethical puzzle. Was Father Gabriel (Irons) correct in his passive resistance to the European troops or was Father Mendoza (DeNiro) right in attempting armed resistance? Berrigan praises the film for leaving this ethical conundrum a little ambiguous at the end by having both Gabriel and Mendoza die.[19] He writes that "the film celebrates memory, the present, the prisoners of conscience, the martyrs, all who renounce pernicious well-being and the middle way."[20] Ever since Christ's death there has been a theological

---

18. Saegar, "*Mission* and Historical Missions," 63.

19. Berrigan, *Mission*, 11–12 and 19–20.

20. Ibid., 21. Contrast this with his questioning of the violence of contemporary films on 30–31 and 55–56.

conversation on how to comprehend the reality of warfare. Was Mendoza doing God's will in joining the Guarani in fighting against the Europeans, or was Gabriel faithful to the non-violent testimony of Jesus by presenting the mission to the European army like lambs to the slaughter? Again, since the director had both characters die we the viewers are left to answer this question. If showing the film to your history or theology class, this might be an appropriate place to bring in writers like Arendt, LaCapra, Fanon, and Ellacuría, providing their thoughts on violence.[21]

Berrigan was brought in as a consultant on the history of the Jesuits; he does not hold back criticism of European domination of the Americas even by the agency of the Catholic Church.[22] Berrigan's ideas on the film illustrate the nature of group "research" in historical filmmaking, which cannot be boiled down to the solitary work of the director.[23] The historian in general works alone, whereas it takes a community to make a movie. Throughout Berrigan's journaling there is thoughtful consideration among the film crew that it would not become "a kind of wide-screen National Geographic series: 'Innocent Savages Brought to Your Coffee Table in Three Issues.'"[24] It is up to the viewer on whether or not the film is successful in not presenting these events as an activity in third world pity or of a another depiction of the white saviors.[25]

The movie opens by stating that what happens in the film corresponds to true historical events. It actually is a smorgasbord of historical events and fiction, a point I try to make transparent to my students. As a tool for teaching history in the classroom, I focus on the following three points. First, the film illustrates the rise of the modern, secular European nation state. One of the motivations for Spain and Portugal to take the mission territories is their regressive influence in global power in relation to the rising British power. The diplomats mention how Spanish (Catholic) law prevent

---

21. Arendt, *On Violence*; LaCapra, *History and Its Limits*, 90–122; Fanon, *Wretched of the Earth*, 1–62; Ellacuría, *Freedom Made Flesh*, 165–231.

22. Berrigan, *Mission*, 113–14. For all of his declarations against the corruption of the church, he positions himself as a faithful member, reserving criticism for what he sees as some of the excesses of Latin American liberation theology; see 143–46.

23. Davis, *Slaves on Screen*, 12–13.

24. Berrigan, *Mission*, 100.

25. One example of criticism of the perceived European paternalism in the film is Saeger, "*The Mission* and Historical Missions." Saegar's criticism of the film is pretty severe, seeing it as too Eurocentric, even in the films source material. He provides an annotated bibliography for research on the historical Guarani.

slavery of the indigenous, yet note how the more secular state of Portugal condones slavery. The Catholic church's ethical problem is to either stand in the way of allowing the Portuguese to seize the territories and enslave the indigenous, or attempt to hold on to its influence in Europe. The Church decides to ultimately sacrifice the missions, and in some sense, the Jesuit order. The students begin to sense a pattern about the rise of European nation state power by seeing it used for violent ends. They are able to then conceptualize and make sense of this narrative of conquest that started back with Columbus in 1492. Nevertheless, there is a case to be made that the Spanish come across as cardboard villains in the film.[26]

The second point applauds just how well the Jesuits are depicted in the movie. The viewer sees how these priests were able to travel to Asia and the Americas, navigating through difficult terrain, and establishing successful missions throughout the world. These figures are the star athletes and soldiers that were inspired by Ignatius's vision. The Jesuits show that they really believe in the meaning of the missions for the indigenous by travelling the way they do through a foreign environment, and for attempting to defend the native peoples, realizing that even their eternal souls hang in the balance by this subversive act.

The third point considers the agency given to indigenous history. The Guarani both accept and reject the Jesuits at different times. They will also decide to go to war with the Europeans on their own volition. The subversive Jesuits follow the Guarani in their decision. In addition, the film does a good job not portraying the indigenous as too exotic or ritualistic, but a group of people essentially on an equal level with the Europeans. In fact, it is because the colonizers believe in the Guarani racial inferiority that they brutally massacre them. The indigenous do not show such an attitude at all, but are even accepting of the former mercenary and slave trader.

My third point remains one that needs to be held with a nuanced perspective. In a way the film cannot help but present its material in the context of white saviors (the Jesuits) to the Guarani. There are at times featured a dialectic between a passive and active agency from the Guarani, whom James Schofield Saegar claims serve as "cultural ciphers" in the movie.[27]

---

26. There are elements of the "Black Legend" in the depiction of the bloodthirsty Spanish in the film. The Black Legend was English and French propaganda against Spain, depicting their conquest as innocuous while Spain's was demonic to the core. Here is a further good example of history as propaganda. For more information on the Black Legend see the various books by Walter Mignolo. Also see, Elizondo, *Future is Mestizo*, 29–45.

27. Saegar, "*Mission* and Historical Missions," 74. Again, his biggest complaint is that

The movie contains a not so subtle romanticism of paradise, a Garden of Eden, featuring a tribe of noble savages. Since the film was released in the 1980s, after the death of Romero, the clamping down on liberation theology by a conservative Vatican establishment, and the stories of priests joining revolutionary movements, it cannot be helped to interpret the movie in the context of a Cold War dynamic. Are the historical Jesuits meant to represent the so-called freedom fighters of the twentieth century? Does this aspect of European priests as militant defenders of the oppressed take away from the film's accuracy? Indeed, the connection between communism and liberation theology is not something that is universally considered righteous even by activists on the progressive left.[28] Much like Eurocentric philosophies and their radical historicism has no place for indigenous stories, myths, and cultures in their agenda, the Guarani in the film always need a white interpreter, if, in fact, their words are interpreted at all.

Finally, if the passivity of the Guarani remains open for questioning, the role of women in the film is definitely minor and passive. The Guarani women have two roles to play in the film: welcoming the priests to the community, while oftentimes coddling their babies, and cannon fodder at the end of the movie.[29] The Guarani women have few, if any, speaking parts. The one crucial woman in the movie has a love affair with Mendoza's younger brother, while he is off doing the hard work of slave trading, which leads him to murder his beloved brother in a duel because of jealousy. Mendoza's brother and his lover never object to Mendoza's occupation as slave trader, so she does not dump him because she finds his work appalling. She more or less, gets between the brothers because suddenly Mendoza does not fit her emotional needs. Therefore, this character is hardly sympathetic especially since her part concludes with weeping over her murdered love. At this point, the audience moves on from wondering what happens to her since we now become invested in Mendoza's purgatory and redemption. I cannot help but wonder what a close contemporary to the historical events in the film, the nun Sor Juana Ines de la Cruz, would think about the way

---

the Guarani are depicted through typical Indian tropes, whereas the historical Guarani were a lot more diverse and technologically advanced than seen in the film.

28. See Tinker, *Spirit and Resistance*; Comblin, *Called for Freedom*, 214.

29. Saegar, "*Mission* and Historical Missions," 69. Here I cannot help but agree with his critique.

this woman leads to the tearing apart of fraternal bond and the eventual redemption of the male figure.[30]

The Mission serves as a good example of how even a film striving for historical faithfulness is set with a number of problems. On the one hand, the theologian may bypass these problems and use the film to discuss non-violence, the lengths some will go to share the gospel, or the way the film showcases the theology of grace and forgiveness. This is a theme orientated viewing. On the other hand, the historian may appreciate some aspects of the films narrating of his historical events, yet will criticize the largely interpretive, fictional elements of the movie. I know that when I saw the film for the first time at a younger age, it taught me that Catholics are also Christian (since I was raised in an evangelical Protestant home), and that the power of the nation-state is a dangerous thing. In some sense, this is a point I still share with my evangelical students. This is a lesson that speaks to their experience. However, I can see that indigenous groups would be disturbed at the Guarani representation.

I am raising only some slight criticisms of the film. Perhaps what might be a major problem, one I will be discussing below about the power of the photograph, is the dimension of voyeurism. Does the film at the end attempt to present the unpresentable? With the closing scenes of the eradication of the priests and the indigenous does the film wander into the category of spectacle? What are the viewers of this difficult scene supposed to leave with? Other historical films made around this time like *Romero, Cry Freedom, Salvador,* and *The Killing Fields* (also directed by Joffé) tend to follow the same format. In fact, in all cases, those with social-political power, and mostly of European heritage, are the ones committing atrocities and torturing the victims. The so-called savages in the films are depicted as mostly witnesses to the horrors of violence, testifying to the audience of their innocence. Using terminology by Dussel, we might categorize this as seeing the underside of modernity experiencing the barbarism of the European project. However, the problem continues in that most of these films tend to tell their story through the eyes of a white, Anglo-American or European protagonist. This is a sober fact of how Eurocentrism is not only in the textbooks.

I continue to use *The Mission* in the classroom. It asks important historical-theological questions. In fact, its problematic representations are the kind of sample to engage the students critically. Do the Indians in the film seem a little docile? What do you think about the way most of the

---

30. See Gonzalez, *Sor Juana*; Yugar, *Sor Juana*.

indigenous never have their words directly translated? What purpose do women serve in the film? The same thing applies to the theological themes of missions, violence, the imago Dei, grace, and forgiveness. It might be a good place to ask questions about the nature of missions for both the Europeans and the indigenous groups in the Americas. Questions that guide the film help prevent a passive, voyeuristic type viewing. However, whether or not I raise intentional and direct questions about the film, the students are already processing the movie, comparing the narrative to their own experiences and grasp of human history. Therefore, I agree with Davis that the time has come to reject the idea of the passive spectator:

> The passive spectator, naively accepting what comes off the movie screen, has disappeared from film theory, and should also disappear from historical criticism of films. Spectators may delight in a historical film, be interested in it or repelled by it. But they do not believe automatically what they see in a historical film: rather, they ask about it, argue about it, and write letters of protest about it.[31]

Some of the images of *The Mission* can make the viewer uncomfortable, much like snapshots of historical images of violence and pain in a history textbook. In what ways do the visual images of the photograph and film produce empathy in the viewer and not pity? We have read about the oftentimes difficult life of those on the margins. History is scattered with catastrophes. However, we live in a time where these experiences are immortalized by the camera. How are we supposed to ethically handle these historical sources? We will close the book with this question.

Only Reading Books with Pictures

> "To remember is, more and more, not to recall a story but to be able to call up a picture."—Susan Sontag[32]

> "Globalization is not about a slide show viewed in the comfort of middle-class living rooms where photographic depiction serves to domesticate oppressive reality."—Harold Recinos[33]

31. Davis, *Slaves on Screen*, 15.
32. Sontag, *Regarding the Pain of Others*, 89.
33. Recinos, *Jesus Weeps*, 54.

A narrative text provides insight to the human imagination. A photograph is a captured image in human time and space that prevents the viewer from doubting its veracity. It is one thing to make a case to a classroom of students that European racism expanded after the Enlightenment era. It is an entirely different presentation that is formed when you can illustrate through photographs what this racism actually looked like. The power of the photograph captures the viewer. For example, one can insist that the El Niño famine in India in the late nineteenth century was horrible and that the genocide in the Congo, including the chopping off of hands, was gruesome. However, point to an image from a textbook or from a Prezi presentation and suddenly witness the renewed focus that students give to these grisly images.

I remember when I was a student in junior college watching a documentary video on the 1911 Triangle Shirtwaist Factory fire in Manhattan where 146 young women, mostly immigrants, died because the escape exits were blocked. The video and its images were so powerful that they have stayed with me ever since. I now show the video to my U.S. History classes in light of labor reform history and women's history. The power of this documentary video and the images of the lifeless bodies on the pavement have the capacity to influence the viewer in a sense like it would affect an eyewitness. I acknowledge the emotional impact I am trying to get from the student viewing this video. Is this the purpose of historical images? Is it empathy that we seek as instructors? Is this evidence of the way pictures being worth one thousand words?

One of the best recent examples of the use of images in a historical study is Simon Gikandi's book *Slavery and the Culture of Taste*. The book contains pictures illustrating the changing dynamic of racial understanding among whites toward blacks, prominently displayed in portraits of white aristocrats with black slaves, who are standing in an inferior position. Gikandi's thesis is that "slavery and the culture of taste were connected by the theories and practices that emerged in the modern period."[34] In other words, Gikandi illustrates that it was during the eighteenth-century Enlightenment period, the same time when democracy was the new buzz word, the moment when revolutions based on universal freedom rocked the European world, that modern ideas of beauty (philosophy of aesthetics) was formed in relation to the African slave trade.

---

34. Gikandi, *Slavery and the Culture of Taste*, xiii.

The shock of the difference between time and space occurs when viewing these images in the present, especially when juxtaposed by the racist sentiment of Enlightenment thinkers like David Hume and Immanuel Kant, realizing that modern theories of beauty are haunted by "the ghosts of slavery."[35] The black figures in the paintings look up toward the white master as looking into the face of God.[36] The roots of Social Darwinism and the historical proof of the espousal of the racial superiority of white Anglo-Americans and Europeans are framed in images that are available in either books on the subject, like Gikandi's, or a quick search on the internet. Now Gikandi's text provides enough information to argue his thesis, yet the images inside the book take his argument to a whole other level. In fact, I have taught this racial aspect of modernity relying on Gikandi's outline and the images he provides. Therefore, the instructor may point out the racist comments of such Enlightenment philosophers like Hume and Kant, but by also providing these images illustrates perfectly these ideas and their consequences. A picture is worth a thousand words, but these pictures along with clear statements of white superiority by European philosophers provide exhaustive evidence of the problem of Eurocentric thinking.

Susan Sontag's fantastic little book *Regarding the Pain of Others* compliments Gikandi's connection of slavery and aesthetics, especially as witnessed through the medium of the photograph. Sontag exclaims that over other media, including cinema, photos of suffering have a "deeper bite" with its ability to be captured in our memories.[37] When looking at the images of "real horror" there is a response of both "shame" and "shock" because most of us lack the influence and ability to alleviate such suffering.[38] This is exactly the type of responses that Haitian writer Michel-Rolph Trouillot provides over a debate about a proposed exhibition at EuroDisney of Disney's America, which includes Afro-American slavery.[39] The exhibition was sacked but the debate over history and suffering continues. Empathy is the emotion I have sought to preach about in this book, yet the powerlessness one feels exposed to a harsh historical reality, in the past, the present, and

---

35. Ibid., 281. For a sample of these readings see Eze, *Race and the Enlightenment*.

36. Also see similar images in Buck-Morss, *Hegel, Haiti, and Universal History*, 30–31. She points out that the fruit the black figures in these portraits represent are the fruits of labor from the colonies.

37. Sontag, *Regarding the Pain of Others*, 22.

38. Ibid., 42. Also see Sacks, *Dignity of Difference*, 30.

39. Trouillot, *Silencing the Past*, 141–53.

most definitely in the future, provides the place to ask the ethical question about in what little or grand ways is it possible to prevent such violence?

Sontag, speaking as a North American thinker, points out that Eurocentrism even affects the way *we* in the West perceive pictures of recent horrors. She writes that "the grievously injured bodies shown in published photographs are from Asia or Africa. This journalistic custom inherits the centuries-old practice of exhibiting exotic—that is, colonized—human beings.... The exhibition in photographs of cruelties inflicted on those with darker complexions in exotic countries continues this offering, oblivious to the considerations that deter such displays of our own victims of violence; for the other, even when not an enemy, is regarded only as someone to be seen, not someone (like us) who also sees."[40] Here Sontag raises this issue especially in exposing the lack of historical understanding among her American readers. She points out that the first way to critically understand an image is to know the history behind the image. Photos of this nature without some type of textual information ultimately force the imagination of the viewer to provide an explanation. If it is accomplished in this way then the result is most probably pure fantasy, a misguided projection of the ego. In addition, part of the role empathy plays is in trying to see the situation of the photo from the other person's point of view. Again, this is really difficult to comprehend without a good grasp of history, and potentially ends up leading into a fantastic leap into a world that remains alien to us. However, one question to raise is, what if a photographic image is accompanied by ideological texts? Puar, for example, raises the point on the way images of Abu Ghraib have been used by different parties, even the way American exceptionalism finds excuses for them.[41]

Sontag suggests that the "atrocious images" still serve a "vital function" in that they declare to the viewer: "This is what human beings are capable of doing—may volunteer to do, enthusiastically, self-righteously. Don't forget."[42] Historical events of ethnic cleansing, political purges, and genocides in recent memory provide the context for Sontag's statement. The idea of "never again" after the Holocaust was supposed to be a historical, concrete warning of the capacity of violence, but recent history has proven that humanity has not heeded the call. In most cases, the people committing

---

40. Sontag, *Regarding the Pain of Others*, 72.

41. Puar, *Terrorist Assemblages*, 79–113. Puar's book uses a number of images that corresponds to her theoretical work.

42. Sontag, *Regarding the Pain of Others*, 115.

the atrocities rationalized the rapes and murders. *The Mission* makes this point well, at the final moments of the film, when after the Guarani and the Jesuits are slaughtered, the Spanish ambassador self-righteously claims that he had no qualms about sending his troops to massacre them. Even though the film's portrayal of the Spanish is heavy handed, there is a historical truth behind their use of force to modernize the countryside. Nations still remove people from their place in order to keep up with the times. Moreover, every teacher or writer of history realizes in a short amount of time that some of their readers or students refused to be moved by the horrors of history, or at least found ways to justify it.[43] They too will someday either ignore or rationalize the disappearance or the invisibility of the Other. The Portuguese ambassador in *The Mission* at least claims a deterministic view of history, stating that violence is at the heart of human history. Is there an alternative view? The Cardinal claims responsibility, but how much agency did he really have in this instance? In what ways do we have agency if we really gain empathy from the history of the oppressed?

One aspect of agency contains the act of recording the historical event for memory. European theologians like Johann Baptist Metz, Henri Nouwen, and Dorothee Soelle chronicled their time in Latin America to raise awareness about the violence, and the first world's responsibility for causing much of it since 1492.[44] For example, Metz describes the children he saw in Peru with "eyes without dreams, the faces without tears, as it were the unhappiness beyond wishing," hiding the fact of a hidden strength that perseveres day after day in miserable conditions.[45] Nouwen writes similar thoughts when he states that "in a poor country the children always suffer the most" or that "the naked King on the Cross and the naked kids in Cochabamba belong together. The God who is love stands with the children who crave love."[46]

Much like Metz, Nouwen, and Soelle, American writer Joan Didion's *Salvador* opens stating that "terror is the given of the place."[47] Didion visited

43. Ibid., 111.

44. Soelle, *Stations of the Cross*, 141–46; Nouwen, *¡Gracias!*; Metz, "With the Eyes." These theologians write against Eurocentrism in light of the 500 year anniversary of Colombus's voyage. In his journal written while he stayed in Latin America, Nouwen talks about such things as meeting liberation theologians Gustavo Gutierrez and Jon Sobrino. His thoughts on liberation theology and spirituality are still important; see 39–40.

45. Metz, "With the Eyes," 113–14.

46. Nouwen, *¡Gracias!*, 50; also see, 9, 93–95, and 122–23.

47. Didion, *Salvador*, 14.

El Salvador soon after the assassination of Archbishop Romero, pointing out the futility of American interests in this country. What makes these writers different from others is that they actually visited Latin America with open eyes and with a historical consciousness. These European and American writers provide historical texts that correspond to the violence in places like El Salvador. Soelle, Metz, Nouwen, and Didion at the very least were able to comprehend the violence of the photographs adorning the pages of newspapers. They also chastise their North American and European readers for their sense of innocence and detachment from third-world violence. Moreover, they provided the theological detractors of liberation theology with a nuanced perspective of how horrible the violence was in many parts of Latin America.

Recall from the Introduction, that theologian James Cone exhort us in the present to not forget the horrors of lynching. This is a role historians play in not allowing the present and future generations to forget a nation's sins. In fact, Sontag thinks that the United States is still incapable of dealing with its past. She asserts that having a museum dedicated to the history of slavery in the United States is almost impossible to conceive. She declares why: "That this country, like every other country, has its tragic past does not sit well with the founding, and still all-powerful, belief in American exceptionalism. The national consensus on American history as a history of progress is a new setting for distressing photographs—one that focuses our attention on wrongs, both here and elsewhere, for which America sees itself as the solution and cure."[48] Perhaps we can envision a day that Sontag's words about American exceptionalism will be proven wrong. The challenge will only come from a sober historical consciousness, matched with a deepened empathy for the Other, suspicious of all exclusive theologies of history like American exceptionalism. Faith traditions might be one place where this begins, yet they must be the type that takes history, even the most uncomfortable, seriously.

For all of Sontag's musings on the shocking photograph, she does bring up an important idea about the video camera and the role it plays in shaping opinions. She writes: "The war America waged in Vietnam, the first to be witnessed day after day by television cameras, introduced the home

---

48. Sontag, *Regarding the Pain of Others*, 88. The view of the United States as a Redeemer Nation and above reproach is critiqued by Latin American liberation theology; see Nessan, *Vitality of Liberation Theology*, 126–27.

front to new tele-intimacy with death and destruction."[49] Unfortunately this intimacy has not stopped the waging of war in the present day. Instead, the postmodern era has moved into a time of fear and security, with wars of terror waged across the globe, and the spectacle of hyper-violent acts staged for the camera. For those living in North American or Western European states, even when the violent act is committed, there is general outcry, followed by the rush to return things to normalcy. However, in the third world, normalcy is oftentimes this drama of continual violence.

A good book to link our current discussion on historical images with the overall focus of *Remembering Lived Lives* is Jean Franco's recent book *Cruel Modernity*. She studies the horrific use of torture by Latin American regimes, especially the brutal attacks against women. She provides the type of historical text that agrees with Sontag's work in illustrating the volitional nature of these violent crimes. The *machismo* culture oftentimes ridiculed in Latin American liberation theology, mostly from women theologians, is seen crystal clear in Franco's detail of these tortures. The amount of clarity she provides for these events, the depraved enjoyment by the perpetrators, makes it difficult to naively talk about a general human decency in this history. Raw violence has become the norm. She opens her book with this thought: "Cruelty leaves long-lasting memory traces—hence the recurrent theme of buried books, faded photographs, fragmented testimonies, exhumed bodies, harvest of bones."[50]

In her chapter "The Ghostly Arts," Franco writes about the iconographic use of headshots used by mothers and grandmothers as representing the disappeared people in Argentina. She suggests: "In the absence of their narratives, photographs, films, and art installations are ghostly hauntings. The silence of the disappeared is absolute."[51] This thought matches well with Didion's musings on the "unrecognizable" bodies of the dead in El Salvador that are "taken for granted as in a nightmare, or a horror movie."[52] Franco correctly points out that the photo of the disappeared, which often appear as forever young, serves as a link to the past whereas the bodies that

---

49. Ibid., 21.

50. Franco, *Cruel Modernity*, 9. Franco's book features a number of fictional and non-fictional accounts of the violent history in Latin America in the twentieth century, including a number of films that I would recommend.

51. Ibid., 195. Also see Cavarero, *Horrorism* for more on this theme.

52. Didion, *Salvador*, 16 and 19.

suffered "atrocities" lose their ties to humanity.⁵³ The name of El Mozote in El Salvador is infamous in this regard. It is hard not to view the pictures by Susan Meiselas in Franco's book and fall into the trap of spectatorship. However, the images and the narrative of the book are so powerful it is almost impossible not to be touched by these events. This is a key point that connects well to Sontag's argument that images need a historical description to provide a context. Without Franco's text we almost unconsciously supply the meaning to the photos based on our own experiences.

Books, photographs, and movies are left to history for human memory to take hold of. A spectacular event of violence like 9/11 will forever be memorialized in the pages of American history textbooks. I call it spectacular because of the spectacle of the event in the focus of video cameras. It is perhaps this element of spectacle in New York City that makes it an event that stands out in comparison to a bombing in a third-world nation. There is an assumption throughout the texts looked at in this chapter that the violence in places like El Salvador have become a way of life. Does the US media not spend enough time on suicide bombs that detonate in Pakistan, Iraq, Nigeria, and other places outside of Europe? Are they assuming that this is because violence has become a way of life? Is it safe to guess that images of 9/11 will be the focus of history textbooks of the present future, whereas dead Iraq children will be missing? Who makes these decisions? And what if the photos of dead people from terrorist attack across the Middle East were included? The fact the biggest body count from Islamic terrorism remains Muslims! What about the accusation of spectatorship of the Oriental Other that might arise?

If we pealed back the layers to present day reality in every society we would be shocked to see pictures of violence that would haunt our memories. Reality is structured in such a way to present to general human history a normative sense of being. However, this normality is interrupted by the spectacular. It is the spectacular image that grabs the pages of the history textbooks.

---

53. Franco, *Cruel Modernity*, 208.

Conclusion

"However profound the impression left on them by the testimonies, readers are still at a distance and free to be in some other place. And that is a huge problem that no scholar can evade." —Jean Franco[54]

"As long as we bear in mind the differences between film and professional prose, we can take film seriously as a source of valuable and even innovative historical vision. We can then ask questions of historical films that are parallel to those we ask of historical books. Rather than being poachers on the historian's preserve, filmmakers can be artists for whom history matters." —Natalie Zemon Davis[55]

As a child I liked books with pictures. I guess that makes me like any other kid. My favorite Bible was the great big family Bible, which included some of the great baroque era art by Rembrandt, Rubens, and Caravaggio. These pictures were stuck in my imagination, and I cannot help seeing them when hearing these biblical passages in a sermon. Pictures have a way to free the imagination for a better appreciation of a text.

Photos of history coming from societies wracked with violence and war are a different story. For people living a pretty mundane life, pictures of genocide look like they took place in another world. There seems an almost alien and somewhat exotic dimension to the subject matter. Framing the discussion in this manner presents us with the problem of what societies we might label as civilized versus the barbaric. For example, this is what Aimé Césaire meant when he scolded Europe on how Hitler had brought the type of colonial barbarism so familiar to the third world to Europe's backyard.[56] The barbaric can be found in any part of the world, yet sometimes the violence is so rampant that the eye of the photographer or the movie director captures moments of great terror for all eternity. Before recent years we could only rely on the chronicler or the poet to articulate such events. Everything has changed with the camera.

There is an amazing distance between the photograph and the viewer. One cannot magically make the viewer empathic to an image. However, there

54. Ibid., 251.
55. Davis, *Slaves on Screen*, 15.
56. Césaire, *Discourse on Colonialism*, 36.

remains a perverted draw that comes from the horrific image.[57] Here Berrigan's condemnation of our comfortable fascination with violence and its banality is on full display: "*The Battle of Algiers* must surely rank as one of the noblest examinations on record of the conquest of the oppressor by the moral superiority of the oppressed. Yet when I last saw the film in my neighborhood, the Columbia University students in the theater raised a gross cheer every time a bomb went off in restaurant or market. And when the film was ended, these ersatz warriors in Plato's cave returned beyond doubt to their stereos and pot sessions."[58] This example shows the type of indiscriminate revolutionary violence that Franco illustrates in her book when guerillas, particularly the example of the Shining Path in Peru, can assassinate a fellow companion simply because the person is slowing down the movement by his or her existence. However, Berrigan words carry a lot of meaning because the value of human life is sacrificed for ideology on a conscious level. This is human empathy trumped for the universal cause. It also features the type of poseur revolutionary feeling made by those in the middle-class. The response by what seems like bored students toward the rush of revolutionary violence brings the question of empathy to a new level. One would perhaps expect a better ethical compass among these students especially considering that bombs detonating in a restaurant and market are probably sending children to their graves. However, perhaps this is a better illustration on the hidden barbarism in what we consider the most civilized societies.

On the ten-year anniversary of Archbishop Oscar Romero's death, Dorothee Soelle asks a poignant question that relates to this chapter: "*Who will think about Oscar Romero in these days? How many cinemas will show the film about him? What church congregations will request it?*"[59] Indeed, what churches are watching *Romero*? We live in an age, at least in North America, where many Christian films depict sentimental conversions to evangelical Christianity or a reactionary apologetic fueled by a growing sense of social-political persecution. Seen in the light of a film like *Romero*, Christian cinema presents itself as disingenuous and without a historical consciousness. Perhaps movies focused on recent Latin American history like *Romero*, *For Greater Glory*, and even *In the Time of Butterflies* would introduce church audiences to what real persecution looks like.

57. Franco, *Cruel Modernity*, 212.

58. Berrigan, *Mission*, 31. Also see Davis, *Slaves on Screen*, 8–9 on Gillo Pontecorvo's technique in making *Battle of Algiers*.

59. Soelle, *Stations of the Cross*, 76.

Conclusion

"The practice of Christianity does not entail historical-theological optimism; victory is not promised to us. What is promised is a God who goes with us into poverty, torture, political powerlessness. The experiences that people have with this God cannot be domesticated."—Dorothee Soelle[1]

"The ruin of history visited on a people does not wipe out the steadfastness of beauty."—Dionne Brand[2]

Remembering Lived Lives might be accused of privileging ethnic minorities outside of the Anglo-American and European world. It does this out of the sole purpose of exposing the trend to ignore these figures in the past or to section them off as contextual thinkers on the periphery of the central argument of so-called Western canon thinkers. As Aboriginal historian Jackie Huggins notes, the silence is often forced: "Aboriginal people have been excluded from the pages of white history, and denied access to the records of their own people."[3] This is a historical point that we in the present need constant reminders about, which is why I encourage my students to read James Baldwin's essays.[4] Consequently, Huggins suggests that there are more examples today of the oppressed writing about the marginalized, illustrating that liberation movements from these narratives are growing.[5]

1. Soelle, *Stations of the Cross*, 50–51.
2. Brand, *A Map*, 193.
3. Huggins, *Sister Girl*, 2.
4. I recommend Baldwin's *The Fire Next Time* as the best example.
5. Huggins, *Sister Girl*, 47, and 108–19. In fact, see pp. 120–30 for her autobiographical

Thus it might be thought a rare occurrence to see a book on the history of Christian thought that does not reference a person of color, but unfortunately books like this are still being published. One of my fears remains that once assumed that enough acknowledgment of minority groups has been accomplished, Eurocentric books will return as the status quo. Perhaps even with the last few decades of the attention toward the culture wars, this clouded our vision that this status quo has remained. In fact, not too long ago, Dale Irvin argued for a diverse understanding of Christianity, what he called "faithful histories," in order to stop the privileging of European history.[6] Would Irvin be correct to say that in the twenty-first century, we still need to recognize this privilege?

One of my main theses is that historically minded people interested in the study of religion should study contextual theologies as a form of micro-history. These books should be considered primary sources dealing with religious matters. However, because these works are concerned with historical context they also contain autobiographies, biographies, testimonies, experiences, and even fictional writing that are worth historical study. Sometimes the best of this genre are the history books. These books display narratives that present voices from the margins. Because these writings were composed at the same time as postcolonial writings, they both tend to feature attention to matters of gender, race, class, and language.[7] The multiple views towards each of these categories get away from the European tradition of privileging reason or class as the universal category. Therefore, *Remembering Lived Lives* also highlighted a number of postcolonial literatures along with what is considered contextual and liberation theologies.

One of my book's main arguments is it that major European theologians like Karl Barth and Paul Tillich are somewhat responsible for setting the Eurocentric precedent in the early to mid-twentieth century.[8] Barth

---

history writing in the chapter titled "Experience and Identity: Writing History."

6. Irvin, *Christian Histories, Christian Traditioning*, 1–14. The irony of this book is that it contains mostly European thinkers. However, his intention for diversity in Christian history finds a connection in the focus on multiplicity and border thinking by Latin American theorists like Mayra Rivera and Walter Mignolo.

7. For a recent example see the essays in Isasi-Díaz and Medieta, *Decolonizing Epistemologies*.

8. Tillich, *History of Christian Thought*. Tillich manages not just to exclude ethnic minorities from his account of church history, but also most of North American thought. In some sense, both Barth's and Tillich's historical accounts are historical relics, full of useful information but somewhat dated.

CONCLUSION

in particular shows traces of understanding the problems of Eurocentric thought, yet leaves it to the next generation to ameliorate such accounts. In fact, I have highlighted some of the moments where they theorized about events outside of Europe. Unfortunately not everyone from this next generation realizes that Eurocentrism is much of a problem and thus continue practicing this trend in the spirit of Barth and Tillich. Cornel West argues that these great "neo-orthodox" thinkers of the past spoke to a different time, and that it is unfortunate today many of their "insights" are ignored today by people suspicious of Eurocentric theology.[9] The point is not to ignore Barth and Tillich just because they have Eurocentric tendencies, but upon realizing this about them, move forward in historical-theological theory by embracing the diversity of thought. In many ways, Michael Eric Dyson's words from about twenty years ago still ring true:

> Multicultural education, whether in the seminary or the wider academic community, does not require a wholesale repudiation of European culture or traditional values, but it does entail a rigorous and honest examination of the ways in which the worst aspects of Eurocentrism and narrow traditionalism have trashed cultures, traditions, and peoples not of European heritage. Barth, Tillich, and Niebuhr remain as theological icons and resources. But Cone, Ruether, Cannon, Gutierrez, and a host of others have been added to the list, and further questions about who makes the list are now entertained.[10]

Remembering Lived Lives is part of a movement to focus on "neglected" persons from history books, especially religious thinkers, unfortunately not so strangely absent until about thirty-five to forty years ago in the United States.[11] The hostility sometimes evident in the so-called "history wars" (or cultural wars) seems so fresh because historically it is in our recent past. Again, my point is not that we must cease to read Barth and Tillich because

---

9. West, *Prophetic Fragments*, 274. In the same essay, he asserts that theology is in desperate need of historians.

10. Dyson, *Reflecting Black*, 321. In this short essay, Dyson claims that being PC is not the problem, but SOS (same old stuff) is. Sadly this discussion continues to rear its ugly head in the academy and the media.

11. See Foner, *Who Owns History*, ix–xix. I came to Foner late in writing this book, which served as a comfort for me because he also quotes James Baldwin at the start of his book and mentions the Hollywood trend of history themed movies, illustrating the public fascination with history. Moreover, the first chapter is autobiographical as he answers the question why he became a historian.

they are Europeans, and we must only read Gutiérrez and Dussel because they are not. I quote Dyson once more because he basically states the goal of my book:

> The point is not that we must trash everything European. Nothing exists in cultural, racial, or even national purity. Neither is the point to indiscriminately valorize everything non-European. The point is to *tell the truth*, as clearly and intelligently as we are able. Only then will we be able to counter the forces of genocide, racism, and historical amnesia, the effects of which still linger in our contemporary cultural, religious, and national practices.[12]

The truth of the matter is that it has only been about thirty to forty years that the perspectives of the underside of modernity has challenged Eurocentric history and theology. This will only continue if future historians and theologians continue to glean from both Barth and Cone.

One idea that came late as I was finishing this book, leaving the issue of the color line in abeyance for the moment, is that historians in general are a neglected class of intellectuals. The names of George Marsden and Mark Noll feature in the world of American evangelical academia but are these historians read among the American populist tradition often at the center of their analysis? In fact, Noll's account of American race and religion issues offers a readable account every mature American should read, featuring a short historical narrative with an even shorter theological conclusion.[13] Noll's book presents a great example of a historical-theological work, heavy on the history, short on the theology (one small chapter to close the book). Moreover, American historians such as Richard Hofstadter, Reinhold Niebuhr, Arthur Schlesinger Jr., and Nathan Huggins represent a sample of historians and cultural critics that would provide important analysis for our contemporary moment in history. Indeed, W. E. B. DuBois, as a historian, is especially ignored at the peril of present day thought. American historians continually remind their readers of American historical amnesia. Perhaps instead of writing books about taking the latest European intellectual into the American evangelical congregation we should be reading historians who have written about both the sins and hopes of the United States. Since I started teaching modern United States history for the first

---

12. Ibid., 166.

13. Noll, *God and Race in American Politics*, 1. With regards to the subject of religion, Karen Armstrong and Huston Smith have written a number of introductory studies of many of the great world religions.

CONCLUSION

time at the tail end of completing this book, I realized how much I loved this history and how many wonderful historical-theological lessons are found there. Even though I have dedicated the last couple of years studying Latin American history and theology, and that I have attended a Spanish speaking Baptist church for over a decade, this history does not seem as existentially penetrating to me as the United States history I have recently encountered. Much of this has to do with going to school in the US during the eighties before the impact of cultural studies, not having even a first grade knowledge of Spanish until high school, and coming from an interracial marriage. Perhaps this illustrates the type of border thinker reality of my own existence, my own ambiguous, mixed-race identity growing up in Los Angeles, and the various historical roots of my being. This is personally an existential struggle that I negotiate with myself and in addition with my near and far neighbors.

The honest reminder of my difference throughout my childhood, and frankly even now, was my last name. Almost any time my mispronounced last name was discovered, it was usually followed with how they did not realize I was Mexican. When, after I first suggested the correct pronunciation of my name, I usually told them that my father was from Costa Rica (not Puerto Rico, which for some reason was what half of these people heard me say). Existentially I feel sometimes like a charlatan utilizing the methodology of Latin American thinkers. However, part of my own academic journey has been to discover my father's side of the family narrative because that has formed a part of me. The consequences of my own autobiography resulted in a growing appreciation of the historical-theological thinking of Latin Americans, and other third-world writers. The beauty and depth of this literature is enough for me to not want to go back to a Eurocentric view. It is my hope that my book would encourage the reader to do the same. Moreover, this existential awareness continues to guide my theology. Following Father Elizondo's work, the foundation of the faith is the fact that Christ identified as a Galilean on the borderlands, among the underside of history, rejecting all accounts of purity.[14] This is both a historical message faithful to the flesh and blood historical Jesus, and the core of the faith that continues to inspire and unite people across the globe.

I did not want to get sidetracked by being a cheerleader for historians (albeit this is often the role I play in general education history courses) in this book, even though the temptation is strong. The message about the role

14. Elizondo, *Future is Mestizo*, 74–86.

of historians in general especially on religious matters is due for another day. Recalling the historiography books mentioned in the opening of this book about why history matters, we are at a crisis point when history teachers spend an inordinate amount of time trying to wake up students from their dogmatic slumbers (sometimes literal slumbers), children dreaming of fantasies detached from the historical past. My fear is that their awakening will be in a world of their worst nightmares.

The recent trend in movies shows that we are very good in depicting nightmare scenarios. In fact, sooner than later, historians will study why our generation liked to watch apocalyptic films and TV shows so much! Whether we admit it or not, movies are often the only history students pay attention to. This fact is a little scary, considering movies still carry with them some of the familiar stereotypes of minorities, not to mention also their underrepresentation. I am always a little encouraged when a student speaks up in class to tell me about a documentary that is worth watching on the History Channel or PBS. However, we should encourage the viewing of movies like *Selma* and *The Mission* as well. These movies deal with such powerful historical-theological themes that watching these movies is as good a project as reading a selection from Dr. King or St. Ignatius (okay, not as good as hearing the real Martin Luther King Jr. talk). Of course maximum efficiency would be to watch *Selma* and read King. However, I have to admit I am perplexed at the lack of students, often the students I teach at Christian colleges, in my classes who have actually seen *Selma*. This is more of a personal observation. I leave it to the reader to ask why out of a class of thirty-five students that only two students on average have seen the film. I reflect on this point since Christian apologists oftentimes publicly lament the lack of Christian faith films produced for the big screen. Here is a history based film on a Christian icon, yet Christian students do not seem that interested. Again, I leave it to reader to decide why.

For the reader interested in further reading, I would recommend scanning the bibliography at the end of the book. Many of the books listed were read for my dissertation work on modernity, which led to my privileging of the importance of the historical consequences of 1492. Some of these books and essays in the bibliography were referenced in the construction of *Remembering Lived Lives*, but are not highlighted in its pages. For the historical-theological study of Latin America in particular, the work of Justo González and Enrique Dussel is a good place to start.

CONCLUSION

With the attention toward Islam in the media for the last couple of decades, followed by speeches of the importance of not stereotyping Muslims, one would expect better engagement between religious scholars from the interfaith community. As we have seen in this book, a number of scholars like Dabashi, Djaït, Sayyid, and others have challenged the Eurocentric view of history. I cannot recommend their work more highly especially in the analysis of Islamophobia and Eurocentrism. Thankfully there is a growing literature on the nature of Islamophobia (a topic I wish I had the space and time to discuss here), along the remaining problem of Orientalism.[15] These books matter greatly in our current social-political world, and even though one may not be a specialist in Islam, they deserve more attention especially from non-Muslims. Probably nothing is more frustrating to read than the continual flaming of the fires by Christian theologians and historians over the so-called clash of civilizations against a monolithic Islam. Moreover, Dabashi is correct to sense the double standard regarding Islamic thinkers and other non-English texts located in the Western canon. If it is okay to read an English translation of Heidegger, why not one by Qutb or Al-Azmeh?[16] In fact, I would argue that more attention should be given to Al-Azmeh than Taylor or Habermas in our day and age. There is so much misinformation and sensationalist literature on Islam that attempting to read this topic might seem daunting. It is up to the reader to consult the experts, from the best academic presses, in order to initiate contact.

One main reason for the so-called "return of the religions" in the academic and public sphere is the rise of religious fundamentalisms across the globe. As I am finishing this book, there has been a string of terrorist acts across the earth in 2016. Paying attention to both the history and the theology of some of these movements will help the public to differentiate between the good and the bad religions. It is ridiculous that a sensationalist media can prop up a political ideologue who can condemn a whole religion in xenophobic terms and not be laughed off the platform. I am not an optimistic idealist in the sense that there are numerous books written on each major faith tradition, including many on the theme of reconciliation, justice, and care for the Other, yet the stereotypes of all religions flow throughout the public without much challenge. In academia where we are preached on the ideal of tolerance, and have the educational grounding to have the access to more information than the average person, we are often

---

15. See Ramadan, *What I Believe*, 28.
16. Dabashi, *Can Non-Europeans Think*, 37–38.

ignored by the public (and frankly some of our students). I know that there are many times I have seen a political talk show or a religious service where someone is trying to sell their book, probably without the historical rigor of scholarly citation, or the nuance understanding of the history of religions, and that book will sell much better than the aforementioned books stressing historical consciousness and concern for the Other.

History writing was once the place where nationalism was the norm. Theology was also the place where triumphalism was the norm. This was the norm for at least modern European society, which was then blindsided by the imperialist wars at the start of the twentieth century, followed by the postcolonial wars of independence across the third world. A historical-theological literature is necessary to deconstruct both nationalist and triumphalist myths. I argue that empathy must be at the basis of good history and good theology. The more ignorance is removed and empathy established, will help maintain a better public sphere for all religious voices seeking a better global community. In fact, Muslim writers like Tariq Ramadan, with his analogy of windows, are leading the world into this discussion:

> By recognizing the existence of one's window, and then taking the risk of moving away from it and becoming decentered, one will, thanks to the essence of debates about one notion, gain access to the shared fate and hopes of subjects, men and women from all walks of life, throughout the whole of history.[17]

In addition, he writes what could be the subtext for my book:

> The challenge of diversity requires practical solutions and compels citizens, intellectuals, and religious representatives to develop a balanced critical mind, always open to evolution, analysis, empathy, and of course self-criticism. Voicing one's own needs while also listening to and hearing the other, accepting compromise without yielding on essentials, challenging deep-set beliefs and rigid or dogmatic minds on all sides and particularly within one's own cultural and religious family: that it is not easy and it requires time, patience, empathy, and determination.[18]

Not everyone that I cite in this book is someone I would generally agree with on all matters of faith and even historical interpretation. I attempt to provide a diverse set of writers because I truly agree with Ramadan's

---

17. Ramadan, *Quest for Meaning*, xi.
18. Ramadan, *What I Believe*, 13–14.

window symbol. Therefore, if I truly affirm this message then it is up to me as a teacher and a reader to get to know those near and far neighbors by actually listening to their voices in a way that acknowledges the power is knowledge framework. To know is not to master; to know is to empathize.

The place for historians as simply chroniclers of impending doom locates them outside historical events, wagging their finger at the sleeping masses from a transcendent vantage point. On the contrary, one point I have tried to make here is that historians prove their value to society since they continually point backwards to historical events that happened in time and space. They oftentimes refuse to paint current events in Manichean light versus darkness terms, a favorite pastime of some theologians. The idea of examining events from a historical context rather than through some metaphysical or ideological pronouncements means historians are not as sexy in their analysis. In fact, opening the book with Barth was my way of framing a sober view of history. What I hope was revealed, by starting with Barth, is a type of pessimism with regards to a philosophy or theology of history. Great strides have been made to incorporate neglected persons into the narrative of history. However, whatever progress that has been made needs to be chastened by a realist pessimism that things will never be perfect. In fact, a historical-theological position must remain vigilant to not return to a Eurocentric view or to be captured by a regressive, religious triumphalism.

Barth's pessimism toward a concrete philosophy of history does not mean he had a negative view of history. In fact, he posits a neighborliness method of history that features an openness to the Other of history. This openness is at the heart of a historical-theological method concerned with empathy. Empathy will get us to listen to the Other's readings of history, yet the violence often found in these narratives may actually be debilitating. What if the end result of a historical-theological reading leads to nihilism? In order for this reading of history to matter an essential element is needed. That idea is hope. Theologian C. S. Song articulates the importance of hope for history:

> Whether short or long, whether brief or lasting, history is history because it has a beginning and an end. It is a process, a duration of time. But more important, history is history not because it consists merely of dates and places, but because it is moved by a promise to achieve a purpose, even the most elemental promise and purpose of being alive and of carrying life forward for posterity. In other words, history itself has a history. It is a history of how a promise

is made and unmade, how it is carried out and aborted, and how it reaches or fails to reach a destination. History consists of a series of promises and goals. At the heart of history is hope, the power that moves history from promise to reality, the energy that enables something to emerge from promise. History, then, consists of hopes conceived and miscarried, hopes realized and frustrated, hopes born and dead. History is, thus, the history of hope.[19]

One may have finished this book exasperated by my attention to postcolonial theorists or historical-theological thinkers from across the globe. On the contrary, perhaps the reader experiences the challenge of these historical-theological accounts and looks to learn more. Because of Eurocentrism, I have found that I must be purposefully intentional in choosing books and movies produced by ethnic minorities. This is not some type of PC reflex or personal affirmative action on my part. I am intentional, and I suggest to the reader as well, because the norm tends to still be Eurocentric. The worst thing about this is that we oftentimes miss great works of amazing quality. Moreover, the biggest danger is to simply pass by very recent dark history, especially experienced by colonized or oppressed peoples, pushing the discussion immediately to reconciliation. Reconciliation is a noble idea, yet justice must be on the agenda first. As womanist theologian Karen Baker-Fletcher poignantly declares: "We have no right to demand anyone to forgive, because this request is God's right alone in loving spiritual relationship with each individual as God in empathy heals each of us."[20] It is in this spirit that I recommend to first learn to listen. As Native American theologian Randy Woodley warns "when our stories are not heard, or when they are disrupted, it is perhaps the ultimate sign of disrespect, and it adds insult to injury."[21] We continue to show disrespect when we ignore the obvious diversity within the historical-theological evidence. As the writers, featured in this book, illustrated in their accounts, we can no longer write (in fact, never should have) about God divorced from the oftentimes messy, uncomfortable history. Reading these historical-theological works instills

---

19. Song, *Believing Heart*, 134.
20. Baker-Flectcher, *Dancing with God*, 114.
21. Woodley, *Living in Color*, 165. This quote is part of an excellent chapter, "Getting Beyond 'Getting Along,'" that deals with the difficult issues of real, concrete reconciliation. Also see Woodley, *Shalom and the Community of Creation*, 148–51.

It should be noted that at a certain point the tireless asking of questions toward minority writers needs to be corrected with some real silent, soul searching by the questioner. See Huggins, *Sister Girl*, x, for more on this.

CONCLUSION

an empathic response to not just the figures of the past but to the continual struggle of peoples across the globe today and in the future. Empathy produces love—the kind of love James Baldwin speaks about, the one that perhaps can "change the history of the world."[22]

---

22. Baldwin, *Fire Next Time*, 105.

Bibliography

Adichie, Chimamanda Ngozi. "The Danger of a Single Story." Online: https://www.youtube.com/watch?v=D9Ihs241zeg.
Ahmed, Sara. "'Liberal Multiculturalism is the Hegemony—Its an Empirical Fact—A Response to Slavoj Žižek." Online: http://www.darkmatter101.org/site/2008/02/19/%e2%80%98liberal-multiculturalism-is-the-hegemony-%e2%80%93-its-an-empirical-fact%e2%80%99-a-response-to-slavoj-zizek/.
Alfred, Taiaiake. *Peace, Power, Righteousness: An Indigenous Manifesto*. New York: Oxford University Press, 2009.
Althaus-Reid, Marcella. "From Liberation Theology to Indecent Theology: The Trouble with Normality in Theology." In *Latin American Liberation Theology: The Next Generation*, edited by Ivan Petrella, 20–38. Maryknoll, NY: Orbis, 2005.
Amin, Samir. *Eurocentrism*. Translated by Russell Moore and James Membrez. New York: Monthly Review, 2009.
———. *Global History: A View From the South*. Oxford: Pambazuka, 2011.
Anidjar, Gil. *Semites: Race, Religion, Literature*. Stanford: Stanford University Press, 2008.
Anzaldúa, Gloria. *Borderlands/La Frontera: The New Mestiza*. San Francisco: Aunt Lute, 2007.
Arendt, Hannah. *On Violence*. New York: Harvest, 1970.
Ateek, Naim Stifan. *Justice, and Only Justice: A Palestinian Theology of Liberation*. Maryknoll, NY: Orbis, 1989.
Baker-Fletcher, Karen. *Dancing with God: The Trinity from a Womanist Perspective*. St. Louis, Missouri: Chalice, 2006.
Baldwin, James. *The Devil Finds Work*. New York: Vintage, 1976.
———. *The Fire Next Time*. New York: Vintage, 1963.
Balthasar, Hans Urs von. *A Theology of History*. New York: Communio, 1994.
Bañuelas, Arturo J., ed. *Mestizo Christianity: Theology from the Latino Perspective*. Maryknoll, NY: Orbis, 1995.
Barber, Michael D. *Ethical Hermeneutics: Rationalism in Enrique Dussel's Philosophy of Liberation*. New York: Fordham, 1998.
Barker, John. *The Superhistorians: Makers of Our Past*. New York: Scribners, 1982.
Barth, Karl. *Church Dogmatics*, III/4. Translated and edited by Geoffrey W. Bromiley and Thomas F. Torrance. Edinburgh: T. & T. Clark, 1961.
———. *Ethics*. Edinburgh: T. & T. Clark, 1981.

BIBLIOGRAPHY

———. *Protestant Theology in the Nineteenth Century: Its Background and History*. Translated by Brian Cozens and John Bowden. Grand Rapids: Eerdmans. 2001.

Bass, Diana Butler. *A People's History of Christianity: The Other Side of the Story*. New York: HarperOne, 2009.

Bedford, Nancy E. "To Speak of God from More Than One Place: Theological Reflections from the Experience of Migration." In *Latin American Liberation Theology: The Next Generation*, 95-118, edited by Ivan Petrella. Maryknoll, NY: Orbis, 2005.

Benjamin, Walter. *Illuminations: Essays and Reflections*. Translated by Harry Zohn. New York: Schocken, 1968.

Berrigan, Daniel. *The Mission: A Film Journal*. San Francisco: Harper & Row, 1986.

Berryman, Phillip. *Liberation Theology: The Essential Facts About the Revolutionary Movement in Latin America and Beyond*. Illinois: Meyer Stone, 1987.

Bigo, Pierre. *The Church and Third World Revolution*. Translated by Jeanne Marie Lyons. Maryknoll, NY: Orbis, 1977.

Blaut, J. M. *The Colonizer's Model of the World: Geographical Diffusionism and Eurocentric History*. New York: Guilford, 1993.

———. *Eight Eurocentric Historians*. New York: Guilford, 2000.

Boff, Leonardo. *Francis of Assisi: A Model for Human Liberation*. Translated by John W. Diercksmeier. Maryknoll, NY: Orbis, 2006.

———. *Fundamentalism, Terrorism and the Future of Humanity*. Translated by Alexander Guilherme. Great Britain: SPCK, 2006.

Boff, Leonardo, and Virgil Elizondo, eds. *1492-1992: The Voice of the Victims*. London: SCM, 1991.

Bonhoeffer, Dietrich. *Letters and Papers from Prison*, edited by Eberhard Bethge. New York: Macmillan, 1971.

Borg, Marcus J. *The Heart of Christianity: How We Can Be Passionate Believers Today*. San Francisco: HarperSanFrancisco, 2004.

Boyarin, Daniel. *Border Lines: The Partition of Judaeo-Christianity*. Philadelphia: University of Pennsylvania Press, 2004.

Brand, Dionne. *A Map to the Door of No Return: Notes to Belonging*. Toronto: Vintage, 2002.

Breisach, Ernst. *Historiography: Ancient, Medieval, and Modern*. Chicago, IL: University of Chicago Press, 1994.

Brock, Rita Nakashima and Parker, Rebecca Ann. *Saving Paradise: How Christianity Traded Love of this World for Crucifixion and Empire*. Boston: Beacon, 2008.

Brown, Colin. *History and Faith: A Personal Exploration*. Grand Rapids: Zondervan, 1987.

Brown, Robert McAfee. "Good News from Karl Barth." In *How Karl Barth Changed My Mind*, edited by Donald K. McKim, 94-101. Grand Rapids: Eerdmans, 1986.

Burke, Kevin. *The Ground Beneath the Cross: The Theology of Ignacio Ellacuría*. Washington, DC: Georgetown University Press, 2000.

Buck-Morss, Susan. *Hegel, Haiti, and Universal History*. Pittsburgh: University of Pittsburgh Press, 2009.

Burke, Peter. *Cultural Hybridity*. Malden, Massachusetts: Polity, 2009.

Busch, Eberhard. *Karl Barth: His Life from Letters and Autobiographical Texts*. Grand Rapids: Eerdmans, 1994.

Cannon, Katie G. *Black Womanist Ethics*. Atlanta, Georgia: Scholars, 1988.

Carrigan, Ann. *Salvador Witness: The Life and Calling of Jean Donovan*. Maryknoll, New York: Orbis, 2005.

BIBLIOGRAPHY

Carter, J. Kameron. "An Unlikely Convergence: W. E. B. Du Bois, Karl Barth, and the Problem of the Imperial God-Man." *The New Centennial Review* 11 (2011) 167–224.
———. *Race: A Theological Account.* Oxford: Oxford University Press, 2008.
Cavarero, Adriana. *Horrorism: Naming Contemporary Violence.* Translated by William McCuaig. New York: Columbia University Press, 2009.
Césaire, Aimé. *Discourse on Colonialism.* Translated by John Pinkham. New York: Monthly Review, 2000.
Chakrabarty, Dipesh. *Provincializing Europe: Postcolonial Thought and Historical Difference.* Princeton, NJ: Princeton University Press, 2000.
Chasteen, John Charles. *Born in Blood and Fire: A Concise History of Latin America.* New York: W. W. Norton, 2011.
Chaves, João B. *Evangelicals and Liberation Revisited: An Inquiry into the Possibility of an Evangelical Liberationist Theology.* Eugene, OR: Wipf and Stock, 2013.
Chomsky, Noam. *Year 501: The Conquest Continues.* Boston: South End, 1993.
Chopp, Rebecca S. *The Praxis of Suffering: An Interpretation of Liberation and Political Theologies.* Maryknoll, NY: Orbis, 1986.
Cimino, Richard. "'No God in Common:' American Evangelical Discourse on Islam after 9/11." *Review of Religious Research* 47.2 (2005) 162–74.
Clarke, Sathianathan. *Dalits and Christianity: Subaltern Religion and Liberation Theology in India.* Oxford: Oxford University Press, 1999.
Cleveland, Christena. *Disunity in Christ: Uncovering the Hidden Forces that Keep Us Apart.* Downers Grove, IL: InterVarsity, 2013.
Comblin, José. *Called for Freedom: The Changing Context of Liberation Theology.* Translated by Phillip Berryman. New York: Orbis, 1998.
Cone, James H. *The Cross and the Lynching Tree.* Maryknoll, NY: Orbis, 2012.
———. *Martin & Malcolm & America: A Dream or a Nightmare.* Maryknoll, NY: Orbis, 1991.
———. *The Spirituals and the Blues: An Interpretation.* Maryknoll, New York: Orbis, 1992.
Copeland, M. Shawn. *Enfleshing Freedom: Body, Race, and Being.* Minneapolis: Fortress, 2009.
Costello, Damian. *Black Elk: Colonialism and Lakota Catholicism.* New York: Orbis, 2005.
Coulthard, Glen Sean. *Red Skin, White Masks: Rejecting the Colonial Politics of Recognition.* Minnesota: University of Minnesota Press, 2014.
Dabashi, Hamid. *Brown Skin, White Masks.* London: Pluto, 2011.
———. *Can Non-Europeans Think?* London: Zed, 2015.
———. *Islamic Liberation Theology: Resisting the Empire.* New York: Routledge, 2008.
Dancer, Anthony. *An Alien in a Strange Land: Theology in the Life of William Stringfellow.* Eugene, OR: Cascade, 2011.
Davaney, Sheila Greeve. *Historicism: The Once and Future Challenge for Theology.* Minneapolis: Fortress, 2006.
Davis, Angela. *Women, Race, and Class.* New York: Vintage, 1983.
Davis, Natalie Zemon. *Slaves on Screen: Film and Historical Vision.* Cambridge, MA: Harvard University Press, 2000.
De La Torre, Miguel A., and Edwin David Aponte. *Introducing Latino/a Theologies.* Maryknoll, NY: Orbis, 2001.
Deloria, Vine, Jr. *Custer Died for Your Sins: An Indian Manifesto.* Norman: University of Oklahoma Press, 1988.

BIBLIOGRAPHY

Diaz, Miguel H. *On Being Human: U.S. Hispanic and Rahnerian Perspectives*. Maryknoll, NY: Orbis, 2001.
Didion, Joan. *Salvador*. New York: Vintage, 1994.
Djaït, Hichem. *Europe and Islam*. Translated by Peter Heinegg. Berkley, CA: University of California Press, 1985.
Douglas, Kelly Brown. *The Black Christ*. New York: Orbis, 1994.
Du Bois, W. E. B. *Black Reconstruction in America, 1860-1880*. New York: Meridian, 1964.
Dussel, Enrique. *A History of the Church in Latin America: Colonialism to Liberation (1492–1979)*. Translated by Alan Neely. Grand Rapids: Eerdmans, 1981.
———. *History and the Theology of Liberation: A Latin American Perspective*. Translated by John Drury. New York: Orbis, 1976.
———. *The Invention of the Americas: Eclipse of "the Other" and the Myth of Modernity*. Translated by Michael D. Barber. New York: Continuum, 1995.
———. "Philosophy of Liberation, the Postmodern Debate, and Latin American Studies." In *Coloniality at Large: Latin America and the Postcolonial Debate*. Translated by Rosalia Bermúdez, edited by Mabel Moraña, Enrique Dussel, and Carlos A. Jáuregui, 335–49. Durham, NC: Duke University Press, 2008.
———. *The Underside of Modernity: Apel, Ricoeur, Rorty, Taylor and the Philosophy of Liberation*. Translated and edited by Eduardo Mendieta. Amherst, NY: Humanity, 1998.
Dyson, Michael Eric. *I May Not Get There With You: The True Martin Luther King, Jr.* New York: Free Press, 2000.
———. *Making Malcolm: The Myth and Meaning of Malcolm X*. New York: Oxford University Press, 1996.
———. *Reflecting Black: African-American Cultural Criticism*. Minneapolis: University of Minnesota Press, 1993.
Elizondo, Virgilio. *Galilean Journey: The Mexican-American Promise*. Maryknoll, NY: Orbis, 2000.
———. *The Future is Mestizo: Life Where Cultures Meet*. Boulder, CO: University Press of Colorado, 2000.
Ellacuría, Ignacio. *Freedom Made Flesh: The Mission of Christ and His Church*. Translated by John Drury. Maryknoll, NY: Orbis, 1976.
———. "The Challenge of the Poor Majority," in *Towards a Society that Serves its People: The Intellectual Contribution of El Salvador's Murdered Jesuits*. Translated by Phillip Berryman, edited by John Hassett and Hugh Lacey, 171–76. Washington, DC: Georgetown University Press, 1991.
———. "The True Social Place of The Church." In *Towards a Society that Serves its People: The Intellectual Contribution of El Salvador's Murdered Jesuits*. Translated by Phillip Berryman, edited by John Hassett and Hugh Lacey, 283–92. Washington, DC: Georgetown University Press, 1991.
Ellis, Marc H. *Practicing Exile: The Religious Odyssey of an American Jew*. Minneapolis: Fortress, 2002.
———. *Toward a Jewish Theology of Liberation: The Uprising and the Future*. Maryknoll, NY: Orbis, 1989.
Erskine, Noel Leo. *Decolonizing Theology: A Caribbean Perspective*. Maryknoll, NY: Orbis, 1981.
Euben, Roxanne L. *Enemy in the Mirror: Islamic Fundamentalism and the Limits of Modern Rationalism*. Princeton, NJ: Princeton University Press, 1999.

BIBLIOGRAPHY

Eze, Emmanuel Chukwudi. *Race and the Enlightenment: A Reader*. Oxford: Blackwell, 1997.
Fall, Babacar. "Orality and Life Histories: Rethinking the Social and Political History of Senegal." *Africa Today* (2003) 55–65.
Fanon, Frantz. *Black Skin, White Masks*. Translated by Richard Philcox. New York: Grove, 2008.
———. *The Wretched of the Earth*. Translated by Richard Philcox. New York: Grove, 2004.
Fea, John. *Why Study History? Reflecting on the Importance of the Past*. Grand Rapids: Baker Academic, 2013.
Federici, Silvia, *Caliban and the Witch: Women, the Body and Primitive Accumulation*. Brooklyn, NY: Autonomedia, 2004.
Fernandez, Eleazar S. *Toward a Theology of Struggle*. Maryknoll, NY: Orbis, 1994.
Foner, Eric. *Who Owns History? Rethinking the Past in a Changing World*. New York: Hill and Wang, 2002.
Franco, Jean. *Cruel Modernity*. Durham, NC: Duke University Press, 2013.
Frank, Andre Gunder. *ReOrient: Global Economy in the Asian Age*. Berkeley, CA: University of California Press, 1998.
Gibson, Andrew. *Intermittency: The Concept of Historical Reason in Recent French Philosophy*. Edinburgh: Edinburgh University Press, 2012.
Gikandi, Simon. "On Culture and the State: The Writings of Ngũgĩ wa Thiong'o." *Third World Quarterly* 11.1 (1989) 149–56.
———. *Slavery and the Culture of Taste*. Princeton: Princeton University Press, 2011.
Gilderhus, Mark T. *History and Historians: A Historiographical Introduction*. Upper Saddle River, NJ: Prentice Hall, 2003.
Gillespie, Michael Allen. *The Theological Origins of Modernity*. Chicago, Illinois: University of Chicago Press, 2009.
Ginzburg, Carlos. *History, Rhetoric, and Proof*. Hanover, NH: University Press of New England, 1999.
Glaude, Eddie S., Jr. *In a Shade of Blue: Pragmatism and the Politics of Black America*. Chicago: Chicago University Press, 2007.
Goizueta, Roberto S. "Christ of the Borderlands: Faith and Idolatry in an Age of Globalization." In *Religion, Economics, and Culture in Conflict and Conversation*, edited by Laurie M. Cassidy and Maureen H. O'Connell, 177–95. Maryknoll, NY: Orbis, 2011.
González, Justo L. *Church History: An Essential Guide*. Nashville, TN: Abingdon, 1996.
Gonzalez, Michelle A. *Sor Juana: Beauty and Justice in the Americas*. Maryknoll, NY: Orbis, 2003.
Gordon, Lewis R. *Existentia Africana: Understanding Africana Existential Thought*. New York: Routledge, 2000.
Gran, Peter. *Beyond Eurocentrism: A New View of Modern World History*. New York: Syracuse University Press, 1996.
Gregory, Brad S. *The Unintended Reformation: How a Religious Revolution Secularized Society*. Cambridge, MA: Belknap, 2015.
Gutiérrez, Gustavo. *Las Casas: In Search of the Poor of Jesus Christ*. Translated by Robert R. Barr. Maryknoll, NY: Orbis, 1993.
———. *A Theology of Liberation: History, Politics, and Salvation*. Maryknoll, NY: Orbis, 1988.

BIBLIOGRAPHY

Hanke, Lewis. *Aristotle and the American Indians: A Study in Race Prejudice in the Modern World*. Bloomington, IN: Indiana University Press, 1959.

Hanh, Thich Nhat. *The Heart of Buddha's Teaching: Transforming Suffering into Peace, Joy, and Liberation*. New York: Broadway, 1998.

Hart, David Bentley. *The Story of Christianity: A History of 2,000 Years of the Christian Faith*. London: Quercus, 2009.

Hart, William D. *Edward Said and the Religious Effects of Culture*. New York: Cambridge University Press, 2000.

Heaney, Sharon E. *Contextual Theology for Latin America: Liberation Themes in Evangelical Perspective*. Eugene, OR: Wipf and Stock, 2008.

Henry, Paget. *Caliban's Reason: Introducing Caribbean Philosophy*. New York: Routledge, 2000.

Hill, Johnny Bernard. *Prophetic Rage: A Postcolonial Theology of Liberation*. Grand Rapids: Eerdmans, 2013.

Hobson, John M. *The Eastern Origins of Western Civilizations*. Cambridge: Cambridge University Press, 2004.

Huggan, Graham. "Decolonising the Map: Post-Colonialism, Post-Structuralism, and the Cartographic Connection." *Ariel* 20.4 (1989) 115–31.

Huggins, Jackie. *Sister Girl: The Writings of Aboriginal Activist and Historian Jackie Huggins*. St. Lucia, Queensland: University of Queensland Press, 1998.

Inchausti, Robert. *Subversive Orthodoxy: Outlaws, Revolutionaries, and Other Christians in Disguise*. Grand Rapids: Brazos, 2005.

Irvin. Dale T. *Christian Histories, Christian Traditioning: Rendering Accounts*. Maryknoll, NY: Orbis, 1998.

Isasi-Díaz, Ada Maria. *Mujerista Theology: A Theology for the Twenty-First Century*. Maryknoll, NY: Orbis, 1996.

Isasi-Díaz, Ada Maria, and Eduardo Mendieta, eds. *Decolonizing Epistemologies: Latino/a Theology and Philosophy*. New York: Fordham University Press, 2011.

Jenkins, Philip. *The Next Christendom: The Coming of Global Christianity*. Oxford: Oxford University Press, 2011.

Jenkins, Willis, and Jennifer M. McBride, eds. *Bonhoeffer and King: The Legacies and Import for Christian Social Thought*. Minneapolis: Fortress, 2010.

Jeyifo, Biodun. *Wole Soyinka: Politics, Poetics and Postcolonialism*. Cambridge: Cambridge University Press, 2004.

Jimenez, Michael. "Power Corrupts: Karl Barth's Use of Jacob Burckhardt's Philosophy of History." *Journal for the History of Modern Theology/Zeitschrift für Neuere Theologiegeschicte*. 21:1–2 (2014).

Joh, Wonhee Anne. *Heart of the Cross: A Postcolonial Christology*. Louisville, KY: Westminster John Knox, 2006.

Kamau-Goro, Nicholas. "Rejection or Reappropriation? Christian Allegory and the Critique of Postcolonial Public Culture in the Early Novels of Ngũgĩ wa Thiong'o." In *Christianity and Public Culture in Africa*, edited by Harri Englund, 67–85. Athens, OH: Ohio University Press, 2011.

Keillor, Steven J. *God's Judgments: Interpreting History and the Christian Faith*. Downers Grove, IL: InterVarsity Academic, 2007.

Kelley, Robin D. G. *Yo' Mama's Disfunktional! Fighting the Culture Wars in Urban America*. Boston, MA: Beacon, 1997.

BIBLIOGRAPHY

King, Robert H. *Thomas Merton and Thich Nhat Hanh: Engaged Spirituality in an Age of Globalization.* New York: Continuum, 2011.

King, Thomas. *The Truth About Stories: A Native Narrative.* Minneapolis: University of Minnesota Press, 2008.

Kitamori, Kazoh. *Theology of the Pain of God.* Eugene, OR: Wipf and Stock, 2005.

Knitter, Paul F. *Jesus and the Other Names: Christian Mission and Global Responsibility.* Maryknoll, NY: Orbis, 1996.

Koyama, Kosuke. *Water Buffalo Theology.* Maryknoll, NY: Orbis, 1999.

Kyung, Chung Hyun. *Struggle to be the Sun Again: Introducing Asian Women's Theology.* Maryknoll, NY: Orbis, 1990.

LaCapra, Dominick. *History and Its Limits: Human, Animal, Violence.* Ithaca, NY: Cornell University Press, 2009.

Lardas, Jon. *The Bop Apocalypse: The Religious Visions of Kerouac, Ginsberg, and Burroughs.* Chicago: University of Illinois Press, 2001.

Lassalle-Klein, Robert. *Blood and Ink: Ignacio Ellacuría, Jon Sobrino, and the Jesuit Martyrs of the University of Central America.* Maryknoll, NY: Orbis, 2014.

Lau, Lisa. "Re-Orientalism: The Perpetration and Development of Orientalism by Orientals." *Modern Asian Studies* 43 (2009) 571–90.

Lazier, Benjamin. *God Interrupted: Heresy and the European Imagination Between the World Wars.* Princeton, NJ: Princeton University Press, 2008.

Lee, Jung Young. *Marginality: The Key to Multicultural Theology.* Minneapolis: Fortress, 1995.

Lee, Krys. *Drifting House.* New York: Viking, 2012.

Linebaugh, Peter, and Marcus Rediker. *The Many-Headed Hydra: Sailors, Slaves, Commoners, and the Hidden History of the Revolutionary Atlantic.* Boston, MA: Beacon, 2000.

Llosa, Maria Vargas. *Wellsprings.* Cambridge: Harvard University Press, 2008.

Löwy, Michael. *The War of Gods: Religion and Politics in Latin America.* New York: Verso, 1996.

Mahbubani, Kishore. *Can Asians Think? Understanding the Divide Between East and West.* South Royalton, VT: Steerforth, 2002.

Mahtani, Minelle. *Mixed Race Amnesia: Resisting the Romanticization of Multiraciality.* Seattle: University of Washington Press, 2014.

Maldonado-Torres, Nelson. *Against War: Views from the Underside of Modernity.* Durham, NC: Duke University Press, 2008.

———. "Liberation Theology and the Search for the Lost Paradigm: From Radical Orthodoxy to Radical Diversality." In *Latin American Liberation Theology: The Next Generation*, edited by Ivan Petrella, 39–61. Maryknoll, NY: Orbis, 2005.

———. "Secularism and Religion in the Modern/Colonial World-System: From Secular Postcoloniality to Postsecular Transmodernity." In *Coloniality at Large: Latin America and the Postcolonial Debate*, edited by Mabel Moraña et al., 360–84. Durham, NC: Duke University Press, 2008.

Marks, Robert B. *The Origins of the Modern World: A Global and Environmental Narrative from the Fifteenth to the Twenty-First Century.* New York: Rowman and Littlefield, 2015.

Marsh, Charles. *God's Long Summer: Stories of Faith and Civil Rights.* Princeton, NJ: Princeton University Press, 1997.

Martínez, Elizabeth. *De Colores Means All of Us: Latina Views for a Multi-Colored Century*. Cambridge, MA: South End, 1998.

Martinez, Gaspar. *Confronting the Mystery of God: Political, Liberation, and Public Theologies*. New York: Continuum, 2001.

McCann, Dennis P. *Christian Realism and Liberation Theology: Practical Theologies in Creative Conflict*. Maryknoll, NY: Orbis, 1982.

McClendon, James W., Jr. *Biography as Theology: How Life Stories Can Remake Today's Theology*. Nashville, TN: Abingdon, 1974.

McIntyre, C. T., ed. *God, History, and Historians: An Anthology of Modern Christian Views of History*. New York: Oxford University Press, 1977.

———. "The Ongoing Task of Christian Historiography." In *A Christian View of History*, edited by George Marsden and Frank Roberts, 51–74. Grand Rapids: Eerdmans, 1975.

McKittrick, Katherine, ed. *Sylvia Wynter: On Being Human as Praxis*. Durham, NC: Duke University Press, 2015.

Menchu, Rigoberta. *I, Rigoberta Menchu: An Indian Woman in Guatemala*. Translated by Ann Wright. New York: Verso, 2010.

Menon, Nivedita. "The Two Žižeks." Online: http://kafila.org/2010/01/07/the-two-zizeks/.

Metz, Johann Baptist. "With the Eyes of a European Theologian." In *1492–1992: The Voice of the Victims*, edited by Leonardo Boff and Virgil Elizondo, 113–19. London: SCM Press, 1991.

Mignolo, Walter D. "The Geopolitics of Knowledge and the Colonial Difference." In *Coloniality at Large: Latin America and the Postcolonial Debate*, 225-258, edited by Mabel Moraña et al. Durham, NC: Duke University Press, 2008.

———. "Islamophobia/Hispanophobia: The (Re)Configuration of the Racial Imperial/Colonial Matrix." *Human Architecture: Journal of the Sociology of Self-Knowledge* 5 (2006) 13–28.

———. *Local Histories/Global Designs: Coloniality, Subaltern Knowledges, and Border Thinking*. Princeton: Princeton University Press, 2012.

Minh-ha, Trinh T. *Woman, Native, Other: Writing Postcoloniality and Feminism*. Bloomington, IN: Indiana University Press, 1989.

Mohanty, Chandra Talpade. *Feminism Without Borders: Decolonizing Theory, Practicing Solidarity*. Durham, NC: Duke University Press, 2003.

Moltmann, Jürgen. *The Coming of God: Christian Eschatology*. Translated by Margaret Kohl. Minneapolis: Fortress, 2004.

Morris, Glenn T. "Vine Deloria Jr., and the Development of a Decolonizing Critique of Indigenous Peoples and International Relations." In *Native Voices: American Indian Identity and Resistance*, edited by Richard A. Grounds et al., 97–154. Lawrence, KS: University Press of Kansas, 2003.

Mosse, George L. *Toward the Final Solution: A History of European Racism*. New York: Howard Fertig, 1985.

Moyn, Samuel. *Origins of the Other: Emmanuel Levinas between Revelation and Ethics*. Ithaca, NY: Cornell University Press, 2005.

Moyn, Samuel, and Andrew Sartori, eds. *Global Intellectual History*. New York: Columbia University Press, 2015.

Musalha, Nur. "Civil Liberation Theology in Palestine: Indigenous, Secular-Humanist, and Post-Colonial Perspectives." In *Theologies of Liberation in Palestine-Israel:*

BIBLIOGRAPHY

Indigenous, Contextual, and Postcolonial Perspectives, edited by Nur Musalha and Lisa Isherwood, 192–214. Eugene, OR: Pickwick, 2014.
Muskus, Eddy José. *The Origins and Early Development of Liberation Theology in Latin America: With Particular Reference to Gustavo Gutiérrez*. Great Britain: Pasternoster, 2002.
Nash, Ronald H. *Christian Faith and Historical Understanding*. Grand Rapids: Zondervan, 1984.
Nava, Alexander. *The Mystical and Prophetic Thought of Simone Weil and Gustavo Gutiérrez: Reflections on the Mystery and Hiddenness of God*. New York: State University of New York Press, 2001.
Nayar, Pramod K. *Postcolonialism: A Guide for the Perplexed*. New York: Continuum, 2010.
Nessan, Craig L. *The Vitality of Liberation Theology*. Eugene, OR: Pickwick, 2012.
Niebuhr, Reinhold. *The Children or Light and the Children of Darkness: A Vindication of Democracy and a Critique of its Traditional Defense*. New York: Charles Scribner's Sons, 1960.
Nigam, Aditya. "End of Postcolonialism and the Challenge for 'Non-European' Thought." *Critical Encounters*, May 19, 2013. Online: https://criticalencounters.net/2013/05/19/end-of-postcolonialism-and-the-challenge-for-non-european-thought/.
Noll, Mark A. *God and Race in American Politics: A Short History*. Princeton, NJ: Princeton University Press, 2008.
———. *Turning Points: Decisive Moments in the History of Christianity*. Grand Rapids: Baker Academic, 2012.
Noone, Judith M. *The Same Fate as the Poor*. Maryknoll, New York: Orbis, 1995.
Nouwen, Henri J. M. *¡Gracias! A Latin American Journal*. Maryknoll, NY: Orbis, 2005.
Nuccetelli, Susana. *Latin American Thought: Philosophical Problems and Arguments*. Boulder, CO: Westview, 2002.
Okihiro, Gary Y. *Margins and Mainstreams: Asians in American History and Culture*. Seattle: University of Washington Press, 1994.
Olson, Gary A. and Lynn Worsham, eds. *Race, Rhetoric, and the Postcolonial*. New York: State University of New York Press, 1999.
Ortega y Gasset, José. *Man and Crisis*. Translated by Mildred Adams. New York: W. W. Norton, 1962.
Partnoy, Alicia. *The Little School: Tales of Disappearance and Survival*. San Francisco, CA: Midnight Editions, 1998.
Pomeranz, Kenneth. *The Great Divergence: China, Europe, and the Making of the Modern World Economy*. Princeton, NJ: Princeton University Press, 2000.
Prashad, Vijay. *The Darker Nations: A People's History of the Third World*. New York: The New Press, 2007.
Pivot, Andrew. "Ignacio Ellacuría and Enrique Dussel, "On the Contributions of Phenomenology to Liberation Theology." In *A Grammar of Justice: The Legacy of Ignacio Ellacuría*, edited by J. Matthew Ashley et al., 119–33. New York: Orbis, 2014.
Puar, Jasbir K. *Terrorist Assemblages: Homonationalism in Queer Times*. Durham, NC: Duke University Press, 2007.
Pui-lan, Kwok. *Postcolonial Imagination and Feminist Theology*. Louisville, KY: Westminster John Knox, 2005.
Rabasa, José. *Inventing America: Spanish Historiography and the Formation of Eurocentrism*. Norman, OK: University of Oklahoma Press, 1993.

BIBLIOGRAPHY

Rah, Soong-Chan. *The Next Evangelicalism: Freeing the Church from Western Cultural Captivity.* Downers Grove, IL: InterVarsity, 2009.

Raheb, Mitri. *Faith in the Face of Empire: The Bible Through Palestinian Eyes.* Maryknoll, NY: Orbis, 2014.

———. *I Am a Palestinian Christian.* Translated by Ruth C. L. Gritsch. Minneapolis: Fortress, 1995.

Ramadan, Tariq. *The Quest for Meaning: Developing a Philosophy of Pluralism.* London: Allen Lane, 2010.

———. *What I Believe.* New York: Oxford University Press, 2010.

Rashkover, Randi. *Revelation and Theopolitics: Barth, Rosenzweig and the Politics of Praise.* New York: T. & T. Clark, 2005.

Rea, Robert F. *Why Church History Matters: An Invitation to Love and Learn from Our Past.* Downers Grove: InterVarsity Academic, 2014.

Recinos, Harold J. *Jesus Weeps: Global Encounters on Our Doorstep.* Nashville, TN: Abingdon, 1992.

Regan, Ethna. *Theology and the Boundary Discourse of Human Rights.* Washington, D.C.: Georgetown University Press, 2010.

Richard, Pablo. *Death of Christendoms, Birth of the Church: Historical Analysis and Theological Interpretation of the Church in Latin America.* Translated by Phillip Berryman. Maryknoll, NY: Orbis, 1987.

Rivera, Mayra. *Poetics of the Flesh.* Durham, NC: Duke University Press, 2015.

———. *The Touch of Transcendence: A Postcolonial Theology of God.* Louisville: Westminster John Knox, 2007.

Rivera-Pagan, Luis N. *A Violent Evangelism: The Political and Religious Conquest of the Americas.* Louisville, KY: Westminster John Knox, 1992.

———. *Essays from the Margins.* Eugene, OR: Cascade, 2014.

Roberts, J. Deotis. *Bonhoeffer and King: Speaking Truth to Power.* Louisville, KY: Westminster John Knox, 2005.

Robinson, Elaine A. *Race and Theology.* Nashville, TN: Abingdon, 2012.

Robinson, Marilynne. *The Death of Adam: Essays on Modern Thought.* New York: Picador, 2005.

Rodríguez, Jeanette. *We Live/Cuentos Que Vivimos: Hispanic Women's Spirituality.* New York: Paulist, 1996.

Rose, Gillian. *Love's Work: A Reckoning with Life.* New York: Schocken, 1995.

Rubenstein, Richard L. *The Cunning of History: The Holocaust and the American Future.* New York: Harper & Row, 1975.

Sacks, Jonathan. *The Dignity of Difference: How to Avoid the Clash of Civilizations.* New York: Continuum, 2002.

Saeger, James Schofield. "The Mission and Historical Missions: Film and the Writing of History." In *Based on a True Story: Latin American History at the Movies,* edited by Donald F. Stevens, 63–84. Lanham, MD: Scholarly Resources, 2005.

Said, Edward W. *Humanism and Democratic Criticism.* New York: Columbia University Press, 2004.

———. *Orientalism.* New York: Vintage, 2003.

———. *Power, Politics, and Culture: Interviews with Edward W. Said,* edited by Gauri Viswanathan. New York: Pantheon, 2001.

Sanneh, Lamin. *Whose Religion is Christianity? The Gospel beyond the West.* Grand Rapids: Eerdmans, 2003.

BIBLIOGRAPHY

Satrapi, Marjane. *The Complete Persepolis*. New York: Pantheon, 2007.
Sayyid, S. *A Fundamental Fear: Eurocentrism and the Emergence of Islamism*. New York: Zed, 2003.
Schutte, Ofelia. *Cultural Identity and Social Liberation*. Albany: State University of New York Press, 1993.
Serequeberhan, Tsenay. *Contested Memory: The Icons of the Occidental Tradition*. Trenton, NJ: Africa World, 2007.
———. *The Hermeneutics of African Philosophy: Horizon and Discourse*. New York: Routledge, 1994.
Shiva, Vandana. *Biopiracy: The Plunder of Nature and Knowledge*. Boston, MA: South End, 1997.
Shohat, Ella and Robert Stam. *Unthinking Eurocentrism: Multiculturalism and the Media*. New York: Routledge, 2013.
Shulman, George. *American Prophecy: Race and Redemption in American Political Culture*. Minneapolis: University of Minnesota Press, 2008.
Smith, Christian. *The Emergence of Liberation Theology: Radical Religion and Social Movement Theory*. Chicago: The University of Chicago Press, 1991.
Smith, Kay Higuera, et al. *Evangelical Postcolonial Conversations: Global Awakenings in Theology and Praxis*. Downers Grove, IL: InterVarsity Academic, 2014.
Sobrino Jon. *No Salvation Outside the Poor: Prophetic-Utopian Essays*. New York: Orbis, 2008.
Soelle, Dorothee. *Stations of the Cross: A Latin American Pilgrimage*. Translated by Joyce Irwin. Minneapolis: Fortress, 1993.
Song, C. S. *The Believing Heart: An Invitation to Story Theology*. Minneapolis: Fortress, 1999.
Sontag, Susan. *Regarding the Pain of Others*. New York: Picador, 2003.
Soulen, R. Kendall. *The God of Israel and Christian Theology*. Minneapolis: Fortress, 1996.
Soyinka, Wole. *The Burden of Memory, the Muse of Forgiveness*. New York: Oxford University Press, 1999.
———. *Climate of Fear: The Quest for Dignity in a Dehumanized World*. New York: Random, 2005.
Sproul, R. C. *The Consequences of Ideas: Understanding the Concepts that Shaped Our World*. Wheaton, IL: Crossway, 2000.
Stannard, David E. *American Holocaust: The Conquest of the New World*. New York: Oxford University Press, 1992.
Sweet, James H. "The Iberian Roots of American Racist Thought." *William and Mary Quarterly* 54.7 (1997) 143–66.
Takaki, Ronald. *A Different Mirror: A History of Multicultural America*. New York: Back Bay, 2008.
———. *Hiroshima: Why America Dropped the Atomic Bomb*. New York: Back Bay, 1996.
Taubes, Jacob. *From Cult to Culture: Fragments Toward a Critique of Historical Reason*. Stanford, California: Stanford University Press, 2010.
———. *Occidental Eschatology*. Translated by David Ratmoko. Stanford, CA: Stanford University Press, 2009.
Tibebu, Teshale. *Hegel and the Third World: The Making of Eurocentrism in World History*. New York: Syracuse University Press, 2010.
Thiong'o, Ngũgĩ wa. *Decolonizing the Mind: The Politics of Language in African Literature*. London: Heinemann, 2011.

BIBLIOGRAPHY

Thornton, Russell. *American Indian Holocaust and Survival: A Population History since 1492*. University of Oklahoma Press, 1987.

Tillich, Paul. *A History of Christian Thought: From its Judaic and Hellenistic Origins to Existentialism*. New York: Touchstone, 1968.

Tinker, George E. *Spirit and Resistance: Political Theology and American Indian Liberation*. Minneapolis: Augsburg Fortress, 2004.

Todorov, Tzvetan. *The Conquest of America: The Question of the Other*. Oklahoma: University of Oklahoma Press, 1999.

Toscano, Alberto. *Fanaticism: On the Uses of an Idea*. New York: Verso, 2010.

Trouillot, Michel-Rolph. *Silencing the Past: Power and the Production of History*. Boston, MA: Beacon, 1995.

Trueman, Carl R. *Histories and Fallacies: Problems Faced in the Writing of History*. Wheaton, IL: Crossway, 2010.

———. "Uneasy Consciences and Critical Minds: What the Followers of Carl Henry Can Learn From Edward Said." *Themelios* 30.2 (2005) 32–45.

Turner, Bryan S. *Marx and the End of Orientalism*. London: Allen and Unwin, 1978.

Twiss, Richard. *One Church, Many Tribes: Following Jesus the Way God Made You*. Ventura, California: Regal, 2000.

———. *Rescuing the Gospel from the Cowboys: A Native American Expression of the Jesus Way*. Downers Grove, IL: InterVarsity, 2015.

Villa-Vicencio, Charles, ed. *On Reading Karl Barth in South Africa*. Grand Rapids: Eerdmans, 1988.

Walia, Shelly. *Edward Said and the Writing of History*. Cambridge: Totem, 2001.

West, Cornel. *Prophetic Fragments*. Grand Rapids: Eerdmans, 1988.

Westhelle, Vitor. *After Heresy: Colonial Practices and Post-Colonial Theologies*. Eugene, OR: Cascade, 2010.

Whitfield, Teresa. *Ignacio Ellacuría and the Martyred Jesuits of El Salvador*. Philadelphia, PA: Temple University Press, 1995.

Williams, Delores S. *Sisters in the Wilderness: The Challenge of Womanist God-Talk*. Maryknoll, NY, 1993.

Williams, Reggie L. *Bonhoeffer's Black Jesus: Harlem Renaissance Theology and an Ethic of Resistance*. Waco, TX: Baylor University Press, 2014.

Wilmore, Gayraud S. *Last Things First*. Philadelphia, PA: Westminster, 1982.

Wong, R. Bin. *China Transformed: Historical Change and the Limits of European Experience*. New York: Cornell University, 1997.

Woodley, Randy S. *Living in Color: Embracing God's Passion for Ethnic Diversity*. Downers Grove, IL: InterVarsity, 2001.

———. *Shalom and the Community of Creation: An Indigenous Vision*. Grand Rapids: Eerdmans, 2012.

Wynter, Sylvia. "Columbus and the Poetics of the Propter Nos." *Annals of Scholarship* 8.2 (1991) 251–86.

———. "1492: A New World View." In *Race, Discourse, and the Origin of the Americas: A New World View*, edited by Vera Lawrence Hyatt and Rex Nettleford, 5–57. Washington, DC: Smithsonian Institution Press, 1995.

———. "Unsettling the Coloniality of Being/Power/Truth/Freedom: Towards the Human after Man, Its Overrepresentation—An Argument." *The New Centennial Review* 3.3 (2003) 257–337.

BIBLIOGRAPHY

Yancey, Philip. *Soul Survivor: How My Faith Survived the Church*. New York: Doubleday, 2001.
Young III, Josiah Ulysses. *No Difference in the Fare: Dietrich Bonhoeffer and the Problem of Racism*. Grand Rapids: Eerdmans, 1998.
Yugar, Theresa A. *Sor Juana Inés de la Cruz: Feminist Reconstruction of Biography and Text*. Eugene, OR: Wipf and Stock, 2014.
Zinn, Howard. *A People's History of the United States*. New York: Harper Perennial, 1980.
Žižek, Slavoj. *The Fragile Absolute: Or Why the Christian Legacy is Worth Fighting For?* New York: Verso, 2000.
———. *First as Tragedy, Then as Farce*. New York: Verso, 2009.
———. *Living in the End Times*. New York: Verso, 2010.
———. *The Universal Exception*. New York: Continuum, 2006.

Index

A Song to Remember, 122
Adichie, Chimamanda Ngozi, 1–2, 6, 12, 116
Ahmed, Sara, 58n41, 63–64
Al-Azmeh, Aziz, 145
Alfred, Taiaiake, 107
Althaus-Reid, Marcella, 80
American Sniper, 122
Amin, Samir, 54n23, 70, 78n106, 112n98
Anidjar, Gil, 8, 49–50, 55, 57, 76
Anzaldúa, Gloria, 34, 38n62, 39–42, 44
Aponte, Edwin David, 72–73
Aquinas, 8, 22–23, 60
Aquino, María Pilar, 73
Arendt, Hannah, 125
Ateek, Naim Stifan, 104
Augustine, 7n16, 22–23, 48, 88

Bainton, Roland, 24n18
Baker-Fletcher, Karen, 148
Baldwin, James, 1, 14, 14n24, 119, 120, 139, 141n11, 149
Balthasar, Hans Urs von, 72, 88n8
Barber, Michael D., 38n64, 76n101
Barker, John, 28
Barth, Karl, ix, 3–4, 7, 10, 15–48, 50, 60, 72, 81, 86, 89, 115, 140–42, 147
Bass, Diane Butler, 91
Bedford, Nancy, 40
Benjamin, Walter, x, 24, 46, 48–49, 82, 106
Berrigan, Daniel, 124–25, 138
Bhabha, Homi K., 38n62, 59, 81n115

biography, 12–13, 86–115
Black Elk, 83
Black Legend, 126n26
Blake, William, 94
Bloch, Ernst, 46n89
Boff, Leonardo, 93, 122–23
Bonhoeffer, Dietrich, 3–4, 12, 16n3, 67, 86, 111
border thinking, x, 10–11, 21, 32–44, 61, 64, 77, 82, 84, 140, 143
Boyarin, Daniel, 43–44
Brand, Dionne, 12, 139
Brock, Rita Nakashima, 91
Brown, Robert McAfee, 34
Brunner, Emil, 72
Buber, Martin, 105n66
Bultmann, Rudolf 15, 72
Burckhardt, Jacob, 25n22, 33n44
Burke, Peter, 37

Cabral, Amilcar, 79n107
Calvin, John 10, 24n18, 104
Camus, Albert, 87
Cannon, Katie, 95, 141
Carter, James Kameron, 5, 28n30, 78n106
Casas, Bartolome De La, 75, 93
Césaire, Aimé, 33
Chakrabarty, Dipesh, 65
Chávez, César, ix
Chomsky, Noam, 70
Chopin, Frédéric, 122
cinema, 118–29
Cisneros, Sandra, 38

165

INDEX

Clarke, Sathianathan, 9, 103n53
Cleveland, Christena, 116
Cone, James, 3–4, 7, 20, 27–28, 103n53, 105, 105n63, 106n67, 109–111, 114n105, 116, 134, 141–42
Cortez, Hernan, 75
Cry Freedom, 128

Dabashi, Hamid, 11, 51, 53n14, 58–63, 66, 72–73, 81, 84, 111–13, 145
Dalits, 100, 103
Dancer, Anthony, 93–94
Davis, Natalie Zemon, 129
DeNiro, Robert, 124
Derrida, Jacques, 87, 116
Dilthey, Wilhelm, 78n107
Dion, Joan, 133–35
Djaït, Hichem, 52, 145
Dostoevsky, Fyodor, 33n44, 88n6
Douglas, Kelly Brown, 7n13, 109–110
Du Bois, W.E.B., 11, 28–30, 142
Dussel, Enrique, 8–9, 11–12, 38, 46, 49, 51, 72–, 78, 81–84, 142, 144
Dyson, Michael Eric, 71, 109, 141–42

El Clon, 122
Elizondo, Virgilio, 38, 40–41, 73, 121n12, 143
Ellacuría, Ignacio, 11–12, 46, 48–49, 51, 72–73, 75–78, 82–83, 95–98, 116, 125
Ellis, Marc H., 86, 105–6
Ellul, Jacques, 94
empathy, 1–5, 13, 21, 86–87, 89, 90, 97, 100, 115, 118, 129–34, 138, 146–49
eschatology, 10, 21, 44–46, 88
Espín, Orlando, 73
Eurocentrism, 7, 11, 17–21, 48–85, 87, 116–17, 119–21, 132–33, 139–49

Fanon, Frantz, 46–47, 53n15, 59, 76n99, 79n108, 113, 125
Fea, John, 5–6, 54
Fernandez, Eleazer, 103n53
Florovsky, Georges, 7, 23n14
Foner, Eric, 141n11

For Greater Glory, 138
Foucault, Michel, 60n44, 87, 116
Francis of Assisi, 93
Franco, Jean, 13, 135–38
Frank, Andre Gunder, 67n60
Freud, Sigmund 33, 59, 80
Frye, Northrop, 94

Gadamer, Hans Georg, 11, 78
Gandhi, 115
Gandhi, 123
Gershwin, George, 122
Gibson, Andrew, 77
Gikandi, Simon, 13, 130–31
Gillespie, Michael Allen, 74
Ginzburg, Carlos, 25n22
Girard, René, 94
Glaude, Eddie S., Jr., 14n24, 89
Glissant, Édouard, 46
Gogarten, Friedrich 15
Goizueta, Robert S., 40
González, Justo, 69n69, 73, 144
Gran, Peter, 67
Gregory, Brad, 74
Gutiérrez, Gustavo, 7, 33n44, 46, 93, 103n53, 105, 106n67, 142, 133n44, 141

Habermas, Jürgen, 145
Hanh, Thich Nhat, 4, 118
Hart, David Bentley, 91
Hauerwas, Stanley, 110n87
Hegel, Georg Friedrich Wilhelm, 59–60, 72, 75, 78, 80
Heidegger, Martin, 11, 33, 64, 78, 145
hermeneutics, 77–82
Hill, Johnny Bernard, 109
Hillesum, Etty, 105n66
historiography, 5–10, 15–32
Hobbes, Thomas, 75
Hofstadter, Richard, 142
Holocaust, 8, 29, 45, 54, 67–68, 104–6, 132
hooks, bell, 13, 121
Hountondji, Paulin J., 79n107
Huggins, Jackie, 139, 148
Huggins, Nathan, 142

166

INDEX

Hume, David, 131
Hurston, Nora Zeale, 95
Husserl, Edmund, 78n107
hybridity, 37, 82

Ibn Rushd, 71
Illich, Ivan, 94
In the Time of Butterflies, 138
Inchausti, Robert, 94–95, 114
Irons, Jeremy, 124
Irvin, Dale, 140
Isasi-Díaz, Ada María, 73
Islamophobia, 74, 123n17, 145

Jefferson, Thomas, 24n18, 90
Joffe, Roland, 13, 124–29
Joh, Wonhee Anne, 37, 122

Kant, Immanuel, 60, 75, 78, 78n106, 80, 131
Keillor, Steven J., 27, 29
Kelley, Robin D. G., 80
Kerouac, Jack, 33n44, 94n26
Khatibi, Abdelkebir, 46
Kierkegaard, Søren, 34, 81, 87
King, Martin Luther, Jr., ix, 7, 12, 27, 90, 93, 95, 109–116, 144
Knitter, Paul, 112
Koyama, Kosuke, 48, 79
Kyung, Chung Hyun, 102–3, 116

Lacan, Jacques, 59
LaCapra, Dominick, 2n3, 125
Lassalle-Klein, Robert, 96–97
Latin America, 37–43, 69–77, 96–98, 124–29
Lee, Jung Young, 92–93
Lee, Krys, 38n62
Lenin, Vladimir, 58–59
Levinas, Emmanuel, 34, 36, 38, 59–60, 76, 81, 84
Lewis, C. S., 7
Lincoln, Abraham, 27, 90
Locke, John, 75
Lonergan, Bernard, 72
Lord Acton, 24n18
Löwith, Karl, 7–8, 33n44, 46n89, 67

Löwy, Michael, 62n46, 73n82, 100n41
Luther, Martin, 22–23, 74, 90, 113–14

Mahbubani, Kishore, 59, 102n50
Mahtani, Minelle, 39n65
Maldonado-Torres, Nelson, 61–62, 76n99,
Mandela, 123
Marsden, George, 142
Martínez, Elizabeth, 13, 121
Marks, Robert, 66–67
Marx, Karl (Marxism), 24n18, 33, 50, 52, 58–59, 60n44, 61–63, 65n53, 67n60, 70n73, 78, 78n106, 80–81, 83, 99, 100n41
Maryknoll sisters, 12, 97n34, 105n63
Massey, James 103
McClendon, James, 12–13, 86, 89, 92–93, 95, 110–11, 113, 115
McIntyre, C. T., 6–7, 9, 46, 88
McLuhan, Marshall, 94
Meiselas, Susan, 136
Menchu, Rigoberta, 12
Menon, Nivedita,
Merton, Thomas 4n5, 94n26
mestizaje, 20, 37–44
Metz, Johann Baptist, 45, 133–34
Mignolo, Walter, 12, 34, 39–40, 44, 46, 51, 59–61, 63–65, 69, 72–74, 84, 106, 126n26, 140n6
Mitterand, Danielle, 48n3
Moltmann, Jürgen, 18n6, 45–46
Moraga, Cherrie, 39n67
Mosse, George, 68, 78n106
Moyn, Samuel, 34
Musalha, Nur, 53n16

Nayar, Pramod K., 50n9, 77
neighbor, 32–47
Niebuhr, Reinhold, 3, 7, 15, 72, 141–42
Nietzsche, Friedrich, 25n22, 33n44, 64, 80, 86–87, 90, 99, 100n41
Nigam, Aditya, 60–61
Nkrumah, Kwame, 79n107
Noll, Mark, 27n27, 91, 142
Nouwen, Henri, 88n6, 133–34

167

INDEX

Orientalism, 51–57, 111, 120–21, 145
Ortega y Gasset, José, 33, 118

Parker, Rebecca Ann, 91
periodization, 23, 30–32, 42, 77
Pineda, Nancy, 73
Pomeranz, Kenneth, 67n60
postcolonialism, 48–85
Prashad, Vjay, x, 48, 50,
Puar, Jasbir, 121, 132
Pui-lan, Kwok, 53n15, 102n46

Qutb, Sayyid, 111n93, 145

Rabasa, José, 70
Rahner, Karl, 42n83, 48, 72, 96
Raheb, Mitri, 98, 104–5, 116
Recinos, Harold, 129
Ramadan, Tariq, 37–38, 54n23, 113, 146
Rancière, Jacques, 15, 120
Rea, Robert, 6, 54
Recinos, Harold, 100–102, 113, 129
Regan, Ethna, 73
Rhapsody in Blue, 122
Richard, Pablo, 70, 105
Rivera, Mayra, x, 20, 34, 42, 44, 140n6
Rivera-Pagan, Luis, 4n6, 69–70,
Roberts, J. Deotis, 110n87, 111
Robinson, Marilynne, 22, 24
Romero, 128, 138
Romero, Oscar, ix, 12, 96–98, 127, 134, 138
Rose, Gillian, 105n63
Rosenzweig, Franz, 46n89
Rousseau, Jean Jacques, 75
Rubenstein, Richard, 68

Saeger, James Schofield, 124–29
Said, Edward, 11, 51–57, 59, 61, 120
Salvador, 128
Sand, George, 122
Sandoval, Chela, x
Satrapi, Marjanie, 113
Sayyid, S., 54, 57, 66, 145
Schlesinger, Arthur M., Jr., 142
Schleiermacher, Friedrich, 23, 78n107,

Scholem, Gershom, 46n89
Schutte, Ofelia, 76n101, 77
Segovia, Fernando, 73
Selma, 122, 144
Senghor, Leopold Sedar, 79n107
Serequeberhan, Tsenay, 11, 52, 78–81
Shohat, Ella, 119
Socrates, 114
Sobrino, Jon, 76, 97, 133n44
Soelle, Dorothee, 45, 105, 105n63, 133–34, 138–39
Song, C.S., 91, 147
Sontag, Susan, 13, 129, 131–32, 134–36
Sor Juana Ines de la Cruz, 127
Soyinka, Wole, 48, 67–68, 79, 80n114, 82
Spengler, Oswald, 33
Stam, Robert, 119
Stringfellow, William, 86, 93–94

Taubes, Jacob, 25–26, 44, 46, 67
Takaki, Ronald, 18
Tanner, Kathryn, 23n13
Taylor, Charles, 145
The Battle of Algiers, 138
The Imitation Game, 122
The Killing Fields, 128
The Mission, 13, 124–29, 133, 144
The Theory of Everything, 122
Thiong'o, Ngũgĩ wa, 35
Thurman, Howard, 95
Tillich, Paul, 72, 114–15, 140–41
Tinker, George, 83
Tolstoy, 33n44, 88n6
Torre, Miguel A. De La, 39n65, 72–73
Toscano, Alberto, 66n56
Toynbee, Alfred, 33
Triangle Shirtwaist Factory fire, 130
Trouillot, Michel-Rolph, 57, 69n68, 74n88, 98, 118, 121, 131
Trueman, Carl, 53–54
12 Years a Slave, 122
Twiss, Richard, 71, 83, 86, 98, 106–8, 116

Vattino, Gianni, 78n107
Villafañe, Eldín, 73
Vitoria, Francisco De, 75

INDEX

Walia, Shelly, 56
Weber, Max, 24n18, 67n60,
Wesley, John, 10
West, Cornel, 141
Whitfield, Teresa, 96–97
Wiesel, Elie 48n3
Wong, R. Bin, 67n60
Wood, Lawrence, 7
Woodley, Randy, 70–71, 83, 148
Wynter, Sylvia, 11–12, 64, 79, 84

X, Malcolm, 27, 62n48, 90, 93, 109–116

Yancey, Philip, 88

Zabala, Santiago, 59n43
Zinn, Howard, 18n6, 91
Žižek, Slavoj, 11, 50–52, 57–67, 69, 80–84
Zubiri, Xavier, 96

www.ingramcontent.com/pod-product-compliance
Lightning Source LLC
Chambersburg PA
CBHW030113170426
43198CB00009B/605